MODERN ESSAYS

SELECTED BY
CHRISTOPHER MORLEY

NEW YORK
HARCOURT, BRACE AND COMPANY

PRINTED IN THE U. S. A. BY
THE QUINN & BODEN COMPANY
RAHWAY, N. J.

PREFACE

It had been my habit, I am now aware, to speak somewhat lightly of the labors of anthologists: to insinuate that they led lives of bland sedentary ease. I shall not do so again. When the publisher suggested a collection of representative contemporary essays, I thought it would be the most lenient of tasks. But experience is a fine aperitive to the mind.

Indeed the pangs of the anthologist, if he has conscience, are burdensome. There are so many considerations to be tenderly weighed; personal taste must sometimes be set aside in view of the general plan; for every item chosen half a dozen will have been affectionately conned and sifted; and perhaps some favorite pieces will be denied because the authors have reasons for withholding permission. It would be enjoyable (for me, at any rate) to write an essay on the things I have lingered over with intent to include them in this little book, but have finally sacrificed for one reason or another. How many times—twenty at least —I have taken down from my shelf Mr. Chesterton's *The Victorian Age in Literature* to reconsider whether his ten pages on Dickens, or his glorious summing-up of Decadents and Æsthetes, were not absolutely essential. How many times I have palpitated upon certain passages in *The Education of Henry Adams* and in Mr. Wells's *Outline of History,* which, I assured myself, would legitimately stand as essays if shrewdly excerpted.

But I usually concluded that would not be quite fair. I have not been overscrupulous in this matter, for the essay is a mood rather than a form; the frontier between the essay and the short story is as imperceptible as is at present the once famous Mason and Dixon line. Indeed, in that pleasant lowland country between the two empires lie (to my way of thinking) some of the most fertile fields of prose—fiction that expresses feeling and character and setting rather than action and plot; fiction beautifully ripened by the lingering mild sunshine of the essayist's mood. This is fiction, I might add, extremely unlikely to get into the movies. I think of short stories such as George Gissing's, in that too little known volume *The House of Cobwebs,* which I read again and again at midnight with unfailing delight; fall asleep over; forget; and again re-read with undiminished satisfaction. They have no brilliance of phrase, no smart surprises, no worked-up 'situations' which have to be taken at high speed to pass without breakdown over their brittle bridgework of credibility. They have only the modest and faintly melancholy savor of life itself.

Yet it is a mere quibble to pretend that the essay does not have easily recognizable manners. It may be severely planned, or it may ramble in ungirdled mood, but it has its own point of view that marks it from the short story proper, or the merely personal memoir. That distinction, easily felt by the sensitive reader, is not readily expressible. Perhaps the true meaning of the word *essay*—an attempt—gives a clue. No matter how personal or trifling the topic may be, there is always a tendency to generalize, to walk round the subject or the experience, and view it from several vantages; instead of (as in the short story) cutting a carefully landscaped path through a chosen tract of human complication. So an essay can never be more than an attempt, for it is an excursion into the endless. Any student of fiction will admit that in the composition of a short story many entertaining and valuable elaborations may rise in the mind of the author which must be strictly rejected because they do not forward the essential motive. But in the essay (of an informal sort) we ask not relevance to plot, but relevance to mood. That is why there are so many essays that are mere marking time. The familiar essay is easier to write than the short story, but it imposes equal restraints on a scrupulous author. For in fiction the writer is controlled and limited and swept along by his material; but in the essay, the writer rides his pen. A good story, once clearly conceived, almost writes itself; but essays are written.

There also we find a pitfall of the personal essay—the temptation to become too ostentatiously quaint, too deliberately 'whimsical' (the word which, by loathsome repetition, has become emetic). The fine flavor and genius of the essay—as in Bacon and Montaigne, Lamb, Hazlitt, Thackeray, Thoreau; perhaps even in Stevenson—is the rich bouquet of personality. But soliloquy must not fall into monologue. One might put it thus: that the perfection of the familiar essay is a conscious revelation of self done inadvertently.

The art of the anthologist is the art of the host: his tact is exerted in choosing a congenial group; making them feel comfortable and at ease; keeping the wine and tobacco in circulation; while his eye is tenderly alert down the bright vista of tablecloth, for any lapse in the general cheer. It is well, also, for him to hold himself discreetly in the background, giving his guests the pleasure of clinching the jape, and seeking only, by innocent wiles, to draw each one into some characteristic and felicitous vein. I think I can offer you, in this parliament of philomaths, entertainment of the most genuine sort; and having said so much, I might well retire and be heard no more.

But I think it is well to state, as even the most bashful host may do, just why this particular company has been called together. My intention is not merely to please the amiable dilettante, though I hope to do that too. I made my choices, first and foremost, with a view to stimulating those who are themselves interested in the arts of writing. I have, to be frank, a secret ambition that a book of this sort may even be used as a small but useful weapon in the classroom. I wanted to bring it home to the student that as brilliant and sincere work is being done to-day in the essay as in any period of our literature. Accordingly the pieces reprinted here are very diverse. There is the grand manner; there is foolery; there is straightforward literary criticism; there is pathos, politics, and the picturesque. But every selection is, in its own way, a work of art. And I would call the reader's attention to this: that the greater number of these essays were written not by retired æsthetes, but by practising journalists in the harness of the daily or weekly press. The names of some of the most widely bruited essayists of our day are absent from this roster, not by malice, but because I desired to include material less generally known.

I should apologize, I suppose, for the very informal tone of the introductory notes on each author. But I conceived the reader in the rôle of a friend spending the evening in happy gossip along the shelves. Pulling out one's favorites and talking about them, now and then reading a chosen extract aloud, and ending (some time after midnight) by choosing some special volume for the guest to take to bed with him—in the same spirit I have compiled this collection. Perhaps the editorial comments have too much the manner of dressing gown and slippers; but what a pleasant book this will be to read in bed!

And perhaps this collection may be regarded as a small contribution to Anglo-American friendliness. Of course when I say Anglo-, I mean Brito-, but that is such a hideous prefix. Journalists on this side are much better acquainted with what their professional colleagues are doing in Britain, than they with our concerns. But surely there should be a congenial fraternity of spirit among all who use the English tongue in print. There are some of us who even imagine a day when there may be regular international exchanges of journalists, as there have been of scholars and students. The contributions to this book are rather evenly divided between British and American hands; and perhaps it is not insignificant that two of the most pleas-

ing items come from Canada, where they often combine the virtues of both sides.

It is a pleasant task to thank the authors and publishers who have assented to the reprinting of these
pieces. To the authors themselves, and to the following publishers, I admit my sincere gratitude for the use
of material copyrighted by them:—Doubleday Page
and Company for the extracts from books by John
Macy, Stewart Edward White and Pearsall Smith;
Charles Scribner's Sons for Rupert Brooke's *Niagara
Falls;* the New York *Sun* for Don Marquis's *Almost
Perfect State;* the George H. Doran Company for the
essays by Joyce Kilmer and Robert Cortes Holliday;
Mr. James B. Pinker for permission to reprint Mr.
Conrad's Preface to *A Personal Record;* Alfred A.
Knopf, Inc., for the essays by H. M. Tomlinson, A. P.
Herbert and Philip Guedalla; Lady Osler for the essay
by the late Sir William Osler; Henry Holt and Com-
pany for Thomas Burke's *The Russian Quarter;* E. P.
Dutton and Company for *A Word for Autumn,* by
A. A. Milne; the New York *Evening Post* for the
essays by Stuart P. Sherman and Harry Esty Dounce;
Harper and Brothers for Marian Storm's *A Wood-
land Valentine;* Dodd, Mead and Company for Simeon
Strunsky's *Nocturne,* from his volume *Post-Impressions;* the Macmillan Company for *Beer and Cider,*

from Professor Saintsbury's *Notes on a Cellar Book;*
Longmans Green and Company for Bertrand Russell's
A Free Man's Worship, from *Mysticism and Logic;*
Robert M. McBride and Company for the selection
from James Branch Cabell; Harcourt, Brace and
Company for the essay by Heywood Broun; *The
Weekly Review* for the essays by O. W. Firkins, Harry
Morgan Ayres and Robert Palfrey Utter. The present ownership of the copyright of the essay by Louise
Imogen Guiney I have been unable to discover. It
was published in *Patrins* (Copeland and Day, 1897),
which has long been out of print. Knowing the purity
of my motives I have used this essay, hoping that it
might introduce Miss Guiney's exquisite work to the
younger generation that knows her hardly at all.

CHRISTOPHER MORLEY

OCTOBER, *1921.*

CONTENTS

		PAGE
PREFACE		iii
AMERICAN LITERATURE	John Macy	3
MARY WHITE	William Allen White	22
NIAGARA FALLS	Rupert Brooke	30
THE ALMOST PERFECT STATE	Don Marquis	39
"THE MAN O' WAR'S 'ER 'US-BAND"	David W. Bone	49
THE MARKET	William McFee	60
HOLY IRELAND	Joyce Kilmer	67
A FAMILIAR PREFACE	Joseph Conrad	81
ON DRAWING	A. P. Herbert	94
O. HENRY	O. W. Firkins	100
THE MOWING OF A FIELD	Hilaire Belloc	113
THE STUDENT LIFE	William Osler	128
THE DECLINE OF THE DRAMA	Stephen Leacock	145
AMERICA AND THE ENGLISH TRADITION	Harry Morgan Ayres	153
THE RUSSIAN QUARTER	Thomas Burke	160
A WORD FOR AUTUMN	A. A. Milne	173
"A CLERGYMAN"	Max Beerbohm	177
SAMUEL BUTLER	Stuart P. Sherman	187
BED-BOOKS AND NIGHT-LIGHTS	H. M. Tomlinson	210
THE PRECEPT OF PEACE	Louise Imogen Guiney	219
ON LYING AWAKE AT NIGHT	Stewart Edward White	229
A WOODLAND VALENTINE	Marian Storm	236
THE ELEMENTS OF POETRY	George Santayana	241
NOCTURNE	Simeon Strunsky	246
BEER AND CIDER	George Saintsbury	253
A FREE MAN'S WORSHIP	Bertrand Russell	263
SOME HISTORIANS	Philip Guedalla	278
WINTER MIST	Robert Palfrey Utter	291
TRIVIA	Logan Pearsall Smith	297
BEYOND LIFE	James Branch Cabell	304
THE FISH REPORTER	Robert Cortes Holliday	316
SOME NONSENSE ABOUT A DOG	Harry Esty Dounce	331
THE FIFTY-FIRST DRAGON	Heywood Broun	338

MODERN ESSAYS

AMERICAN LITERATURE

By JOHN MACY

This vigorous survey of American letters is the first chapter of John Macy's admirable volume *The Spirit of American Literature,* published in 1913—a book shrewd, penetrating and salty, which has unfortunately never reached one-tenth of the many readers who would find it permanently delightful and profitable. Mr. Macy has no skill in vaudeville tricks to call attention to himself: no shafts of limelight have followed him across the stage. But those who have an eye for criticism that is vivacious without bombast, austere without bitterness, keen without malice, know him as one of the truly competent and liberal-minded observers of the literary scene.

Mr. Macy was born in Detroit, 1877; graduated from Harvard in 1899; did editorial service on the *Youth's Companion* and the Boston *Herald;* and nowadays lives pensively in Greenwich Village, writing a good deal for *The Freeman* and *The Literary Review.* Perhaps, if you were wandering on Fourth Street, east of Sixth Avenue, you might see him treading thoughtfully along, with a wide sombrero hat, and always troubled by an iron-gray forelock that droops over his brow. You would know, as soon as you saw him, that he is a man greatly lovable. I like to think of him as I first saw him, some years ago, in front of the bright hearth of the charming St. Botolph Club in Boston, where he was usually the center of an animated group of nocturnal philosophers.

The essay was written in 1912, before the very real reawakening of American creative work that began in the 'teens of this century. The reader will find it interesting to consider how far Mr. Macy's remarks might be modified if he were writing to-day.

The Spirit of American Literature has been reissued in an inexpensive edition by Boni and Liveright. It is a book well worth owning.

AMERICAN literature is a branch of English literature, as truly as are English books written in Scotland or South Africa. Our literature lies almost entirely in the nineteenth century when the ideas and books of

3

the western world were freely interchanged among the nations and became accessible to an increasing number of readers. In literature nationality is determined by language rather than by blood or geography. M. Maeterlinck, born a subject of King Leopold, belongs to French literature. Mr. Joseph Conrad, born in Poland, is already an English classic. Geography, much less important in the nineteenth century than before, was never, among modern European nations, so important as we sometimes are asked to believe. Of the ancestors of English literature "Beowulf" is scarcely more significant, and rather less graceful, than our tree-inhabiting forebears with prehensile toes; the true progenitors of English literature are Greek, Latin, Hebrew, Italian, and French.

American literature and English literature of the nineteenth century are parallel derivatives from preceding centuries of English literature. Literature is a succession of books from books. Artistic expression springs from life ultimately but not immediately. It may be likened to a river which is swollen throughout its course by new tributaries and by the seepages of its banks; it reflects the life through which it flows, taking color from the shores; the shores modify it, but its power and volume descend from distant headwaters and affluents far up stream. Or it may be likened to the race-life which our food nourishes or impoverishes, which our individual circumstances foster or damage, but which flows on through us, strangely impersonal and beyond our power to kill or create.

It is well for a writer to say: "Away with books! I will draw my inspiration from life!" For we have too many books that are simply better books diluted by John Smith. At the same time, literature is not born spontaneously out of life. Every book has its literary parentage, and students find it so easy to trace genealogies that much criticism reads like an Old Testament chapter of "begats." Every novel was suckled at the breasts of older novels, and great mothers are often prolific of anæmic offspring. The stock falls off and revives, goes a-wandering, and returns like a prodigal. The family records get blurred. But of the main fact of descent there is no doubt.

American literature is English literature made in this country. Its nineteenth-century characteristics are evident and can be analyzed and discussed with some degree of certainty. Its "American" characteristics—no critic that I know has ever given a good account of them. You can define certain peculiarities of American politics, American agriculture, American public schools, even American religion. But what is uniquely American in American literature? Poe is just as American as Mark Twain; Lanier is just as

American as Whittier. The American spirit in literature is a myth, like American valor in war, which is
precisely like the valor of Italians and Japanese. The
American, deluded by a falsely idealized image which
he calls America, can say that the purity of Longfellow
represents the purity of American home life. An Irish
Englishman, Mr. Bernard Shaw, with another falsely
idealized image of America, surprised that a face does
not fit his image, can ask: "What is Poe doing in
that galley?" There is no answer. You never can
tell. Poe could not help it. He was born in Boston,
and lived in Richmond, New York, Baltimore, Philadelphia. Professor van Dyke says that Poe was a
maker of "decidedly un-American cameos," but I do
not understand what that means. Facts are uncom-
fortable consorts of prejudices and emotional generalities; they spoil domestic peace, and when there is a
separation they sit solid at home while the other party
goes. Irving, a shy, sensitive gentleman, who wrote
with fastidious care, said: "It has been a matter of
marvel, to European readers, that a man from the
wilds of America should express himself in tolerable
English." It is a matter of marvel, just as it is a
marvel that Blake and Keats flowered in the brutal
city of London a hundred years ago.

The literary mind is strengthened and nurtured, is
influenced and mastered, by the accumulated riches of

literature. In the last century the strongest thinkers in our language were Englishmen, and not only the traditional but the contemporary influences on our thinkers and artists were British. This may account for one negative characteristic of American literature —its lack of American quality. True, our records must reflect our life. Our poets, enamored of nightingales and Persian gardens, have not altogether forgotten the mocking-bird and the woods of Maine. Fiction, written by inhabitants of New York, Ohio, and Massachusetts, does tell us something of the ways of life in those mighty commonwealths, just as English fiction written by Lancashire men about Lancashire people is saturated with the dialect, the local habits and scenery of that county. But wherever an English-speaking man of imagination may dwell, in Dorset or Calcutta or Indianapolis, he is subject to the strong arm of the empire of English literature; he cannot escape it; it tears him out of his obscure bed and makes a happy slave of him. He is assigned to the department of the service for which his gifts qualify him, and his special education is undertaken by drill-masters and captains who hail from provinces far from his birthplace.

Dickens, who writes of London, influences Bret Harte, who writes of California, and Bret Harte influences Kipling, who writes of India. Each is intensely local in subject matter. The affinity between them is a matter of temperament, manifested, for example, in the swagger and exaggeration characteristic of all three. California did not "produce" Bret Harte; the power of Dickens was greater than that of the Sierras and the Golden Gate. Bret Harte created a California that never existed, and Indian gentlemen, Caucasian and Hindoo, tell us that Kipling invented an army and an empire unknown to geographers and war-offices.

The ideas at work among these English men of letters are world-encircling and fly between book and brain. The dominant power is on the British Islands, and the prevailing stream of influence flows west across the Atlantic. Sometimes it turns and runs the other way. Poe influenced Rossetti; Whitman influenced Henley. For a century Cooper has been in command of the British literary marine. Literature is reprehensibly unpatriotic, even though its votaries are, as individual citizens, afflicted with local prides and hostilities. It takes only a dramatic interest in the guns of Yorktown. Its philosophy was nobly uttered by Gaston Paris in the Collège de France in 1870, when the city was beleaguered by the German armies: "Common studies, pursued in the same spirit, in all civilized countries, form, beyond the restrictions of diverse and often hostile nationalities, a great country which no war profanes, no conqueror menaces, where souls find that refuge and unity which in former times was offered them by the city of God." The catholicity of English language and literature transcends the temporal boundaries of states.

What, then, of the "provincialism" of the American province of the empire of British literature? Is it an observable general characteristic, and is it a virtue or a vice? There is a sense in which American literature is not provincial enough. The most provincial of all literature is the Greek. The Greeks knew nothing outside of Greece and needed to know nothing. The Old Testament is tribal in its provinciality; its god is a local god, and its village police and sanitary regulations are erected into eternal laws. If this racial localism is not essential to the greatness of early literatures, it is inseparable from them; we find it there. It is not possible in our cosmopolitan age and there are few traces of it in American books. No American poet has sung of his neighborhood with naïve passion, as if it were all the world to him. Whitman is pugnaciously American, but his sympathies are universal, his vision is cosmic; when he seems to be standing in a city street looking at life, he is in a trance, and his spirit is racing with the winds.

The welcome that we gave Whitman betrays the lack of an admirable kind of provincialism; it shows us

defective in local security of judgment. Some of us
have been so anxiously abashed by high standards of
European culture that we could not see a poet in our
own back yard until European poets and critics told
us he was there. This is queerly contradictory to a
disposition found in some Americans to disregard
world standards and proclaim a third-rate poet as the
Milton of Oshkosh or the Shelley of San Francisco.
The passage in Lowell's "Fable for Critics" about
"The American Bulwers, Disraelis and Scotts" is a
spoonful of salt in the mouth of that sort of gaping
village reverence.

Of dignified and self-respecting provincialism, such
as Professor Royce so eloquently advocates, there
might well be more in American books. Our poets
desert the domestic landscape to write pseudo-Eliza-
bethan dramas and sonnets about Mont Blanc. They
set up an artificial Tennyson park on the banks of the
Hudson. Beside the shores of Lake Michigan they
croon the love affairs of an Arab in the desert and his
noble steed. This is not a very grave offence, for poets
live among the stars, and it makes no difference from
what point of the earth's surface they set forth on
their aerial adventures. A Wisconsin poet may write
very beautifully about nightingales, and a New England Unitarian may write beautifully about cathedrals;
if it is beautiful, it is poetry, and all is well.

The novelists are the worst offenders. There have been few of them; they have not been adequate in numbers or in genius to the task of describing the sections of the country, the varied scenes and habits from New Orleans to the Portlands. And yet, small band as they are, with great domestic opportunities and responsibilities, they have devoted volumes to Paris, which has an able native corps of story-makers, and to Italy, where the home talent is first-rate. In this sense American literature is too globe-trotting, it has too little savor of the soil.

Of provincialism of the narrowest type American writers, like other men of imagination, are not guilty to any reprehensible degree. It is a vice sometimes imputed to them by provincial critics who view literature from the office of a London weekly review or from the lecture rooms of American colleges. Some American writers are parochial, for example, Whittier. Others, like Mr. Henry James, are provincial in outlook, but cosmopolitan in experience, and reveal their provinciality by a self-conscious internationalism. Probably English and French writers may be similarly classified as provincial or not. Mr. James says that Poe's collection of critical sketches "is probably the most complete and exquisite specimen of *provincialism* ever prepared for the edification of men." It is nothing like that. It is an example of what happens when a hack reviewer's work in local journals is collected into a volume because he turns out to be a genius. The list of Poe's victims is not more remarkable for the number of nonentities it includes than "The Lives of the Poets" by the great Doctor Johnson, who was hack for a bookseller, and "introduced" all the poets that the taste of the time encouraged the bookseller to print. Poe was cosmopolitan in spirit; his prejudices were personal and highly original, usually against the prejudices of his *moment* and *milieu*. Hawthorne is less provincial, in the derogatory sense, than his charming biographer, Mr. James, as will become evident if one compares Hawthorne's American notes on England, written in long ago days of national rancor, with Mr. James's British notes on America ("The American Scene"), written in our happy days of spacious vision.

Emerson's ensphering universality overspreads Carlyle like the sky above a volcanic island. Indeed Carlyle (who knew more about American life and about what other people ought to do than any other British writer earlier than Mr. Chesterton) justly complains that Emerson is not sufficiently local and concrete; Carlyle longs to see "some Event, Man's Life, American Forest, or piece of creation which this Emerson loves and wonders at, well *Emersonized*." Longfellow would not stay at home and write more about the excellent village blacksmith; he made poetical tours of Europe and translated songs and legends from several languages for the delight of the villagers who remained behind. Lowell was so heartily cosmopolitan that American newspapers accused him of Anglomania —which proves their provincialism but acquits him. Mr. Howells has written a better book about Venice than about Ohio. Mark Twain lived in every part of America, from Connecticut to California, he wrote about every country under the sun (and about some countries beyond the sun), he is read by all sorts and conditions of men in the English-speaking world, and he is an adopted hero in Vienna. It is difficult to come to any conclusion about provincialism as a characteristic of American literature.

American literature is on the whole idealistic, sweet, delicate, nicely finished. There is little of it which might not have appeared in the *Youth's Companion*. The notable exceptions are our most stalwart men of genius, Thoreau, Whitman, and Mark Twain. Any child can read American literature, and if it does not make a man of him, it at least will not lead him into forbidden realms. Indeed, American books too seldom come to grips with the problems of life, especially the books cast in artistic forms. The essayists, expounders, and preachers attack life vigorously and wrestle with the meaning of it. The poets are thin, moonshiny, meticulous in technique. Novelists are few and feeble.

and dramatists are non-existent. These generalities, subject to exceptions, are confirmed by a reading of the first fifteen volumes of the *Atlantic Monthly,* which are a treasure-house of the richest period of American literary expression. In those volumes one finds a surprising number of vigorous, distinguished papers on politics, philosophy, science, even on literature and art. Many talented men and women, whose names are not well remembered, are clustered there about the half dozen salient men of genius; and the collection gives one a sense that the New England mind (aided by the outlying contributors) was, in its one Age of Thought, an abundant and diversified power. But the poetry is not memorable, except for some verses by the few standard poets. And the fiction is naïve. Edward Everett Hale's "The Man Without a Country" is almost the only story there that one comes on with a thrill either of recognition or of discovery.

It is hard to explain why the American, except in his exhortatory and passionately argumentative moods, has not struck deep into American life, why his stories and verses are, for the most part, only pretty things, nicely unimportant. Anthony Trollope had a theory that the absence of international copyright threw our market open too unrestrictedly to the British product, that the American novel was an unprotected infant industry; we printed Dickens and the rest without paying royalty and starved the domestic manufacturer. This theory does not explain. For there were many American novelists, published, read, and probably paid for their work. The trouble is that they lacked genius; they dealt with trivial, slight aspects of life; they did not take the novel seriously in the right sense of the word, though no doubt they were in another sense serious enough about their poor productions. "Uncle Tom's Cabin" and "Huckleberry Finn" are colossal exceptions to the prevailing weakness and superficiality of American novels.

Why do American writers turn their backs on life, miss its intensities, its significance? The American Civil War was the most tremendous upheaval in the world after the Napoleonic period. The imaginative reaction on it consists of some fine essays, Lincoln's addresses, Whitman's war poetry, "Uncle Tom's Cabin" (which came before the war but is part of it), one or two passionate hymns by Whittier, the second series of the "Biglow Papers," Hale's "The Man Without a Country"—and what else? The novels laid in war-time are either sanguine melodrama or absurd idyls of maidens whose lovers are at the front—a tragic theme if tragically and not sentimentally conceived. Perhaps the bullet that killed Theodore Winthrop deprived us of our great novelist of the Civil War, for he was on the right road. In a general speculation such a might-have-been is not altogether futile; if Milton had died of whooping cough there would not have been any "Paradise Lost"; the reverse of this is that some geniuses whose works ought inevitably to have been produced by this or that national development may have died too soon. This suggestion, however, need not be gravely argued. The fact is that the American literary imagination after the Civil War was almost sterile. If no books had been written, the failure of that conflict to get itself embodied in some masterpieces would be less disconcerting. But thousands of books were written by people who knew the war at first hand and who had literary ambition and some skill, and from all these books none rises to distinction.

An example of what seems to be the American habit of writing about everything except American life, is the work of General Lew Wallace. Wallace was one of the important secondary generals in the Civil War, distinguished at Fort Donelson and at Shiloh. After the war he wrote "Ben-Hur," a doubly abominable book, because it is not badly written and it shows a lively imagination. There is nothing in it so valuable, so dramatically significant as a week in Wallace's war experiences. "Ben-Hur," fit work for a country clergyman with a pretty literary gift, is a ridiculous inanity to come from a man who has seen the things that

Wallace saw! It is understandable that the man of experience may not write at all, and, on the other hand, that the man of secluded life may have the imagination to make a military epic. But for a man crammed with experience of the most dramatic sort and discovering the ability and the ambition to write—for him to make spurious oriental romances which achieve an enormous popularity! The case is too grotesque to be typical, yet it is exceptional in degree rather than in kind. The American literary artist has written about everything under the skies except what matters most in his own life. General Grant's plain autobiography, not art and of course not attempting to be, is better literature than most of our books in artistic forms, because of its intellectual integrity and the profound importance of the subject-matter.

Our dreamers have dreamed about many wonderful things, but their faces have been averted from the mightier issues of life. They have been high-minded, fine-grained, eloquent in manner, in odd contrast to the real or reputed vigor and crudeness of the nation. In the hundred years from Irving's first romance to Mr. Howells's latest unromantic novel, most of our books are eminent for just those virtues which America is supposed to lack. Their physique is feminine; they are fanciful, dainty, reserved; they are literose, sophisticated in craftsmanship, but innocently unaware of the profound agitations of American life, of life everywhere. Those who strike the deeper notes of reality, Whitman, Thoreau, Mark Twain, Mrs. Stowe in her one great book, Whittier, Lowell and Emerson at their best, are a powerful minority. The rest, beautiful and fine in spirit, too seldom show that they are conscious of contemporaneous realities, too seldom vibrate with a tremendous sense of life.

The Jason of western exploration writes as if he had passed his life in a library. The Ulysses of great rivers and perilous seas is a connoisseur of Japanese prints. The warrior of 'Sixty-one rivals Miss Marie Corelli. The mining engineer carves cherry stones. He who is figured as gaunt, hardy and aggressive, conquering the desert with the steam locomotive, sings of a pretty little rose in a pretty little garden. The judge, haggard with experience, who presides over the most tragi-comic divorce court ever devised by man, writes love stories that would have made Jane Austen smile.

Mr. Arnold Bennett is reported to have said that if Balzac had seen Pittsburgh, he would have cried: "Give me a pen!" The truth is, the whole country is crying out for those who will record it, satirize it, chant it. As literary material, it is virgin land, ancient as life and fresh as a wilderness. American literature is one occupation which is not over-crowded, in which, indeed, there is all too little competition for the new-comer to meet. There are signs that some earnest young writers are discovering the fertility of a soil that has scarcely been scratched.

American fiction shows all sorts of merit, but the merits are not assembled, concentrated; the fine is weak, and the strong is crude. The stories of Poe, Hawthorne, Howells, James, Aldrich, Bret Harte, are admirable in manner, but they are thin in substance, not of large vitality. On the other hand, some of the stronger American fictions fail in workmanship; for example, "Uncle Tom's Cabin," which is still vivid and moving long after its tractarian interest has faded: the novels of Frank Norris, a man of great vision and high purpose, who attempted to put national economics into something like an epic of daily bread; and Herman Melville's "Moby Dick," a madly eloquent romance of the sea. A few American novelists have felt the meaning of the life they knew and have tried sincerely to set it down, but have for various reasons failed to make first-rate novels; for example, Edward Eggleston, whose stories of early Indiana have the breath of actuality in them; Mr. E. W. Howe, author of "The Story of a Country Town"; Harold Frederic, a man of great ability, whose work was growing deeper, more significant when he died; George W. Cable, whose novels are unsteady and sentimental, but who gives a genuine impression of having portrayed a city and its people; and Stephen Crane, who, dead at thirty, had given in "The Red Badge of Courage" and "Maggie" the promise of better work. Of good short stories America has been prolific. Mrs. Wilkins-Freeman, Mrs. Annie Trumbull Slosson, Sarah Orne Jewett, Rowland Robinson, H. C. Bunner, Edward Everett Hale, Frank Stockton, Joel Chandler Harris, and "O. Henry" are some of those whose short stories are perfect in their several kinds. But the American novel, which multiplies past counting, remains an inferior production.

On a private shelf of contemporary fiction and drama in the English language are the works of ten British authors, Mr. Galsworthy, Mr. H. G. Wells, Mr. Arnold Bennett, Mr. Eden Phillpotts, Mr. George Moore, Mr. Leonard Merrick, Mr. J. C. Snaith, Miss May Sinclair, Mr. William De Morgan, Mr. Maurice Hewlett, Mr. Joseph Conrad, Mr. Bernard Shaw, yes, and Mr. Rudyard Kipling. Beside them I find but two Americans, Mrs. Edith Wharton and Mr. Theodore Dreiser. There may be others, for one cannot pretend to know all the living novelists and dramatists. Yet for every American that should be added, I would agree to add four to the British list. However, a contemporary literature that includes Mrs. Wharton's "Ethan Frome" and Mr. Dreiser's "Jennie Gerhardt" both published last year, is not to be despaired of.

In the course of a century a few Americans have said in memorable words what life meant to them. Their performance, put together, is considerable, if not imposing. Any sense of dissatisfaction that one feels in contemplating it is due to the disproportion between a limited expression and the multifarious immensity of the country. Our literature, judged by the great literatures contemporaneous with it, is insufficient to the opportunity and the need. The American Spirit may be figured as petitioning the Muses for twelve novelists, ten poets, and eight dramatists, to be delivered at the earliest possible moment.

MARY WHITE

By WILLIAM ALLEN WHITE

Mary White—one seems to know her after reading this sketch
written by her father on the day she was buried—would surely
have laughed unbelievingly if told she would be in a book of
this sort, together with Joseph Conrad, one of whose books lay
on her table. But the pen, in the honest hand, has always been
mightier than the grave.

This is not the sort of thing one wishes to mar with clumsy
comment. It was written for the Emporia *Gazette,* which William Allen White has edited since 1895. He is one of the best-
known, most public-spirited and most truly loved of American
journalists. He and his fellow-Kansan, E. W. Howe of Atchison,
are two characteristic figures in our newspaper world, both
masters of that vein of canny, straightforward, humane and
humorous simplicity that seems to be a Kansas birthright.

Mr. White was born in Emporia in 1868.

THE Associated Press reports carrying the news of
Mary White's death declared that it came as the
result of a fall from a horse. How she would have
hooted at that! She never fell from a horse in her
life. Horses have fallen on her and with her—"I'm
always trying to hold 'em in my lap," she used to say.
But she was proud of few things, and one was that
she could ride anything that had four legs and hair.
Her death resulted not from a fall, but from a blow
on the head which fractured her skull, and the blow
came from the limb of an overhanging tree on the
parking.

The last hour of her life was typical of its happiness. She came home from a day's work at school, topped off by a hard grind with the copy on the High School Annual, and felt that a ride would refresh her. She climbed into her khakis, chattering to her mother about the work she was doing, and hurried to get her horse and be out on the dirt roads for the country air and the radiant green fields of the spring. As she rode through the town on an easy gallop she kept waving at passers-by. She knew everyone in town. For a decade the little figure with the long pig-tail and the red hair ribbon has been familiar on the streets of Emporia, and she got in the way of speaking to those who nodded at her. She passed the Kerrs, walking the horse, in front of the Normal Library, and waved at them; passed another friend a few hundred feet further on, and waved at her. The horse was walking and, as she turned into North Merchant Street she took off her cowboy hat, and the horse swung into a lope. She passed the Tripletts and waved her cowboy hat at them, still moving gaily north on Merchant Street. A *Gazette* carrier passed—a High School boy friend—and she waved at him, but with her bridle hand; the horse veered quickly, plunged into the parking where the low-hanging limb faced her, and, while she still looked back waving, the blow came. But she did not fall from the horse; she slipped off, dazed a bit, staggered and fell in a faint. She never quite recovered consciousness.

But she did not fall from the horse, neither was she riding fast. A year or so ago she used to go like the wind. But that habit was broken, and she used the horse to get into the open to get fresh, hard exercise, and to work off a certain surplus energy that welled up in her and needed a physical outlet. That need has been in her heart for years. It was back of the impulse that kept the dauntless, little brown-clad figure on the streets and country roads of this community and built into a strong, muscular body what had been a frail and sickly frame during the first years of her life. But the riding gave her more than a body. It released a gay and hardy soul. She was the happiest thing in the world. And she was happy because she was enlarging her horizon. She came to know all sorts and conditions of men; Charley O'Brien, the traffic cop, was one of her best friends. W. L. Holtz, the Latin teacher, was another. Tom O'Connor, farmer-politician, and Rev. J. H. J. Rice, preacher and police judge, and Frank Beach, music master, were her special friends, and all the girls, black and white, above the track and below the track, in Pepville and Stringtown, were among her acquaintances. And she brought home riotous stories of her adventures. She loved to rollick; persiflage was her natural expression at home.

Her humor was a continual bubble of joy. She seemed to think in hyperbole and metaphor. She was mischievous wtihout malice, as full of faults as an old shoe. No angel was Mary White, but an easy girl to live with, for she never nursed a grouch five minutes in her life.

With all her eagerness for the out-of-doors, she loved books. On her table when she left her room were a book by Conrad, one by Galsworthy, "Creative Chemistry" by E. E. Slosson, and a Kipling book. She read Mark Twain, Dickens and Kipling before she was ten—all of their writings. Wells and Arnold Bennett particularly amused and diverted her. She was entered as a student in Wellesley in 1922; was assistant editor of the High School Annual this year, and in line for election to the editorship of the Annual next year. She was a member of the executive committee of the High School Y. W. C. A.

Within the last two years she had begun to be moved by an ambition to draw. She began as most children do by scribbling in her school books, funny pictures. She bought cartoon magazines and took a course— rather casually, naturally, for she was, after all, a child with no strong purposes—and this year she tasted the first fruits of success by having her pictures accepted by the High School Annual. But the thrill of delight she got when Mr. Ecord, of the Normal An-

nual, asked her to do the cartooning for that book this
spring, was too beautiful for words.   She fell to her
work with all her enthusiastic heart.   Her drawings
were accepted, and her pride—always repressed by a
lively sense of the ridiculousness of the figure she was
cutting—was a really gorgeous thing to see.   No successful artist ever drank a deeper draught of satisfaction than she took from the little fame her work was
getting among her schoolfellows.   In her glory, she
almost forgot her horse—but never her car.

For she used the car as a jitney bus.   It was her
social life.   She never had a "party" in all her nearly
seventeen years—wouldn't have one; but she never
drove a block in the car in her life that she didn't begin
to fill the car with pick-ups!   Everybody rode with
Mary White—white and black, old and young, rich
and poor, men and women.   She liked nothing better
than to fill the car full of long-legged High School
boys and an occasional girl, and parade the town.   She
never had a "date," nor went to a dance, except once
with her brother, Bill, and the "boy proposition" didn't
interest her—yet.   But young people—great spring-
breaking, varnish-cracking, fender-bending, door-
sagging carloads of "kids" gave her great pleasure.
Her zests were keen.   But the most fun she ever had
in her life was acting as chairman of the committee
that got up the big turkey dinner for the poor folks

at the county home; scores of pies, gallons of slaw; jam, cakes, preserves, oranges and a wilderness of turkey were loaded in the car and taken to the county home. And, being of a practical turn of mind, she risked her own Christmas dinner by staying to see that the poor folks actually got it all. Not that she was a cynic; she just disliked to tempt folks. While there she found a blind colored uncle, very old, who could do nothing but make rag rugs, and she rustled up from her school friends rags enough to keep him busy for a season. The last engagement she tried to make was to take the guests at the county home out for a car ride. And the last endeavor of her life was to try to get a rest room for colored girls in the High School. She found one girl reading in the toilet, because there was no better place for a colored girl to loaf, and it inflamed her sense of injustice and she became a nagging harpie to those who, she thought, could remedy the evil. The poor she had always with her, and was glad of it. She hungered and thirsted for righteousness; and was the most impious creature in the world. She joined the Congregational Church without consulting her parents; not particularly for her soul's good. She never had a thrill of piety in her life, and would have hooted at a "testimony." But even as a little child she felt the church was an agency for helping people to more of life's abundance, and she wanted to help. She never wanted help for herself. Clothes meant little to her. It was a fight to get a new rig on her; but eventually a harder fight to get it off. She never wore a jewel and had no ring but her High School class ring, and never asked for anything but a wrist watch. She refused to have her hair up; though she was nearly seventeen. "Mother," she protested, "you don't know how much I get by with, in my braided pigtails, that I could not with my hair up." Above every other passion of her life was her passion not to grow up, to be a child. The tom-boy in her, which was big, seemed to loathe to be put away forever in skirts. She was a Peter Pan, who refused to grow up.

Her funeral yesterday at the Congregational Church was as she would have wished it; no singing, no flowers save the big bunch of red roses from her Brother Bill's Harvard classmen—Heavens, how proud that would have made her! and the red roses from the *Gazette* force—in vases at her head and feet. A short prayer, Paul's beautiful essay on "Love" from the Thirteenth Chapter of First Corinthians, some remarks about her democratic spirit by her friend, John H. J. Rice, pastor and police judge, which she would have deprecated if she could, a prayer sent down for her by her friend, Carl Nau, and opening the service the slow, poignant movement from Beethoven's Moonlight Sonata, which she loved, and closing the service a cutting from the joyously melancholy first movement of Tschaikowski's Pathetic Symphony, which she liked to hear in certain moods on the phonograph; then the Lord's Prayer by her friends in the High School.

That was all.

For her pall-bearers only her friends were chosen; her Latin teacher—W. L. Holtz; her High School principal, Rice Brown; her doctor, Frank Foncannon; her friend, W. W. Finney; her pal at the *Gazette* office, Walter Hughes; and her brother Bill. It would have made her smile to know that her friend, Charley O'Brien, the traffic cop, had been transferred from Sixth and Commercial to the corner near the church to direct her friends who came to bid her good-by.

A rift in the clouds in a gray day threw a shaft of sunlight upon her coffin as her nervous, energetic little body sank to its last sleep. But the soul of her, the glowing, gorgeous, fervent soul of her, surely was flaming in eager joy upon some other dawn.

NIAGARA FALLS

By RUPERT BROOKE

The poet usually is the best reporter, for he is an observer not
merely accurate but imaginative, self-trained to see subtle suggestions, relations and similarities. This magnificent bit of de-
scription was written by Rupert Brooke as one of the letters
sent to the *Westminster Gazette* describing his trip in the United
States and Canada in 1913. It is included in the volume *Letters
from America* to which Henry James contributed so affectionate
and desperately unintelligible a preface—one of the last things
James wrote. Brooke's notes on America are well worth reading: they are full of delightful and lively comments, though
sometimes much (oh, very much!) too condescending. The last
paragraph in this essay is interesting in view of subsequent
history.

Brooke was born in 1887, son of a master at Rugby School;
was at King's College, Cambridge; died of blood-poisoning in
the Ægean, April 23, 1915.

SAMUEL BUTLER has a lot to answer for. But for
him, a modern traveler could spend his time peacefully
admiring the scenery instead of feeling himself bound
to dog the simple and grotesque of the world for the
sake of their too-human comments. It is his fault if
a peasant's *naïveté* has come to outweigh the beauty
of rivers, and the remarks of clergymen are more
than mountains. It is very restful to give up all effort
at observing human nature and drawing social and
political deductions from trifles, and to let oneself
relapse into wide-mouthed worship of the wonders of
nature. And this is very easy at Niagara. Niagara

means nothing. It is not leading anywhere. It does not result from anything. It throws no light on the effects of Protection, nor on the Facility for Divorce in America, nor on Corruption in Public Life, nor on Canadian character, nor even on the Navy Bill. It is merely a great deal of water falling over some cliffs. But it is very remarkably that. The human race, apt as a child to destroy what it admires, has done its best to surround the Falls with every distraction, incongruity, and vulgarity. Hotels, powerhouses, bridges, trams, picture post-cards, sham legends, stalls, booths, rifle-galleries, and side-shows frame them about. And there are Touts. Niagara is the central home and breeding-place for all the touts of earth. There are touts insinuating, and touts raucous, greasy touts, brazen touts, and upper-class, refined, gentlemanly, take-you-by-the-arm touts; touts who intimidate and touts who wheedle; professionals, amateurs, and *dilettanti,* male and female; touts who would photograph you with your arm round a young lady against a faked background of the sublimest cataract, touts who would bully you into cars, char-à-bancs, elevators, or tunnels, or deceive you into a carriage and pair, touts who would sell you picture post-cards, moccasins, sham Indian beadwork, blankets, tee-pees, and crockery, and touts, finally, who have no apparent object in the world, but just purely, simply, merely, incessantly, in-

defatigably, and ineffugibly to tout. And in the midst
of all this, overwhelming it all, are the Falls. He
who sees them instantly forgets humanity. They are
not very high, but they are overpowering. They are
divided by an island into two parts, the Canadian and
the American.

Half a mile or so above the Falls, on either side, the
water of the great stream begins to run more swiftly
and in confusion. It descends with ever-growing
speed. It begins chattering and leaping, breaking into
a thousand ripples, throwing up joyful fingers of spray.
Sometimes it is divided by islands and rocks, sometimes the eye can see nothing but a waste of laughing,
springing, foamy waves, turning, crossing, even seeming to stand for an instant erect, but always borne impetuously forward like a crowd of triumphant feasters.
Sit close down by it, and you see a fragment of the
torrent against the sky, mottled, steely, and foaming,
leaping onward in far-flung criss-cross strands of
water. Perpetually the eye is on the point of descry-
ing a pattern in this weaving, and perpetually it is
cheated by change. In one place part of the flood
plunges over a ledge a few feet high and a quarter of a
mile or so long, in a uniform and stable curve. It gives
an impression of almost military concerted movement,
grown suddenly out of confusion. But it is swiftly
lost again in the multitudinous tossing merriment.

Here and there a rock close to the surface is marked by a white wave that faces backwards and seems to be rushing madly up-stream, but is really stationary in the headlong charge. But for these signs of reluctance, the waters seem to fling themselves on with some foreknowledge of their fate, in an ever wilder frenzy. But it is no Maeterlinckian prescience. They prove, rather, that Greek belief that the great crashes are preceded by a louder merriment and a wilder gaiety. Leaping in the sunlight, careless, entwining, clamorously joyful, the waves riot on towards the verge.

But there they change. As they turn to the sheer descent, the white and blue and slate color, in the heart of the Canadian Falls at least, blend and deepen to a rich, wonderful, luminous green. On the edge of disaster the river seems to gather herself, to pause, to lift a head noble in ruin, and then, with a slow grandeur, to plunge into the eternal thunder and white chaos below. Where the stream runs shallower it is a kind of violet color, but both violet and green fray and frill to white as they fall. The mass of water, striking some ever-hidden base of rock, leaps up the whole two hundred feet again in pinnacles and domes of spray. The spray falls back into the lower river once more; all but a little that fines to foam and white mist, which drifts in layers along the air, graining it, and wanders out on the wind over the trees and gardens and houses, and so vanishes.

The manager of one of the great power-stations on the banks of the river above the Falls told me that the center of the riverbed at the Canadian Falls is deep and of a saucer shape. So it may be possible to fill this up to a uniform depth, and divert a lot of water for the power-houses. And this, he said, would supply the need for more power, which will certainly soon arise, without taking away from the beauty of Niagara. This is a handsome concession of the utilitarians to ordinary sight-seers. Yet, I doubt if we shall be satisfied. The real secret of the beauty and terror of the Falls is not their height or width, but the feeling of colossal power and of unintelligible disaster caused by the plunge of that vast body of water. If that were taken away, there would be little visible change, but the heart would be gone.

The American Falls do not inspire this feeling in the same way as the Canadian. It is because they are less in volume, and because the water does not fall so much into one place. By comparison their beauty is almost delicate and fragile. They are extraordinarily level, one long curtain of lacework and woven foam. Seen from opposite, when the sun is on them, they are blindingly white, and the clouds of spray show dark against them. With both Falls the color of the water is the ever-altering wonder. Greens and blues, purples and whites, melt into one another, fade, and come again, and change with the changing sun. Sometimes they are as richly diaphanous as a precious stone, and glow from within with a deep, inexplicable light. Sometimes the white intricacies of dropping foam become opaque and creamy. And always there are the rainbows. If you come suddenly upon the Falls from above, a great double rainbow, very vivid, spanning the extent of spray from top to bottom, is the first thing you see. If you wander along the cliff opposite, a bow springs into being in the American Falls, accompanies you courteously on your walk, dwindles and dies as the mist ends, and awakens again as you reach the Canadian tumult. And the bold traveler who attempts the trip under the American Falls sees, when he dare open his eyes to anything, tiny baby rainbows, some four or five yards in span, leaping from rock to rock among the foam, and gamboling beside him, barely out of hand's reach, as he goes. One I saw in that place was a complete circle, such as I have never seen before, and so near that I could put my foot on it. It is a terrifying journey, beneath and behind the Falls. The senses are battered and bewildered by the thunder of the water and the assault of wind and spray; or rather, the sound is not of falling water, but merely of falling; a noise of unspecified ruin. So, if you are close behind the endless clamor, the sight cannot recognize liquid in the masses that hurl past. You are dimly and pitifully aware that sheets of light and darkness are falling in great curves in front of you. Dull omnipresent foam washes the face. Farther away, in the roar and hissing, clouds of spray seem literally to slide down some invisible plane of air.

Beyond the foot of the Falls the river is like a slipping floor of marble, green with veins of dirty white, made by the scum that was foam. It slides very quietly and slowly down for a mile or two, sullenly exhausted. Then it turns to a dull sage green, and hurries more swiftly, smooth and omnious. As the walls of the ravine close in, trouble stirs, and the waters boil and eddy. These are the lower rapids, a sight more terrifying than the Falls, because less intelligible. Close in its bands of rock the river surges tumultuously forward, writhing and leaping as if inspired by a demon. It is pressed by the straits into a visibly convex form. Great planes of water slide past. Sometimes it is thrown up into a pinnacle of foam higher than a house, or leaps with incredible speed from the crest of one vast wave to another, along the shining curve between, like the spring of a wild beast. Its motion continually suggests muscular action. The power manifest in these rapids moves one with a different sense of awe and terror from that of the Falls. Here the inhuman life and strength are spontaneous, active, almost resolute; masculine vigor compared with the passive gigantic power, female, helpless and overwhelming, of the Falls. A place of fear.

One is drawn back, strangely, to a contemplation of the Falls, at every hour, and especially by night, when the cloud of spray becomes an immense visible ghost, straining and wavering high above the river, white and pathetic and translucent. The Victorian lies very close below the surface in every man. There one can sit and let great cloudy thoughts of destiny and the passage of empires drift through the mind; for such dreams are at home by Niagara. I could not get out of my mind the thought of a friend, who said that the rainbows over the Falls were like the arts and beauty and goodness, with regard to the stream of life—caused by it, thrown upon its spray, but unable to stay or direct or affect it, and ceasing when it ceased. In all comparisons that rise in the heart, the river, with its multitudinous waves and its single current, likens itself to a life, whether of an individual or of a community. A man's life is of many flashing moments, and yet one stream; a nation's flows through all its citizens, and yet is more than they. In such places, one is aware, with an almost insupportable and yet comforting certitude, that both men and nations are hurried onwards to their ruin or ending as inevitably as this dark flood. Some go down to it unreluctant, and meet it, like the river, not without nobility. And as incessant, as inevitable, and as unavailing as the spray that hangs over the Falls, is the white cloud of human crying. . . . With some such thoughts does the platitudinous heart win from the confusion and thunder of a Niagara peace that the quietest plains or most stable hills can never give.

THE ALMOST PERFECT STATE

By Don Marquis

Don Marquis is a real name, not a pseudonym; it is pronounced *Markwiss*, not *Markee*. I reprint here two of Mr. Marquis's amiable meditations on the "Almost Perfect State," which have appeared in the column (*The Sun Dial*) conducted by him for ten years in the New York *Sun*. According to the traditional motto of sun-dials, Mr. Marquis's horologe usually numbers only the serene hours; but sometimes, when the clear moonlight of his Muse is shining, it casts darker and even more precious shadows of satire and mysticism. His many readers know by this time the depth and reach of his fun and fancy. Marquis is a true philosopher and wit, his humor adorns a rich and mellow gravity. When strongly moved he sometimes utters an epigram that rings like steel leaving the scabbard.

There are many things to be said against American newspapers, but much of the indictment is quashed when one considers that every now and then they develop a writer like Don Marquis. The violent haste, pressure and instancy of newspaper routine, purgatorial to some temperaments, is a genuine stimulus to others—particularly if they are able, as in the case of the columnist, to fall back upon outside contributors in their intervals of pessimism or sloth.

Mr. Marquis's *The Old Soak*, a post-prohibition portrait of a genial old tippler, is perhaps the most vital bit of American humor since *Mr. Dooley*—some say since Mark Twain. His *Prefaces* and his poems will also be considered by the judicious. He was born in Illinois in 1878, and did newspaper work in Philadelphia and Atlanta before coming to the *Sun* in 1912.

I

No matter how nearly perfect an Almost Perfect State may be, it is not nearly enough perfect unless the individuals who compose it can, somewhere between death and birth, have a perfectly corking time for a few years. The most wonderful governmental system

in the world does not attract us, as a system; we are
after a system that scarcely knows it is a system; the
great thing is to have the largest number of individuals
as happy as may be, for a little while at least, some
time before they die.

Infancy is not what it is cracked up to be. The
child seems happy all the time to the adult, because
the adult knows that the child is untouched by the real
problems of life; if the adult were similarly untouched
he is sure that he would be happy. But children, not
knowing that they are having an easy time, have a
good many hard times. Growing and learning and
obeying the rules of their elders, or fighting against
them, are not easy things to do. Adolescence is certainly far from a uniformly pleasant period. Early
manhood might be the most glorious time of all were
it not that the sheer excess of life and vigor gets a
fellow into continual scrapes. Of middle age the best
that can be said is that a middle aged person has likely
learned how to have a little fun in spite of his troubles.

It is to old age that we look for reimbursement, the
most of us. And most of us look in vain. For the
most of us have been wrenched and racked, in one way
or another, until old age is the most trying time of all.

In the Almost Perfect State every person shall have
at least ten years before he dies of easy, carefree,
happy living . . . things will be so arranged economi-

cally that this will be possible for each individual.

Personally we look forward to an old age of dissipation and indolence and unreverend disrepute. In fifty years we shall be ninety-two years old. We intend to work rather hard during those fifty years and accumulate enough to live on without working any more for the next ten years, for we have determined to die at the age of one hundred and two.

During the last ten years we shall indulge ourself in many things that we have been forced by circumstances to forego. We have always been compelled, and we shall be compelled for many years to come, to be prudent, cautious, staid, sober, conservative, industrious, respectful of established institutions, a model citizen. We have not liked it, but we have been unable to escape it. Our mind, our logical faculties, our observation, inform us that the conservatives have the right side of the argument in all human affairs. But the people whom we really prefer as associates, though we do not approve their ideas, are the rebels, the radicals, the wastrels, the vicious, the poets, the Bolshevists, the idealists, the nuts, the Lucifers, the agreeable good-for-nothings, the sentimentalists, the prophets, the freaks. We have never dared to know any of them, far less become intimate with them.

Between the years of ninety-two and a hundred and two, however, we shall be the ribald, useless, drunken,

outcast person we have always wished to be. We shall
have a long white beard and long white hair; we shall
not walk at all, but recline in a wheel chair and bellow
for alcoholic beverages; in the winter we shall sit before the fire with our feet in a bucket of hot water,
with a decanter of corn whiskey near at hand, and write
ribald songs against organized society; strapped to
one arm of our chair will be a forty-five caliber re-
volver, and we shall shoot out the lights when we
want to go to sleep, instead of turning them off; when
we want air we shall throw a silver candlestick through
the front window and be damned to it; we shall address public meetings to which we have been invited
because of our wisdom in a vein of jocund malice.
We shall . . . but we don't wish to make any one
envious of the good time that is coming to us . . . we
look forward to a disreputable, vigorous, unhonored
and disorderly old age.

(In the meantime, of course, you understand, you
can't have us pinched and deported for our yearn-
ings.)

We shall know that the Almost Perfect State is here
when the kind of old age each person wants is possible
to him. Of course, all of you may not want the kind
we want . . . some of you may prefer prunes and
morality to the bitter end. Some of you may be dissolute now and may look forward to becoming like

one of the nice old fellows in a Wordsworth poem.
But for our part we have always been a hypocrite and
we shall have to continue being a hypocrite for a good
many years yet, and we yearn to come out in our true
colors at last. The point is, that no matter what you
want to be, during those last ten years, that you may
be, in the Almost Perfect State.

Any system of government under which the individual does all the sacrificing for the sake of the general good, for the sake of the community, the State,
gets off on its wrong foot. We don't want things that
cost us too much. We don't want too much strain all
the time.

The best good that you can possibly achieve is not
good enough if you have to strain yourself all the
time to reach it. A thing is only worth doing, and
doing again and again, if you can do it rather easily,
and get some joy out of it.

Do the best you can, without straining yourself too
much and too continuously, and leave the rest to God.
If you strain yourself too much you'll have to ask God
to patch you up. And for all you know, patching
you up may take time that it was planned to use some
other way.

BUT . . . overstrain yourself *now and then*. For
this reason: The things you create easily and joyously
will not continue to come easily and joyously unless

you yourself are getting bigger all the time. And when you overstrain yourself you are assisting in the creation of a new self—if you get what we mean. And if you should ask us suddenly just what this has to do with the picture of the old guy in the wheel chair we should answer: Hanged if we know, but we seemed to sort o' run into it, somehow.

II

Interplanetary communication is one of the persistent dreams of the inhabitants of this oblate spheroid on which we move, breathe and suffer for lack of beer. There seems to be a feeling in many quarters that if we could get speech with the Martians, let us say, we might learn from them something to our advantage. There is a disposition to concede the superiority of the fellows Out There . . . just as some Americans capitulate without a struggle to poets from England, rugs from Constantinople, song and sausage from Germany, religious enthusiasts from Hindustan and cheese from Switzerland, although they have not tested the goods offered and really lack the discrimination to determine their quality. Almost the only foreign importations that were ever sneezed at in this country were Swedish matches and Spanish influenza.

But are the Martians . . . if Martians there be . . . any more capable than the persons dwelling between the Woolworth Building and the Golden Horn, between Shwe Dagon and the First Church, Scientist, in Boston, Mass.? Perhaps the Martians yearn toward earth, romantically, poetically, the Romeos swearing by its light to the Juliets; the idealists and philosophers fabling that already there exists upon it an ALMOST PERFECT STATE—and now and then a wan prophet lifting his heart to its gleams, as a cup to be filled from Heaven with fresh waters of hope and courage. For this earth, it is also a star.

We know they are wrong about us, the lovers in the far stars, the philosophers, poets, the prophets . . . or *are* they wrong?

They are both right and wrong, as we are probably both right and wrong about them. If we tumbled into Mars or Arcturus or Sirius this evening we should find the people there discussing the shimmy, the jazz, the inconstancy of cooks and the iniquity of retail butchers, no doubt . . . and they would be equally disappointed by the way we flitter, frivol, flutter and flivver.

And yet, that other thing would be there too . . . that thing that made them look at our star as a symbol of grace and beauty.

Men could not think of THE ALMOST PERFECT STATE if they did not have it in them ultimately to create THE ALMOST PERFECT STATE.

We used sometimes to walk over the Brooklyn

Bridge, that song in stone and steel of an engineer who was also a great artist, at dusk, when the tides of shadow flood in from the lower bay to break in a surf of glory and mystery and illusion against the tall towers of Manhattan. Seen from the middle arch of the bridge at twilight, New York with its girdle of shifting waters and its drift of purple cloud and its quick pulsations of unstable light is a miracle of splendor and beauty that lights up the heart like the laughter of a god.

But, descend. Go down into the city. Mingle with the details. The dirty old shed from which the "L" trains and trolleys put out with their jammed and mangled thousands for flattest Flatbush and the unknown bourne of ulterior Brooklyn is still the same dirty old shed; on a hot, damp night the pasty streets stink like a paperhanger's overalls; you are trodden and over-ridden by greasy little profiteers and their hopping victims; you are encompassed round about by the ugly and the sordid, and the objectionable is exuded upon you from a myriad candid pores; your elation and your illusion vanish like ingenuous snowflakes that have kissed a hot dog sandwich on its fiery brow, and you say: "Beauty? Aw, h—l! What's the use?"

And yet you *have* seen beauty. And beauty that was created by these people and people like these. . . . You have seen the tall towers of Manhattan, wonderful under the stars. How did it come about that such growths came from such soil—that a breed lawless and sordid and prosaic has written such a mighty hieroglyphic against the sky? This glamor out of a pigsty . . . how come? How is it that this hideous, halfbrute city is also beautiful and a fit habitation for demi-gods? How come?

It comes about because the wise and subtle deities permit nothing worthy to be lost. It was with no thought of beauty that the builders labored; no conscious thought; they were masters or slaves in the bitter wars of commerce, and they never saw as a whole what they were making; no one of them did. But each one had had his dream. And the baffled dreams and the broken visions and the ruined hopes and the secret desires of each one labored with him as he labored; the things that were lost and beaten and trampled down went into the stone and steel and gave it soul; the aspiration denied and the hope abandoned and the vision defeated were the things that lived, and not the apparent purpose for which each one of all the millions sweat and toiled or cheated; the hidden things, the silent things, the winged things, so weak they are easily killed, the unacknowledged things, the rejected beauty, the strangled appreciation, the inchoate art, the submerged spirit—these groped and found each other

and gathered themselves together and worked themselves into the tiles and mortar of the edifice and made
a town that is a worthy fellow of the sunrise and the
sea winds.

Humanity triumphs over its details.

The individual aspiration is always defeated of its
perfect fruition and expression, but it is never lost;
it passes into the conglomerate being of the race.

The way to encourage yourself about the human
race is to look at it first from a distance; look at the
lights on the high spots. Coming closer, you will
be profoundly discouraged at the number of low spots,
not to say two-spots. Coming still closer, you will
become discouraged once more by the reflection that
the same stuff that is in the high spots is also in the
two-spots.

"THE MAN-O'-WAR'S 'ER 'USBAND"

By David W. Bone

Those who understand something of a sailor's feeling for his ship will appreciate the restraint with which Captain Bone describes the loss of the *Cameronia,* his command, torpedoed in the Mediterranean during the War. You will notice (forgive us for pointing out these things) how quietly the quoted title pays tribute to the gallantry of the destroyers that stood by the sinking ship; and the heroism of the chief officer's death is not less moving because told in two sentences. This superb picture of a sea tragedy is taken from *Merchantmen-at-Arms,* a history of the British Merchants' Service during the War; a book of enthralling power and truth, illustrated by the author's brother, Muirhead Bone, one of the greatest of living etchers.

David William Bone was born in Partick (near Glasgow) in 1873; his father was a well-known Glasgow journalist; his great-grandfather was a boyhood companion of Robert Burns. Bone went to sea as an apprentice in the *City of Florence,* an old-time square-rigger, at the age of fifteen; he has been at sea ever since. He is now master of S.S. *Columbia* of the Anchor Line, a well-known ship in New York Harbor, as she has carried passengers between the Clyde and the Hudson for more than twenty years. Captain Bone's fine sea tale, *The Brass-bounder,* published in 1910, has become a classic of the square-sail era; his *Broken Stowage* (1915) is a collection of shorter sea sketches. In the long roll of great writers who have reflected the simplicity and severity of sea life, Captain Bone will take a permanent and honorable place.

A sense of security is difficult of definition. Largely, it is founded upon habit and association. It is induced and maintained by familiar surroundings. On board ship, in a small world of our own, we seem to be contained by the boundaries of the bulwarks, to be sailing beyond the influences of the land and of other ships. The sea is the same we have known for so long. Every item of our ship fitment—the trim arrangement of the decks, the set and rake of mast and funnel, even the furnishings of our cabins—has the power of impressing a stable feeling of custom, normal ship life, safety. It requires an effort of thought to recall that in their homely presence we are endangered. Relating his experiences after having been mined and his ship sunk, a master confided that the point that impressed him most deeply was when he went to his room for the confidential papers and saw the cabin exactly in everyday aspect—his longshore clothes suspended from the hooks, his umbrella standing in a corner as he had placed it on coming aboard.

Soldiers on service are denied this aid to assurance. Unlike us, they cannot carry their home with them to the battlefields. All their scenes and surroundings are novel; they may only draw a reliance and comfort from the familiar presence of their comrades. At sea in a ship there is a yet greater incitement to their disquiet. The movement, the limitless sea, the distance from the land, cannot be ignored. The atmosphere that is so familiar and comforting to us, is to many of them an environment of dread possibilities.

It is with some small measure of this sense of security—tempered by our knowledge of enemy activity in these waters—we pace the bridge. **Anxiety is not**

wholly absent. Some hours past, we saw small flot-
sam that may have come from the decks of a French
mail steamer, torpedoed three days ago. The passing
of the derelict fittings aroused some disquiet, but the
steady routine of our progress and the constant friendly
presence of familiar surroundings has effect in allay-
ing immediate fears. The rounds of the bridge go on
—the writing of the log, the tapping of the glass, the
small measures that mark the passing of our sea-hours.
Two days out from Marseilles—and all well! In
another two days we should be approaching the Canal,
and then—to be clear of 'submarine waters' for a
term. Fine weather! A light wind and sea accom-
pany us for the present, but the filmy glare of the sun,
now low, and a backward movement of the glass fore-
tells a break ere long. We are steaming at high speed
to make the most of the smooth sea. Ahead, on each
bow, our two escorting destroyers conform to the
angles of our zigzag—spurring out and swerving with
the peculiar "thrown-around" movement of their class.
Look-out is alert and in numbers. Added to the watch
of the ship's crew, military signalers are posted; the
boats swung outboard have each a party of troops on
guard.

An alarmed cry from aloft—a half-uttered order
to the steersman—an explosion, low down in the bowels
of the ship, that sets her reeling in her stride!

The upthrow comes swiftly on the moment of impact. Hatches, coal, a huge column of solid water go skyward in a hurtling mass to fall in torrent on the bridge. Part of a human body strikes the awning spars and hangs—watch-keepers are borne to the deck by the weight of water—the steersman falls limply over the wheel with blood pouring from a gash on his forehead. . . . Then silence for a stunned half-minute, with only the thrust of the engines marking the heart-beats of the stricken ship.

Uproar! Most of our men are young recruits: they have been but two days on the sea. The torpedo has gone hard home at the very weakest hour of our calculated drill. The troops are at their evening meal when the blow comes, the explosion killing many outright. We had counted on a proportion of the troops being on the deck, a steadying number to balance the sudden rush from below that we foresaw in emergency. Hurrying from the mess-decks as enjoined, the quick movement gathers way and intensity: the decks become jammed by the pressure, the gangways and passages are blocked in the struggle. There is the making of a panic—tuned by their outcry, *"God! O God! O Christ!"* The swelling murmur is neither excited nor agonized—rather the dull, hopeless expression of despair.

The officer commanding troops has come on the

bridge at the first alarm. His juniors have opportunity to take their stations before the struggling mass reaches to the boats. The impossibility of getting among the men on the lower decks makes the military officers' efforts to restore confidence difficult. They are aided from an unexpected quarter. The bridge-boy makes unofficial use of our megaphone. "Hey! Steady up you men doon therr," he shouts. "Ye'll no' dae ony guid fur yersels croodin' th' ledders!"

We could not have done it as well. The lad is plainly in sight to the crowd on the decks. A small boy, undersized. "Steady up doon therr!" The effect is instant. Noise there still is, but the movement is arrested.

The engines are stopped—we are now beyond range of a second torpedo—and steam thunders in exhaust, making our efforts to control movements by voice impossible. At the moment of the impact the destroyers have swung round and are casting here and there like hounds on the scent: the dull explosion of a depth-charge—then another, rouses a fierce hope that we are not unavenged. The force of the explosion has broken connections to the wireless room, but the aerial still holds and, when a measure of order on the boat-deck allows, we send a message of our peril broadcast. There is no doubt in our minds of the outcome. Our bows, drooping visibly, tell that we shall not float long. We have nearly three thousand on board. There are boats for sixteen hundred—then rafts. Boats—rafts —and the glass is falling at a rate that shows bad weather over the western horizon!

Our drill, that provided for lowering the boats with only half-complements in them, will not serve. We pass orders to lower away in any condition, however overcrowded. The way is off the ship, and it is with some apprehension we watch the packed boats that drop away from the davit heads. The shrill ring of the block-sheaves indicates a tension that is not far from breaking-point. Many of the life-boats reach the water safely with their heavy burdens, but the strain on the tackles—far beyond their working load —is too great for all to stand to it. Two boats go down by the run. The men in them are thrown violently to the water, where they float in the wash and shattered planking. A third dangles from the after fall, having shot her manning out at parting of the forward tackle. Lowered by the stern, she rights, disengages, and drifts aft with the men clinging to the life-lines. We can make no attempt to reach the men in the water. Their life-belts are sufficient to keep them afloat: the ship is going down rapidly by the head, and there remains the second line of boats to be hoisted and swung over. The chief officer, pausing in his quick work, looks to the bridge inquiringly, as though to ask, "How long?" The fingers of two hands suffice to mark our estimate.

The decks are now angled to the deepening pitch of the bows. Pumps are utterly inadequate to make impression on the swift inflow. The chief engineer comes to the bridge with a hopeless report. It is only a question of time. How long? Already the water is lapping at a level of the foredeck. Troops massed there and on the forecastle-head are apprehensive: it is indeed a wonder that their officers have held them for so long. The commanding officer sets example by a cool nonchalance that we envy. Posted with us on the bridge, his quick eyes note the flood surging in the pent 'tween-decks below, from which his men have removed the few wounded. The dead are left to the sea.

Help comes as we had expected it would. Leaving *Nemesis* to steam fast circles round the sinking ship, *Rifleman* swings in and brings up alongside at the forward end. Even in our fear and anxiety and distress, we cannot but admire the precision of the destroyer captain's manœuver—the skilful avoidance of our crowded life-boats and the men in the water—the sudden stoppage of her way and the cant that brings her to a standstill at the lip of our brimming decks. The troops who have stood so well to orders have their reward in an easy leap to safety. Quickly the foredeck is cleared. *Rifleman* spurts ahead in a rush that sets the surrounding life-boats to eddy in her wash. She takes up the circling high-speed patrol and allows her sister ship to swing in and embark a number of our men.

It is when the most of the life-boats are gone we realize fully the gallant service of the destroyers. There remain the rafts, but many of these have been launched over to aid the struggling men in the water. Half an hour has passed since we were struck—thirty minutes of frantic endeavor to debark our men—yet still the decks are thronged by a packed mass that seems but little reduced. The coming of the destroyers alters the outlook. *Rifleman's* action has taken over six hundred. A sensible clearance! *Nemesis* swings in with the precision of an express, and the thud and clatter of the troops jumping to her deck sets up a continuous drumming note of deliverance. Alert and confident, the naval men accept the great risks of their position. The ship's bows are entered to the water at a steep incline. Every minute the balance is weighing, casting her stern high in the air. The bulkheads are by now taking place of keel and bearing the huge weight of her on the water. At any moment she may go without a warning, to crash into the light hull of the destroyer and bear her down. For all the circling

watch of her sister ship, the submarine—if still he
lives—may get in a shot at the standing target. It is
with a deep relief we signal the captain to bear off.
Her decks are jammed to the limit. She can carry
no more. *Nemesis* lists heavily under her burdened
decks as she goes ahead and clears.

Forty minutes! The zigzag clock in the wheel-
house goes on ringing the angles of time and course
as though we were yet under helm and speed. For
a short term we have noted that the ship appears to
have reached a point of arrest in her foundering
droop. She remains upright as she has been since
righting herself after the first inrush of water. Like
the lady she always was, she has added no fearsome
list to the sum of our distress. The familiar bridge,
on which so many of our safe sea-days have been
spent, is canted at an angle that makes foothold uneasy. She cannot remain for long afloat. The end
will come swiftly, without warning—a sudden rup-
ture of the bulkhead that is sustaining her weight.
We are not now many left on board. Striving and
wrenching to man-handle the only remaining boat—
rendered idle for want of the tackles that have parted
on service of its twin—we succeed in pointing her
outboard, and await a further deepening of the bows
ere launching her. Of the military, the officer commanding, some few of his juniors, a group of other

ranks, stand by. The senior officers of the ship, a muster of seamen, a few stewards, are banded with us at the last. We expect no further service of the destroyers. The position of the ship is over-menacing to any approach. They have all they can carry. Steaming at a short distance they have the appearance of being heavily overloaded; each has a staggering list and lies low in the water under their deck encumbrance. We have only the hazard of a quick out-throw of the remaining boat and the chances of a grip on floating wreckage to count upon.

On a sudden swift sheer, *Rifleman* takes the risk. Unheeding our warning hail, she steams across the bows and backs at a high speed: her rounded stern jars on our hull plates, a whaler and the davits catch on a projection and give with the ring of buckling steel—she turns on the throw of the propellers and closes aboard with a resounding impact that sets her living deck-load to stagger.

We lose no time. Scrambling down the life-ropes, our small company endeavors to get foothold on her decks. The destroyer widens off at the rebound, but by clutch of friendly hands the men are dragged aboard. One fails to reach safety. A soldier loses grip and goes to the water. The chief officer follows him. Tired and unstrung as he must be by the devoted labors of the last half-hour, he is in no condition to effect a rescue. A sudden deep rumble from within the sinking ship warns the destroyer captain to go ahead. We are given no chance to aid our shipmates: the propellers tear the water in a furious race that sweeps them away, and we draw off swiftly from the side of the ship.

We are little more than clear of the settling fore-end when the last buoyant breath of *Cameronia* is overcome. Nobly she has held afloat to the debarking of the last man. There is no further life in her. Evenly, steadily, as we had seen her leave the launching ways at Meadowside, she goes down.

THE MARKET

By WILLIAM McFEE

William McFee's name is associated with the sea, but in his writing he treats the life of ships and sailors more as a background than as the essential substance of his tale. I have chosen this brief and colorful little sketch to represent his talent because it is different from the work with which most of his readers are familiar, and because it represents a mood very characteristic of him—an imaginative and observant treatment of the workings of commerce. His interest in fruit is intimate, as he has been for some years an engineer in the sea service of the United Fruit Company, with a Mediterranean interim—reflected in much of his recent writing—during the War.

The publication of McFee's *Casuals of the Sea* in 1916 was something of an event in the world of books, and introduced to the reading world a new writer of unquestionable strength and subtlety. His earlier books, *An Ocean Tramp* and *Aliens* (both republished since), had gone almost unnoticed—which, it is safe to say, will not happen again to anything he cares to publish. His later books are *Captain Macedoine's Daughter, Harbours of Memory,* and *An Engineer's Notebook*. He was born at sea in 1881, the son of a sea-captain; grew up in a northern suburb of London, served his apprenticeship in a big engineering shop, and has been in ships most of the time since 1905.

THERE is a sharp, imperative rap on my outer door; a rap having within its insistent urgency a shadow of delicate diffidence, as though the person responsible were a trifle scared of the performance and on tiptoe to run away. I roll over and regard the clock. Four-forty. One of the dubious by-products of continuous service as a senior assistant at sea is the habit of waking automatically about 4 A. M. This gives one several hours, when ashore, to meditate upon one's sins,

frailties, and (more rarely) triumphs and virtues.
For a man who gets up at say four-thirty is regarded
with aversion ashore. His family express themselves
with superfluous vigor. He must lie still and meditate, or suffer the ignominy of being asked when he
is going away again.

But this morning, in these old Chambers in an
ancient Inn buried in the heart of London City, I
have agreed to get up and go out. The reason for
this momentous departure from a life of temporary
but deliberate indolence is a lady. "Cherchez la
femme," as the French say with the dry animosity of
a logical race. Well, she is not far to seek, being
on the outside of my heavy oak door, tapping, as already hinted, with a sharp insistent delicacy. To
this romantic summons I reply with an articulate growl
of acquiescence, and proceed to get ready. To relieve
the anxiety of any reader who imagines an impend-
ing elopement it may be stated in succinct truthfulness
that we are bound on no such desperate venture. We
are going round the corner a few blocks up the Strand,
to Covent Garden Market, to see the arrival of the
metropolitan supply of produce.

Having accomplished a hasty toilet, almost as prim-
itive as that favored by gentlemen aroused to go on
watch, and placating an occasional repetition of the
tapping by brief protests and reports of progress, I

take hat and cane, and drawing the huge antique bolts of my door, discover a young woman standing by the window looking out upon the quadrangle of the old Inn. She is a very decided young woman, who is continually thinking out what she calls "stunts" for articles in the press. That is her profession, or one of her professions—writing articles for the press. The other profession is selling manuscripts, which constitutes the tender bond between us. For the usual agent's commission she is selling one of my manuscripts. Being an unattached and, as it were, unprotected male, she plans little excursions about London to keep me instructed and entertained. Here she is attired in the flamboyant finery of a London flowergirl. She is about to get the necessary copy for a special article in a morning paper. With the exception of a certain expectant flash of her bright black Irish eyes, she is entirely businesslike. Commenting on the beauty of an early summer morning in town, we descend, and passing out under the ponderous ancient archway, we make our leisurely progress westward down the Strand.

London is always beautiful to those who love and understand that extraordinary microcosm; but at five of a summer morning there is about her an exquisite quality of youthful fragrance and debonair freshness which goes to the heart. The newly-hosed streets are shining in the sunlight as though paved with "patines of bright gold." Early 'buses rumble by from neighboring barns where they have spent the night. And, as we near the new Gaiety Theatre, thrusting forward into the great rivers of traffic soon to pour round its base like some bold Byzantine promontory, we see Waterloo Bridge thronged with wagons, piled high. From all quarters they are coming, past Charing Cross the great wains are arriving from Paddington Terminal, from the market-garden section of Middlesex and Surrey. Down Wellington Street come carts laden with vegetables from Brentwood and Coggeshall, and neat vans packed with crates of watercress which grows in the lush lowlands of Suffolk and Cambridgeshire, and behind us are thundering huge four-horse vehicles from the docks, vehicles with peaches from South Africa, potatoes from the Canary Islands, onions from France, apples from California, oranges from the West Indies, pineapples from Central America, grapes from Spain and bananas from Colombia.

We turn in under an archway behind a theatre and adjacent to the stage-door of the Opera House. The booths are rapidly filling with produce. Gentlemen in long alpaca coats and carrying formidable marbled note-books walk about with an important air. A mountain range of pumpkins rises behind a

hill of cabbages. Festoons of onions are being suspended from rails. The heads of barrels are being
knocked in, disclosing purple grapes buried in cork-
dust. Pears and figs, grown under glass for wealthy
patrons, repose in soft tissue-lined boxes. A broken
crate of tangerine oranges has spilled its contents in
a splash of ruddy gold on the plank runway. A
wagon is driven in, a heavy load of beets, and the
broad wheels crush through the soft fruit so that the
air is heavy with the acrid sweetness.

We pick our way among the booths and stalls until
we find the flowers. Here is a crowd of ladies, young,
so-so and some quite matronly, and all dressed in
this same flamboyant finery of which I have spoken.
They are grouped about an almost overpowering mass
of blooms. Roses just now predominate. There is
a satisfying solidity about the bunches, a glorious
abundance which, in a commodity so easily enjoyed
without ownership, is scarcely credible. I feel no
desire to own these huge aggregations of odorous
beauty. It would be like owning a harem, one imagines. Violets, solid patches of vivid blue in round
baskets, eglantine in dainty boxes, provide a foil to
the majestic blazonry of the roses and the dew-
spangled forest of maiden-hair fern near by.

"And what are those things at all?" demands my
companion, diverted for a moment from the flowers.

She nods towards a mass of dull-green affairs piled on mats or being lifted from big vans. She is a Cockney and displays surprise when she is told those things are bananas. She shrugs and turns again to the musk-roses, and forgets. But to me, as the harsh, penetrating odor of the green fruit cuts across the heavy perfume of the flowers, comes a picture of the farms in distant Colombia or perhaps Costa Rica. There is nothing like an odor to stir memories. I see the timber pier and the long line of rackety open-slatted cars jangling into the dark shed, pushed by a noisy, squealing locomotive. I see the boys lying asleep between shifts, their enormous straw hats covering their faces as they sprawl. In the distance rise the blue mountains; behind is the motionless blue sea. I hear the whine of the elevators, the monotonous click of the counters, the harsh cries of irresponsible and argumentative natives. I feel the heat of the tropic day, and see the gleam of the white waves breaking on yellow sands below tall palms. I recall the mysterious impenetrable solitude of the jungle, a solitude alive, if one is equipped with knowledge, with a ceaseless warfare of winged and crawling hosts. And while my companion is busily engaged in getting copy for a special article about the Market, I step nimbly out of the way of a swarthy gentleman from Calabria, who with his two-wheeled barrow is the last link in the immense chain of transportation connecting the farmer in the distant tropics and the cockney pedestrian who halts on the sidewalk and purchases a banana for a couple of pennies.

HOLY IRELAND

By JOYCE KILMER

This echo of the A.E.F. is probably the best thing Joyce Kilmer ever wrote, and shows the vein of real tenderness and insight that lay beneath his lively and versatile career on Grub Street. In him, as in many idealists, the Irish theme had become legendary, it was part of his religion and his dream-life, and he treated it with real affection and humor. You will find it cropping out many times in his verses. The Irish problem as it is reflected in this country is not always clearly understood. Ireland, in the minds of our poets, is a mystical land of green hills, saints and leprechauns, and its political problems are easy.

Joyce Kilmer was born in New Brunswick in 1886; studied at Rutgers College and Columbia University; taught school; worked on the staff of the Standard Dictionary; passed through phases of socialism and Anglicanism into the Catholic communion, and joined the Sunday staff of the New York *Times* in 1913. He was killed fighting in France in 1918. This sketch is taken from the second of the three volumes in which Robert Cortes Holliday, his friend and executor, has collected Joyce Kilmer's work.

WE had hiked seventeen miles that stormy December day—the third of a four days' journey. The snow was piled high on our packs, our rifles were crusted with ice, the leather of our hob-nailed boots was frozen stiff over our lamed feet. The weary lieutenant led us to the door of a little house in a side street.

"Next twelve men," he said. A dozen of us dropped out of the ranks and dragged ourselves over the threshold. We tracked snow and mud over a spotless stone floor. Before an open fire stood Madame and the three children—a girl of eight years, a boy of five, a boy of three. They stared with round frightened eyes at les soldats Americans, the first they had ever seen. We were too tired to stare back. We at once climbed to the chill attic, our billet, our lodging for the night. First we lifted the packs from one another's aching shoulders: then, without spreading our blankets, we lay down on the bare boards.

For ten minutes there was silence, broken by an occasional groan, an oath, the striking of a match. Cigarettes glowed like fireflies in a forest. Then a voice came from the corner:

"Where is Sergeant Reilly?" it said. We lazily searched. There was no Sergeant Reilly to be found.

"I'll bet the old bum has gone out after a pint," said the voice. And with the curiosity of the American and the enthusiasm of the Irish we lumbered downstairs in quest of Sergeant Reilly.

He was sitting on a low bench by the fire. His shoes were off and his bruised feet were in a pail of cold water. He was too good a soldier to expose them to the heat at once. The little girl was on his lap and the little boys stood by and envied him. And in a voice that twenty years of soldiering and oceans of whisky had failed to rob of its Celtic sweetness, he was softly singing: "Ireland Isn't Ireland Any More." We listened respectfully.

"They cheer the King and then salute him," said Sergeant Reilly.

"A regular Irishman would shoot him," and we all joined in the chorus, "Ireland Isn't Ireland Any More."

"Ooh, la, la!" exclaimed Madame, and she and all the children began to talk at the top of their voices. What they said Heaven knows, but the tones were friendly, even admiring.

"Gentlemen," said Sergeant Reilly from his post of honor, "the lady who runs this billet is a very nice lady indeed. She says yez can all take off your shoes and dry your socks by the fire. But take turns and don't crowd or I'll turn yez all upstairs."

Now Madame, a woman of some forty years, was a true bourgeoise, with all the thrift of her class. And by the terms of her agreement with the authorities she was required to let the soldiers have for one night the attic of her house to sleep in—nothing more; no light, no heat. Also, wood is very expensive in France— for reasons that are engraven in letters of blood on the pages of history. Nevertheless—

"Asseyez-vous, s'il vous plait," said Madame. And she brought nearer to the fire all the chairs the establishment possessed and some chests and boxes to be used as seats. And she and the little girl, whose name was Solange, went out into the snow and came back with heaping armfuls of small logs. The fire blazed merrily—more merrily than it had blazed since August, 1914, perhaps. We surrounded it, and soon the air was thick with steam from our drying socks.

Meanwhile Madame and the Sergeant had generously admitted all eleven of us into their conversation. A spirited conversation it was, too, in spite of the fact that she knew no English and the extent of his French was "du pain," "du vin," "cognac" and "bon jour." Those of us who knew a little more of the language of the country acted as interpreters for the others. We learned the names of the children and their ages. We learned that our hostess was a widow. Her husband had fallen in battle just one month before our arrival in her home. She showed us with simple pride and affection and restrained grief his picture. Then she showed us those of her two brothers —one now fighting at Salonica, the other a prisoner of war—of her mother and father, of herself dressed for First Communion.

This last picture she showed somewhat shyly, as if doubting that we would understand it. But when one of us asked in halting French if Solange, her little daughter, had yet made her First Communion, then Madame's face cleared.

"Mais oui!" she exclaimed, "Et vous, ma foi, vous êtes Catholiques, n'est-ce pas?"

At once rosary beads were flourished to prove our right to answer this question affirmatively. Tattered prayer-books and somewhat dingy scapulars were brought to light. Madame and the children chattered their surprise and delight to each other, and every exhibit called for a new outburst.

"Ah, le bon S. Benoit! Ah, voilà, le Conception Immacule! Ooh la la, le Sacré Cœur!" (which last exclamation sounded in no wise as irreverent as it looks in print).

Now other treasures, too, were shown—treasures chiefly photographic. There were family groups, there were Coney Island snapshots. And Madame and the children were a gratifyingly appreciative audience. They admired and sympathized; they exclaimed appropriately at the beauty of every girl's face, the tenderness of every pictured mother. We had become the intimates of Madame. She had admitted us into her family and we her into ours.

Soldiers—American soldiers of Irish descent—have souls and hearts. These organs (if the soul may be so termed) had been satisfied. But our stomachs remained—and that they yearned was evident to us. We had made our hike on a meal of hardtack and "corned willy." Mess call would sound soon. Should we force our wet shoes on again and plod through the snowy streets to the temporary mess-shack? We knew our supply wagons had not succeeded in climbing the last hill into town, and that therefore bread and unsweetened coffee would be our portion. A great depression settled upon us.

But Sergeant Reilly rose to the occasion.

"Boys," he said, "this here lady has got a good fire going, and I'll bet she can cook. What do you say we get her to fix us up a meal?"

The proposal was received joyously at first. Then some one said:

"But I haven't got any money." "Neither have I —not a damn sou!" said another. And again the spiritual temperature of the room fell.

Again Sergeant Reilly spoke:

"I haven't got any money to speak of, meself," he said. "But let's have a show-down. I guess we've got enough to buy somethin' to eat."

It was long after pay-day, and we were not hopeful of the results of the search. But the wealthy (that is, those who had two francs) made up for the poor (that is, those who had two sous). And among the coins on the table I noticed an American dime, an English half-crown and a Chinese piece with a square hole in the center. In negotiable tender the money came in all to eight francs.

It takes more money than that to feed twelve hungry soldiers these days in France. But there was no harm in trying. So an ex-seminarian, an ex-bookkeeper and an ex-street-car conductor aided Sergeant Reilly in explaining in French that had both a brogue and a Yankee twang that we were hungry, that this was all the money we had in the world, and that we wanted her to cook us something to eat.

Now Madame was what they call in New England a "capable" woman. In a jiffy she had the money in Solange's hand and had that admirable child cloaked and wooden-shod for the street, and fully informed as to what she was to buy. What Madame and the children had intended to have for supper I do not know, for there was nothing in the kitchen but the fire, the stove, the table, some shelves of dishes and an enormous bed. Nothing in the way of a food cupboard could be seen. And the only other room of the house was the bare attic.

When Solange came back she carried in a basket bigger than herself these articles: (1) two loaves of war-bread; (2) five bottles of red wine; (3) three cheeses; (4) numerous potatoes; (5) a lump of fat; (6) a bag of coffee. The whole represented, as was afterward demonstrated, exactly the sum of ten francs, fifty centimes.

Well, we all set to work peeling potatoes. Then with a veritable French trench-knife Madame cut the potatoes into long strips. Meanwhile Solange had put the lump of fat into the big black pot that hung by a chain over the fire. In the boiling grease the potatoes were placed, Madame standing by with a big ladle punched full of holes (I regret that I do not know the technical name for this instrument) and keeping the potato-strips swimming, zealously frustrating any attempt on their part to lie lazily at the bottom of the pot.

We forgot all about the hike as we sat at supper that evening. The only absentees were the two little boys, Michael and Paul. And they were really absent only from our board—they were in the room, in the great built-in bed that was later to hold also Madame and Solange. Their little bodies were covered by the three-foot thick mattress-like red silk quilt, but their tousled heads protruded and they watched us unblinkingly all the evening.

But just as we sat down, before Sergeant Reilly began his task of dishing out the potatoes and starting the bottles on their way, Madame stopped her chattering and looked at Solange. And Solange stopped her chattering and looked at Madame. And they both looked rather searchingly at us. We didn't know what was the matter, but we felt rather embarrassed.

Then Madame began to talk, slowly and loudly, as one talks to make foreigners understand. And the gist of her remarks was that she was surprised to see that American Catholics did not say grace before eating like French Catholics.

We sprang to our feet at once. But it was not Sergeant Reilly who saved the situation. Instead, the ex-seminarian (he is only temporarily an ex-seminarian; he'll be preaching missions and giving retreats yet if a bit of shrapnel doesn't hasten his journey to Heaven) said, after we had blessed ourselves: "Benedicite; nos et quae sumus sumpturi benedicat Deus, Pater et Filius et Spiritus Sanctus. Amen."

Madame and Solange, obviously relieved, joined us in the Amen, and we sat down again to eat.

It was a memorable feast. There was not much conversation—except on the part of Madame and Solange—but there was plenty of good cheer. Also there was enough cheese and bread and wine and potatoes for all of us—half starved as we were when we sat down. Even big Considine, who drains a can of condensed milk at a gulp and has been known to eat an apple pie without stopping to take breath, was satisfied. There were toasts, also, all proposed by Sergeant Reilly—toasts to Madame, and to the children, and to France, and to the United States, and to the Old Gray Mare (this last toast having an esoteric significance apparent only to illuminati of Sergeant Reilly's circle).

The table cleared and the "agimus tibi gratias" duly

said, we sat before the fire, most of us on the floor.
We were warm and happy and full of good food and
good wine. I spied a slip of paper on the floor by
Solange's foot and unashamedly read it. It was an
accounting for the evening's expenditures—totaling
exactly ten francs and fifty centimes.

Now when soldiers are unhappy—during a long,
hard hike, for instance—they sing to keep up their
spirits. And when they are happy, as on the evening now under consideration, they sing to express
their satisfaction with life. We sang "Sweet Rosie
O'Grady." We shook the kitchen-bedroom with the
echoes of "Take Me Back to New York Town." We
informed Madame, Solange, Paul, Michael, in fact,
the whole village, that we had never been a wanderer
and that we longed for our Indiana home. We grew
sentimental over "Mother Machree." And Sergeant
Reilly obliged with a reel—in his socks—to an accomplishment of whistling and handclapping.

Now, it was our hostess's turn to entertain. We
intimated as much. She responded, first by much talk,
much consultation with Solange, and finally by going
to one of the shelves that held the pans and taking
down some paper-covered books.

There was more consultation, whispered this time,
and much turning of pages. Then, after some preliminary coughing and humming, the music began

—the woman's rich alto blending with the child's shrill but sweet notes. And what they sang was "Tantum ergo Sacramentum."

Why she should have thought that an appropriate song to offer this company of rough soldiers from a distant land I do not know. And why we found it appropriate it is harder still to say. But it did seem appropriate to all of us—to Sergeant Reilly, to Jim (who used to drive a truck), to Larry (who sold cigars), to Frank (who tended a bar on Fourteenth Street). It seemed, for some reason, eminently fitting. Not one of us then or later expressed any surprise that this hymn, familiar to most of us since our mothers first led us to the Parish Church down the pavements of New York or across the Irish hills, should be sung to us in this strange land and in these strange circumstances.

Since the gracious Latin of the Church was in order and since the season was appropriate, one of us suggested "Adeste Fideles" for the next item on the evening's program. Madame and Solange and our ex-seminarian knew all the words and the rest of us came in strong with "Venite, adoremus Dominum."

Then, as if to show that piety and mirth may live together, the ladies obliged with "Au Clair de la Lune" and other simple ballads of old France. And after taps had sounded in the street outside our door, and

there was yawning, and wrist-watches were being
scanned, the evening's entertainment ended, by general
consent, with patriotic selections. We sang—as best
we could—the "Star-Spangled Banner," Solange and
her mother humming the air and applauding at the
conclusion. Then we attempted "La Marseillaise."
Of course, we did not know the words. Solange came
to our rescue with two little pamphlets containing the
song, so we looked over each other's shoulders and got
to work in earnest. Madame sang with us, and Solange. But during the final stanza Madame did not
sing. She leaned against the great family bedstead
and looked at us. She had taken one of the babies
from under the red comforter and held him to her
breast. One of her red and toil-scarred hands half
covered his fat little back. There was a gentle dignity
about that plain, hard-working woman, that soldier's
widow—we all felt it. And some of us saw the tears
in her eyes.

There are mists, faint and beautiful and unchang-
ing, that hang over the green slopes of some mountains I know. I have seen them on the Irish hills and
I have seen them on the hills of France. I think that
they are made of the tears of good brave women.

Before I went to sleep that night I exchanged a few
words with Sergeant Reilly. We lay side by side
on the floor, now piled with straw. Blankets, shelter-

halves, slickers and overcoats insured warm sleep.
Sergeant Reilly's hard old face was wrapped round
with his muffler. The final cigarette of the day burned
lazily in a corner of his mouth.

"That was a pretty good evening, Sarge," I said.
"We sure were in luck when we struck this billet."

He grunted affirmatively, then puffed in silence for
a few minutes. Then he deftly spat the cigarette into
a strawless portion of the floor, where it glowed for a
few seconds before it went out.

"You said it," he remarked. "We were in luck is
right. What do you know about that lady, anyway?"

"Why," I answered, "I thought she treated us pretty
white."

"Joe," said Sergeant Reilly, "do you realize how
much trouble that woman took to make this bunch
of roughnecks comfortable? She didn't make a damn
cent on that feed, you know. The kid spent all the
money we give her. And she's out about six francs
for firewood, too—I wish to God I had the money
to pay her. I bet she'll go cold for a week now, and
hungry, too.

"And that ain't all," he continued, after a pause
broken only by an occasional snore from our blissful
neighbors. "Look at the way she cooked them pomme
de terres and fixed things up for us and let us sit
down there with her like we was her family. And

look at the way she and the little Sallie there sung for us.

"I tell you, Joe, it makes me think of old times to hear a woman sing them church hymns to me that way. It's forty years since I heard a hymn sung in a kitchen, and it was my mother, God rest her, that sang them. I sort of realize what we're fighting for now, and I never did before. It's for women like that and their kids.

"It gave me a turn to see her a-sitting there singing them hymns. I remembered when I was a boy in Shangolden. I wonder if there's many women like that in France now—telling their beads and singing the old hymns and treating poor traveling men the way she's just after treating us. There used to be lots of women like that in the Old Country. And I think that's why it was called 'Holy Ireland.' "

A FAMILIAR PREFACE

By Joseph Conrad

This glorious expression of the credo of all artists, in whatever form of creation, lastingly enriches the English tongue. It is from the preface to *A Personal Record*, that fascinating autobiographical volume in which Conrad tells the curious story of a Polish boy who ran away to sea and began to write in English. As a companion piece, those who have the honor of the writer's craft at heart should read Conrad's preface to *The Nigger of the Narcissus*.

"All ambitions are lawful except those which climb upward on the miseries or credulities of mankind." Is it permissible to wonder what some newspaper owners—say Mr. Hearst—would reply to that?

Mr. Conrad's career is too well known to be annotated here. If by any chance the reader is not acquainted with it, it will be to his soul's advantage to go to a public library and look it up.

As a general rule we do not want much encouragement to talk about ourselves; yet this little book * is the result of a friendly suggestion, and even of a little friendly pressure. I defended myself with some spirit; but, with characteristic tenacity, the friendly voice insisted, "You know, you really must."

It was not an argument, but I submitted at once. If one must! . . .

You perceive the force of a word. He who wants to persuade should put his trust not in the right argument, but in the right word. The power of sound

* *A Personal Record.*

has always been greater than the power of sense. I don't say this by way of disparagement. It is better for mankind to be impressionable than reflective. Nothing humanely great—great, I mean, as affecting a whole mass of lives—has come from reflection. On the other hand, you cannot fail to see the power of mere words; such words as Glory, for instance, or Pity. I won't mention any more. They are not far to seek. Shouted with perseverance, with ardor, with conviction, these two by their sound alone have set whole nations in motion and upheaved the dry, hard ground on which rests our whole social fabric. There's "virtue" for you if you like! . . . Of course, the accent must be attended to. The right accent. That's very important. The capacious lung, the thundering or the tender vocal chords. Don't talk to me of your Archimedes' lever. He was an absent-minded person with a mathematical imagination. Mathematics commands all my respect, but I have no use for engines. Give me the right word and the right accent and I will move the world.

What a dream for a writer! Because written words have their accent, too. Yes! Let me only find the right word! Surely it must be lying somewhere among the wreckage of all the plaints and all the exultations poured out aloud since the first day when hope, the undying, came down on earth. It may be there, close by, disregarded, invisible, quite at hand. But it's no good. I believe there are men who can lay hold of a needle in a pottle of hay at the first try. For myself, I have never had such luck.

And then there is that accent. Another difficulty. For who is going to tell whether the accent is right or wrong till the word is shouted, and fails to be heard, perhaps, and goes down-wind, leaving the world unmoved? Once upon a time there lived an emperor who was a sage and something of a literary man. He jotted down on ivory tablets thoughts, maxims, reflections which chance has preserved for the edification of posterity. Among other sayings—I am quoting from memory—I remember this solemn admonition: "Let all thy words have the accent of heroic truth." The accent of heroic truth! This is very fine, but I am thinking that it is an easy matter for an austere emperor to jot down grandiose advice. Most of the working truths on this earth are humble, not heroic; and there have been times in the history of mankind when the accents of heroic truth have moved it to nothing but derision.

Nobody will expect to find between the covers of this little book words of extraordinary potency or accents of irresistible heroism. However humiliating for my self-esteem, I must confess that the counsels of Marcus Aurelius are not for me. They are more fit for a moralist than for an artist. Truth of a modest sort I can promise you, and also sincerity. That complete, praiseworthy sincerity which, while it delivers one into the hands of one's enemies, is as likely as not to embroil one with one's friends.

"Embroil" is perhaps too strong an expression. I can't imagine among either my enemies or my friends a being so hard up for something to do as to quarrel with me. "To disappoint one's friends" would be nearer the mark. Most, almost all, friendships of the writing period of my life have come to me through my books; and I know that a novelist lives in his work. He stands there, the only reality in an invented world, among imaginary things, happenings, and people. Writing about them, he is only writing about himself. But the disclosure is not complete. He remains, to a certain extent, a figure behind the veil; a suspected rather than a seen presence—a movement and a voice behind the draperies of fiction. In these personal notes there is no such veil. And I cannot help thinking of a passage in the "Imitation of Christ" where the ascetic author, who knew life so profoundly, says that "there are persons esteemed on their reputation who by showing themselves destroy the opinion one had of them." This is the danger incurred by an author of fiction who sets out to talk about himself without disguise.

While these reminiscent pages were appearing serially I was remonstrated with for bad economy; as if such writing were a form of self-indulgence wasting the substance of future volumes. It seems that I am not sufficiently literary. Indeed, a man who never wrote a line for print till he was thirty-six cannot bring himself to look upon his existence and his experience, upon the sum of his thoughts, sensations, and emotions, upon his memories and his regrets, and the whole possession of his past, as only so much material for his hands. Once before, some three years ago, when I published "The Mirror of the Sea," a volume of impressions and memories, the same remarks were made to me. Practical remarks. But, truth to say, I have never understood the kind of thrift they recommend. I wanted to pay my tribute to the sea, its ships and its men, to whom I remain indebted for so much which has gone to make me what I am. That seemed to me the only shape in which I could offer it to their shades. There could not be a question in my mind of anything else. It is quite possible that I am a bad economist; but it is certain that I am incorrigible.

Having matured in the surroundings and under the special conditions of sea life, I have a special piety toward that form of my past; for its impressions were vivid, its appeal direct, its demands such as could be responded to with the natural elation of youth and strength equal to the call. There was nothing in them to perplex a young conscience. Having broken away from my origins under a storm of blame from every quarter which had the merest shadow of right to voice an opinion, removed by great distances from such natural affections as were still left to me, and even estranged, in a measure, from them by the totally unintelligible character of the life which had seduced me so mysteriously from my allegiance, I may safely say that through the blind force of circumstances the sea was to be all my world and the merchant service my only home for a long succession of years. No wonder, then, that in my two exclusively sea books —"The Nigger of the Narcissus," and "The Mirror of the Sea" (and in the few short sea stories like "Youth" and "Typhoon")—I have tried with an almost filial regard to render the vibration of life in the great world of waters, in the hearts of the simple men who have for ages traversed its solitudes, and also that something sentient which seems to dwell in ships —the creatures of their hands and the objects of their care.

One's literary life must turn frequently for sustenance to memories and seek discourse with the shades, unless one has made up one's mind to write only in order to reprove mankind for what it is, or praise it for what it is not, or—generally—to teach it how to behave. Being neither quarrelsome, nor a flatterer, nor a sage, I have done none of these things, and I am prepared to put up serenely with the insignificance which attaches to persons who are not meddlesome in some way or other. But resignation is not indifference. I would not like to be left standing as a mere spectator on the bank of the great stream carrying onward so many lives. I would fain claim for myself the faculty of so much insight as can be expressed in a voice of sympathy and compassion.

It seems to me that in one, at least, authoritative quarter of criticism I am suspected of a certain unemotional, grim acceptance of facts—of what the French would call *sécheresse du cœur*. Fifteen years of unbroken silence before praise or blame testify sufficiently to my respect for criticism, that fine flower of personal expression in the garden of letters. But this is more of a personal matter, reaching the man behind the work, and therefore it may be alluded to in a volume which is a personal note in the margin of the public page. Not that I feel hurt in the least. The charge—if it amounted to a charge at all—was made in the most considerate terms; in a tone of regret.

My answer is that if it be true that every novel contains an element of autobiography—and this can hardly

be denied, since the creator can only express himself
in his creation—then there are some of us to whom
an open display of sentiment is repugnant. I would
not unduly praise the virtue of restraint. It is often
merely temperamental. But it is not always a sign of
coldness. It may be pride. There can be nothing
more humiliating than to see the shaft of one's emotion miss the mark of either laughter or tears. Nothing more humiliating! And this for the reason that
should the mark be missed, should the open display
of emotion fail to move, then it must perish unavoid-
ably in disgust or contempt. No artist can be re-
proached for shrinking from a risk which only fools
run to meet and only genius dare confront with im-
punity. In a task which mainly consists in laying one's
soul more or less bare to the world, a regard for
decency, even at the cost of success, is but the regard
for one's own dignity which is inseparably united
with the dignity of one's work.

And then—it is very difficult to be wholly joyous or
wholly sad on this earth. The comic, when it is human,
soon takes upon itself a face of pain; and some of our
griefs (some only, not all, for it is the capacity for
suffering which makes man august in the eyes of men)
have their source in weaknesses which must be recognized with smiling compassion as the common in-
heritance of us all. Joy and sorrow in this world

pass into each other, mingling their forms and their murmurs in the twilight of life as mysterious as an overshadowed ocean, while the dazzling brightness of supreme hopes lies far off, fascinating and still, on the distant edge of the horizon.

Yes! I, too, would like to hold the magic wand giving that command over laughter and tears which is declared to be the highest achievement of imaginative literature. Only, to be a great magician one must surrender oneself to occult and irresponsible powers, either outside or within one's breast. We have all heard of simple men selling their souls for love or power to some grotesque devil. The most ordinary intelligence can perceive without much reflection that anything of the sort is bound to be a fool's bargain. I don't lay claim to particular wisdom because of my dislike and distrust of such transactions. It may be my sea training acting upon a natural disposition to keep good hold on the one thing really mine, but the fact is that I have a positive horror of losing even for one moving moment that full possession of myself which is the first condition of good service. And I have carried my notion of good service from my earlier into my later existence. I, who have never sought in the written word anything else but a form of the Beautiful—I have carried over that article of creed from the decks of ships to the more circumscribed space of my desk, and by that act, I suppose, I have become permanently imperfect in the eyes of the ineffable company of pure esthetes.

As in political so in literary action a man wins friends for himself mostly by the passion of his prejudices and by the consistent narrowness of his outlook. But I have never been able to love what was not lovable or hate what was not hateful out of deference for some general principle. Whether there be any courage in making this admission I know not. After the middle turn of life's way we consider dangers and joys with a tranquil mind. So I proceed in peace to declare that I have always suspected in the effort to bring into play the extremities of emotions the debasing touch of insincerity. In order to move others deeply we must deliberately allow ourselves to be carried away beyond the bounds of our normal sensibility—innocently enough, perhaps, and of necessity, like an actor who raises his voice on the stage above the pitch of natural conversation—but still we have to do that. And surely this is no great sin. But the danger lies in the writer becoming the victim of his own exaggeration, losing the exact notion of sincerity, and in the end coming to despise truth itself as something too cold, too blunt for his purpose—as, in fact, not good enough for his insistent emotion.

From laughter and tears the descent is easy to snivelling and giggles.

These may seem selfish considerations; but you can't, in sound morals, condemn a man for taking care of his own integrity. It is his clear duty. And least of all can you condemn an artist pursuing, however humbly and imperfectly, a creative aim. In that interior world where his thought and his emotions go seeking for the experience of imagined adventures, there are no policemen, no law, no pressure of circumstance or dread of opinion to keep him within bounds. Who then is going to say Nay to his temptations if not his conscience?

And besides—this, remember, is the place and the moment of perfectly open talk—I think that all ambitions are lawful except those which climb upward on the miseries or credulities of mankind. All intellectual and artistic ambitions are permissible, up to and even beyond the limit of prudent sanity. They can hurt no one. If they are mad, then so much the worse for the artist. Indeed, as virtue is said to be, such ambitions are their own reward. Is it such a very mad presumption to believe in the sovereign power of one's art, to try for other means, for other ways of affirming this belief in the deeper appeal of one's work? To try to go deeper is not to be insensible.

A historian of hearts is not a historian of emotions, yet he penetrates further, restrained as he may be, since his aim is to reach the very fount of laughter and tears. The sight of human affairs deserves admiration and pity. They are worthy of respect, too. And he is not insensible who pays them the undemonstrative tribute of a sigh which is not a sob, and of a smile which is not a grin. Resignation, not mystic, not detached, but resignation open-eyed, conscious, and informed by love, is the only one of our feelings for which it is impossible to become a sham.

Not that I think resignation the last word of wisdom. I am too much the creature of my time for that. But I think that the proper wisdom is to will what the gods will without, perhaps, being certain what their will is—or even if they have a will of their own. And in this matter of life and art it is not the Why that matters so much to our happiness as the How. As the Frenchman said, *"Il y a toujours la manière."* Very true. Yes. There is the manner. The manner in laughter, in tears, in irony, in indignations and enthusiasms, in judgments—and even in love. The manner in which, as in the features and character of a human face, the inner truth is foreshadowed for those who know how to look at their kind.

Those who read me know my conviction that the

world, the temporal world, rests on a few very simple ideas; so simple that they must be as old as the hills. It rests notably, among others, on the idea of Fidelity. At a time when nothing which is not revolutionary in some way or other can expect to attract much attention I have not been revolutionary in my writings. The revolutionary spirit is mighty convenient in this, that it frees one from all scruples as regards ideas. Its hard, absolute optimism is repulsive to my mind by the menace of fanaticism and intolerance it contains. No doubt one should smile at these things; but, imperfect Esthete, I am no better Philosopher. All claim to special righteousness awakens in me that scorn and anger from which a philosophical mind should be free.

ON DRAWING

By A. P. HERBERT

A. P. Herbert is one of the most brilliant of the younger English writers, and has done remarkable work in fields apparently incompatible: light verse, humorous drolleries, and a beautifully written tragic novel, *The Secret Battle*. This last was unquestionably one of the most powerful books born of the War, but its sale was tragically small. *The House by the River*, a later book, was also an amazingly competent and original tale, apparently cast along the lines of the conventional "mystery story," but really a study of selfishness and cowardice done with startling irony and intensity.

Mr. Herbert went to Winchester School and New College, Oxford, where he took his degree in 1914. He saw military service at the Dardanelles and in France, and is now on the staff of *Punch*. There is no young writer in England from whom one may more confidently expect a continuance of fine work. This airy and delicious little absurdity is a perfect example of what a genuine humorist can do.

If there is still any one in doubt as to the value of the old-fashioned classical training in forming a lusty prose style, let him examine Mr. Herbert's *The Secret Battle*. This book often sounds oddly like a translation from vigorous Greek—e.g., Herodotus. It is lucid, compact, logical, rich in telling epithet, informal and swift. If these are not the cardinal prose virtues, what are?

IT is commonly said that everybody can sing in the bathroom; and this is true. Singing is very easy. Drawing, though, is much more difficult. I have devoted a good deal of time to Drawing, one way and another; I have to attend a great many committees and public meetings, and at such functions I find that Drawing is almost the only Art one can satisfactorily pursue during the speeches. One really cannot sing during the speeches; so as a rule I draw. I do not say that I am an expert yet, but after a few more meetings I calculate that I shall know Drawing as well as it can be known.

The first thing, of course, is to get on to a really good committee; and by a good committee I mean a committee that provides decent materials. An ordinary departmental committee is no use: generally they only give you a couple of pages of lined foolscap and no white blotting-paper, and very often the pencils are quite soft. White blotting-paper is essential. I know of no material the spoiling of which gives so much artistic pleasure—except perhaps snow. Indeed, if I was asked to choose between making pencil-marks on a sheet of white blotting-paper and making foot-marks on a sheet of white snow I should be in a thing-ummy.

Much the best committees from the point of view of material are committees about business which meet at business premises—shipping offices, for choice. One of the Pacific Lines has the best white blotting-paper I know; and the pencils there are a dream. I am sure the directors of that firm are Drawers; for they always give you two pencils, one hard for doing noses, and one soft for doing hair.

When you have selected your committee and the

speeches are well away, the Drawing begins. Much the best thing to draw is a man.
Not the chairman, or Lord Pommery Quint,
or any member of the committee, but just A
Man. Many novices make the mistake of se-
lecting a subject for their Art before they
begin; usually they select the chairman. And when
they find it is more like Mr. Gladstone they are discouraged. If they had waited a little it could have been
Mr. Gladstone officially.

FIG. 1

As a rule I begin with the forehead and
work down to the chin (Fig. 1).

When I have done the outline I put in the
eye. This is one of the most difficult parts
of Drawing; one is never quite sure where
the eye goes. If, however, it is not a good
eye, a useful tip is to give the man spectacles; this
generally makes him a clergyman, but it helps the
eye (Fig. 2).

FIG. 2

Now you have to outline the rest of the head, and
this is rather a gamble. Personally, I go in
for *strong* heads (Fig. 3).

I am afraid it is not a strong neck; I
expect he is an author, and is not well fed.
But that is the worst of strong heads; they
make it so difficult to join up the chin and
the back of the neck.

FIG. 3

The next thing to do is to put in the ear; and once you have done this the rest is easy. Ears are much more difficult than eyes (Fig. 4).

I hope that is right. It seems to me to be a little too far to the southward. But it is done now. And once you have put in the ear you can't go back; not unless you are on a *very* good committee which provides india-rubber as well as pencils.

Now I do the hair. Hair may either be very fuzzy or black, or lightish and thin. It depends chiefly on what sort of pencils are provided. For myself I prefer black hair, because then the parting shows up better (Fig. 5).

FIG. 4

Until one draws hair one never realizes what large heads people have. Doing the hair takes the whole of a speech, usually, even one of the chairman's speeches.

This is not one of my best men; I am sure the ear is in the wrong place. And I am inclined to think he ought to have spectacles. Only then he would be a clergyman, and I have decided that he is Mr. Philip Gibbs at the age of twenty. So he must carry on with his eye as it is.

FIG. 5

I find that all my best men face to the west; it is a curious thing. Sometimes I draw two men facing each other, but the one facing east is always a dud.

There, you see (Fig. 6)? The one on the right is a Bolshevik; he has a low forehead and beetling brows—a most unpleasant man. Yet he has a powerful face. The one on the left was meant to be another Bolshevik, arguing with him. But he has turned

Fig. 6

out to be a lady, so I have had to give her a "bun." She is a lady solicitor; but I don't know how she came to be talking to the Bolshevik.

When you have learned how to do men, the only other things in Drawing are Perspective and Landscape.

PERSPECTIVE is great fun: the best thing to do is a long French road with telegraph poles (Fig. 7). I have put in a fence as well.

LANDSCAPE is chiefly composed of hills and trees. Trees are the most amusing, especially fluffy trees.

Here is a Landscape (Fig. 8).

Somehow or other a man has got into this landscape; and, as luck would have it, it is Napoleon. Apart from this it is not a bad landscape.

Fig. 7

But it takes a very long speech to get an ambitious piece of work like this through.

Fig. 8

There is one other thing I ought to have said. Never attempt to draw a man front-face. It can't be done.

O. HENRY

By O. W. FIRKINS

Several years ago I turned to *Who's Who in America* in hope of finding some information about O. W. Firkins, whose brilliant reviews—chiefly of poetry—were appearing in *The Nation.* I found no entry, but every few months I would again rummage that stout red volume with the same intention, forgetting that I had done so before without success. It seemed hardly credible that a critic so brilliant had been overlooked by the industrious compilers of that work, which includes hundreds of hacks and fourflushers. When gathering the contents of this book I tried *Who's Who* again, still without result. I wrote to Mr. Firkins pleading for biographical details; modestly, but firmly, he denied me.

So all I can tell you is this, that Mr. Firkins is to my mind one of the half-dozen most sparkling critics in this country. One sometimes feels that he is carried a little past his destination by the sheer gusto and hilarity of his antitheses and paradoxes. That is not so, however, in this essay about O. Henry, an author who has often been grotesquely mispraised (I did not say overpraised) by people incompetent to appreciate his true greatness. Mr. Robert Cortes Holliday, in an essay called "The Amazing Failure of O. Henry," said that O. Henry created no memorable characters. Mr. Firkins suggests the obvious but satisfying answer—New York itself is his triumph. The New York of O. Henry, already almost erased physically, remains a personality and an identity.

Mr. Firkins is professor of English at the University of Minnesota, and a contributing editor of *The Weekly Review,* in which this essay first appeared in September, 1919. The footnotes are, of course, his own.

THERE are two opinions concerning O. Henry. The middle class views him as the impersonation of vigor and brilliancy; part of the higher criticism sees in him little but sensation and persiflage. Between these views there is a natural relation; the gods of the heathens are *ipso facto* the demons of Christianity. Unmixed assertions, however, are commonly mixtures of truth and falsehood; there is room to-day for an estimate which shall respect both opinions and adopt neither.

There is one literary trait in which I am unable to name any writer of tales in any literature who surpasses O. Henry.* It is not primary or even secondary among literary merits; it is less a value *per se* than the condition or foundation of values. But its utility is manifest, and it is rare among men: Chaucer and Shakespeare prove the possibility of its absence in masters of that very branch of art in which its presence would seem to be imperative. I refer to the designing of stories—not to the primary intuition or to skill in development, in both of which finer phases of invention O. Henry has been largely and frequently surpassed, but to the disposition of

---

* William Sidney Porter, 1862-1910, son of Algernon Sidney Porter, physician, was born, bred, and meagerly educated in Greensboro, North Carolina. In Greensboro he was drug clerk; in Texas he was amateur ranchman, land-office clerk, editor, and bank teller. Convicted of misuse of bank funds on insufficient evidence (which he supplemented by the insanity of flight), he passed three years and three months in the Ohio State Penitentiary at Columbus. Release was the prelude to life in New York, to story-writing, to rapid and wide-spread fame. Latterly, his stories, published in New York journals and in book form, were consumed by the public with an avidity which his premature death, in 1910, scarcely checked. The pen-name, O. Henry, is almost certainly borrowed from a French chemist, Etienne-Ossian Henry, whose abridged name he fell upon in his pharmacal researches. See the interesting "O. Henry Biography" by C. Alphonso Smith.

masses, to the blocking-out of plots. That a half-educated American provincial should have been original in a field in which original men have been copyists is enough of itself to make his personality observable.

Illustration, even of conceded truths, is rarely superfluous. I supply two instances. Two lads, parting in New York, agree to meet "After Twenty Years" at a specified hour, date, and corner. Both are faithful; but the years in which their relation has slept in mutual silence and ignorance have turned the one into a dashing criminal, the other into a sober officer of the law. Behind the picturesque and captivating rendezvous lurks a powerful dramatic situation and a moral problem of arresting gravity. This is dealt with in six pages of the "Four Million." The "Furnished Room," two stories further on, occupies twelve pages. Through the wilderness of apartments on the lower West Side a man trails a woman. Chance leads him to the very room in which the woman ended her life the week before. Between him and the truth the avarice of a sordid landlady interposes the curtain of a lie. In the bed in which the girl slept and died, the man sleeps and dies, and the entrance of the deadly fumes into his nostrils shuts the sinister and mournful coincidence forever from the knowledge of mankind. O. Henry gave these tales neither extension nor

prominence; so far as I know, they were received
without bravos or salvos. The distinction of a body
of work in which such specimens are undistinguished
hardly requires comment.

A few types among these stories may be specified.
There are the Sydney Cartonisms, defined in the name;
love-stories in which divided hearts, or simply divided
persons, are brought together by the strategy of chance;
hoax stories—deft pictures of smiling roguery; "prince
and pauper" stories, in which wealth and poverty face
each other, sometimes enact each other; disguise
stories, in which the wrong clothes often draw the
wrong bullets; complemental stories, in which Jim
sacrifices his beloved watch to buy combs for Della,
who, meanwhile, has sacrificed her beloved hair to
buy a chain for Jim.

This imperfect list is eloquent in its way; it smooths
our path to the assertion that O. Henry's specialty is
the enlistment of original method in the service of
traditional appeals. The ends are the ends of fifty
years ago; O. Henry transports us by aeroplane
the old homestead.*

* O Henry's stories have been known to coincide with earlier
work in a fashion which dims the novelty of the tale without
clouding the originality of the author. I thought the brilliant
"Harlem Tragedy" (in the "Trimmed Lamp") unique through
sheer audacity, but the other day I found its motive repeated
with singular exactness in Montesquieu's "Lettres Persanes"
(Letter LI).

Criticism of O. Henry falls into those superlatives and antitheses in which his own faculty delighted. In mechanical invention he is almost the leader of his race. In a related quality—a defect—his leadership is even more conspicuous. I doubt if the sense of the probable, or, more precisely, of the available in the improbable, ever became equally weakened or deadened in a man who made his living by its exercise. The improbable, even the impossible, has its place in art, though that place is relatively low; and it is curious that works such as the "Arabian Nights" and Grimm's fairy tales, whose stock-in-trade is the incredible, are the works which give almost no trouble on the score of verisimilitude. The truth is that we reject not what it is impossible to prove, or even what it is possible to disprove, but what it is impossible to imagine. O. Henry asks us to imagine the unimaginable—that is his crime.

The right and wrong improbabilities may be illustrated from two burglar stories. "Sixes and Sevens" contains an excellent tale of a burglar and a citizen who fraternize, in a comic midnight interview, on the score of their common sufferings from rheumatism. This feeling in practice would not triumph over fear and greed; but the feeling is natural, and everybody with a grain of nature in him can imagine its triumph. Nature *tends* towards that impossibility, and art, lifting, so to speak, the lid which fact drops upon nature, reveals nature in belying fact. In another story, in "Whirligigs," a nocturnal interview takes place in which a burglar and a small boy discuss the etiquette of their mutual relation by formulas derived from short stories with which both are amazingly conversant. This is the wrong use of the improbable. Even an imagination inured to the virtues of burglars and the maturity of small boys will have naught to do with this insanity.

But O. Henry can go further yet. There are inventions in his tales the very utterance of which—not the mere substance but the utterance—on the part of a man not writing from Bedlam or for Bedlam impresses the reader as incredible. In a "Comedy in Rubber," two persons become so used to spectatorship at transactions in the street that they drift into the part of spectators when the transaction is their own wedding. Can human daring or human folly go further? O. Henry is on the spot to prove that they can. In the "Romance of a Busy Broker," a busy and forgetful man, in a freak of absent-mindedness, offers his hand to the stenographer *whom he had married the night before.*

The other day, in the journal of the Goncourts, I came upon the following sentence: "Never will the imagination approach the improbabilities and the antitheses of truth" (II, 9). This is dated February 21, 1862. Truth had still the advantage. O. Henry was not born till September of the same year.

Passing on to style, we are still in the land of antithesis. The style is gross—and fine. Of the plenitude of its stimulus, there can be no question. In "Sixes and Sevens," a young man sinking under accidental morphia, is kept awake and alive by shouts, kicks, and blows. O. Henry's public seems imaged in that young man. But I draw a sharp distinction between the *tone* of the style and its *pattern*. The tone is brazen, or, better perhaps, brassy; its self-advertisement is incorrigible; it reeks with that air of *performance* which is opposed to real efficiency. But the pattern is another matter. The South rounds its periods like its vowels; O. Henry has read, not widely, but wisely, in his boyhood. His sentences are *built*—a rare thing in the best writers of to-day. In conciseness, that Spartan virtue, he was strong, though it must be confessed that the tale-teller was now and then hustled from the rostrum by his rival and enemy, the talker. He can introduce a felicity with a noiselessness that numbers him for a flying second among the sovereigns of English. "In one of the second-floor front windows Mrs. McCaskey awaited her husband. Supper was cooling on the table. Its heat went into Mrs. McCaskey."

I regret the tomfoolery; I wince at the slang. Yet

even for these levities with which his pages are so
liberally besprinkled or bedaubed, some half-apology
may be circumspectly urged. In nonsense his ease is
consummate. A horseman who should dismount to
pick up a bauble would be childish; O. Henry picks
it up without dismounting. Slang, again, is most
pardonable in the man with whom its use is least ex-
clusive and least necessary. There are men who, going
for a walk, take their dogs with them; there are other
men who give a walk to their dogs. Substitute slang
for the dog, and the superiority of the first class to
the second will exactly illustrate the superiority of
O. Henry to the abject traffickers in slang.

In the "Pendulum" Katy has a new patch in her
crazy quilt which the ice man cut from the end of
his four-in-hand. In the "Day We Celebrate," thread-
ing the mazes of a banana grove is compared to "pag-
ing the palm room of a New York hotel for a man
named Smith." O. Henry's is the type of mind to
which images like this four-in-hand and this palm room
are presented in exhaustless abundance and unflagging
continuity. There was hardly an object in the merry-
go-round of civilized life that had not offered at least
an end or an edge to the avidity of his consuming
eyes. Nothing escapes from the besom of his allu-
siveness, and the style is streaked and pied, almost to
monotony, by the accumulation of lively details.

If O. Henry's style was crude, it was also rare; but it is part of the grimness of the bargain that destiny drives with us that the mixture of the crude and the rare should be a crude mixture, as the sons of whites and negroes are numbered with the blacks. In the kingdom of style O. Henry's estates were princely, but, to pay his debts, he must have sold them all.

Thus far in our inquiry extraordinary merits have been offset by extraordinary defects. To lift our author out of the class of brilliant and skilful entertainers, more is needed. Is more forthcoming? I should answer, yes. In O. Henry, above the knowledge of setting, which is clear and first-hand, but subsidiary, above the order of events, which is, generally speaking, fantastic, above the emotions, which are sound and warm, but almost purely derivative, there is a rather small, but impressive body of first-hand perspicacities and reactions. On these his endurance may hinge.

I name, first of all, O. Henry's feeling for New York. With the exception of his New Orleans, I care little for his South and West, which are a boyish South and West, and as little, or even less, for his Spanish-American communities. My objection to his opera-bouffe republics is, not that they are inadequate as republics (for that we were entirely prepared), but that they are inadequate as opera. He lets us see his show from the coulisses. The pretense lacks standing even among pretenses, and a faith must be induced before its removal can enliven us. But his New York has quality. It is of the family of Dickens's London and Hugo's Paris, though it is plainly a cadet in the family. Mr. Howells, in his profound and valuable study of the metropolis in a "Hazard of New Fortunes," is penetrating; O. Henry, on the other hand, is *penetrated*. His New York is intimate and clinging; it is caught in the mesh of the imagination.

O. Henry had rare but precious insights into human destiny and human nature. In these pictures he is not formally accurate; he could never or seldom set his truth before us in that moderation and proportion which truths acquire in the stringencies of actuality. He was apt to present his insight in a sort of parable or allegory, to upraise it before the eyes of mankind on the mast or flagpole of some vehement exaggeration. Epigram shows us truth in the embrace of a lie, and tales which are dramatized epigrams are subject to a like constraint. The force, however, is real. I could scarcely name anywhere a more powerful exposition of fatality than "Roads of Destiny," the initial story in the volume which appropriates its title. It wanted only the skilled romantic touch of a Gautier or Stevenson to enroll this tale among the master-pieces of its kind in contemporary letters.

Now and then the ingredient of parable is hardly perceptible; we draw close to the bare fact. O. Henry, fortunate in plots, is peculiarly fortunate in his renunciation of plot. If contrivance is lucrative, it is also costly. There is an admirable little story called the "Pendulum" (in the "Trimmed Lamp"), the simplicity of whose fable would have satisfied Coppée or Hawthorne. A man in a flat, by force of custom, has come to regard his wife as a piece of furniture. She departs for a few hours, and, by the break in usage, is restored, in his consciousness, to womanhood. She comes back, and relapses into furniture. That is all. O. Henry could not have given us less—or more. Farcical, clownish, if you will, the story resembles those clowns who carry daggers under their motley. When John Perkins takes up that inauspicious hat, the reader smiles, and quails. I will mention a few other examples of insights with the proviso that they are not specially commended to the man whose quest in the short story is the electrifying or the calorific. They include the "Social Triangle," the "Making of a New Yorker," and the "Foreign Policy of Company 99," all in the "Trimmed Lamp," the "Brief Début of Tildy" in the "Four Million," and the "Complete Life of John Hopkins" in the "Voice of the City." I cannot close this summary of good points without a passing reference to the not unsuggestive portrayal of humane and cheerful scoundrels in the "Gentle Grafter." The picture, if false to species, is faithful to genus.

O. Henry's egregiousness, on the superficial side, both in merits and defects, reminds us of those park benches so characteristic of his tales which are occupied by a millionaire at one end and a mendicant at the other. But, to complete the image, we must add as a casual visitor to that bench a seer or a student, who, sitting down between the previous comers and suspending the flamboyancies of their dialogue, should gaze with the pensive eye of Goldsmith or Addison upon the passing crowd.

In O. Henry American journalism and the Victorian tradition meet. His mind, quick to don the guise of modernity, was impervious to its spirit. The specifically modern movements, the scientific awakening, the religious upheaval and subsidence, the socialistic gospel, the enfranchisement of women—these never interfered with his artless and joyous pursuit of the old romantic motives of love, hate, wealth, poverty, gentility, disguise, and crime. On two points a moral record which, in his literature, is everywhere sound and stainless, rises almost to nobility. In an age when sexual excitement had become available and permissible, this worshiper of stimulus never touched with so much as a fingertip that insidious and meretricious fruit. The second point is his feeling for underpaid working-girls. His passionate concern for this wrong derives a peculiar emphasis from the general refusal of his books to bestow countenance or notice on philanthropy in its collective forms. When, in his dream of Heaven, he is asked: "Are you one of the bunch?" (meaning one of the bunch of grasping and grinding employers), the response, through all its slang, is soul-stirring. " 'Not on your immortality,' said I. 'I'm only the fellow that set fire to an orphan asylum and murdered a blind man for his pennies.' " The author of that retort may have some difficulty with the sentries that watch the entrance of Parnassus; he will have none with the gatekeeper of the New Jerusalem.

THE MOWING OF A FIELD

By HILAIRE BELLOC

We **have** not had in our time a more natural-born essayist, **of** the scampering sort, than Hilaire Belloc. He is an infectious fellow: if you read him much you will find yourself trying to imitate him; there is no harm in doing so: he himself caught the trick from Rabelais. I do not propose to rehash here the essay I wrote about him in a book called *Shandygaff*. You can refer to it there, which will be good business all round. I know it is a worthy essay, for much of it was cribbed from an article by Mr. Thomas Seccombe, which an American paper lifted from the English journal which, presumably, paid Mr. Seccombe for it. I wrote it for the Boston *Transcript*, where I knew the theft would be undetected; and in shoveling together some stuff for a book (that was in 1917, the cost of living was rising at an angle of forty-five degrees, as so many graphs have shown) I put it in, forgetting (until too late) that some of it was absolute plunder.

Mr. Chesterton **once** said something like this: "It is a mistake to think that thieves do not respect property. They only wish it to become *their* property, so that they may more perfectly respect it."

And by the way, Max Beerbohm's parody of Belloc, in *A Christmas Garland,* is something not to be missed. It is one of the best proofs that Belloc is a really great artist. Beerbohm does not waste his time mimicking the small fry.

Hilaire Belloc—son of a French father and an English mother; his happy junction of both English and French genius in prose is hereditary—was born in France in 1870. He lived in Sussex as a child; served in the French field artillery; was at Balliol College, Oxford, 1893-95, and sat four years (1906-10) in the House of Commons. Certainly you must read (among his gatherings of essays) *On Nothing, On Everything, On Something, Hills and the Sea, First and Last;* then you can read *The Path to Rome,* and *The Four Men,* and *Caliban's Guide to Letters* and *The Pyrenees* and *Marie Antoinette.* If you desire the bouillon (or bullion) of his charm, there is *A Picked Company,* a selection (by Mr. E. V. Lucas) of his most representative work. It is published by Methuen and Company, 36 Essex Street W. C., London.

Having done so, **come again**: we will go off in a corner and **talk** about Mr. Belloc.

THERE is a valley in South England remote from ambition and from fear, where the passage of strangers is rare and unperceived, and where the scent of the grass in summer is breathed only by those who are native to that unvisited land. The roads to the Channel do not traverse it; they choose upon either side easier passes over the range. One track alone leads up through it to the hills, and this is changeable: now green where men have little occasion to go, now a good road where it nears the homesteads and the barns. The woods grow steep above the slopes; they reach sometimes the very summit of the heights, or, when they cannot attain them, fill in and clothe the coombes. And, in between, along the floor of the valley, deep pastures and their silence are bordered by lawns of chalky grass and the small yew trees of the Downs.

The clouds that visit its sky reveal themselves beyond the one great rise, and sail, white and enormous, to the other, and sink beyond that other. But the plains above which they have traveled and the Weald to which they go, the people of the valley cannot see and hardly recall. The wind, when it reaches such fields, is no longer a gale from the salt, but fruitful and soft, an inland breeze; and those whose blood was nourished here feel in that wind the fruitfulness of our orchards and all the life that all things draw from the air.

In this place, when I was a boy, I pushed through a fringe of beeches that made a complete screen between me and the world, and I came to a glade called No Man's Land. I climbed beyond it, and I was surprised and glad, because from the ridge of that glade, I saw the sea. To this place very lately I returned.

The many things that I recovered as I came up the countryside were not less charming than when a distant memory had enshrined them, but much more. Whatever veil is thrown by a longing recollection had not intensified nor even made more mysterious the beauty of that happy ground; not in my very dreams of morning had I, in exile, seen it more beloved or more rare. Much also that I had forgotten now returned to me as I approached—a group of elms, a little turn of the parson's wall, a small paddock beyond the graveyard close, cherished by one man, with a low wall of very old stone guarding it all round. And all these things fulfilled and amplified my delight, till even the good vision of the place, which I had kept so many years, left me and was replaced by its better reality. "Here," I said to myself, "is a symbol of what some say is reserved for the soul: pleasure of a kind which cannot be imagined save in a moment when at last it is attained."

When I came to my own gate and my own field, and had before me the house I knew, I looked around a

little (though it was already evening), and I saw that
the grass was standing as it should stand when it is
ready for the scythe. For in this, as in everything
that a man can do—of those things at least which are
very old—there is an exact moment when they are
done best. And it has been remarked of whatever rules
us that it works blunderingly, seeing that the good
things given to a man are not given at the precise moment when they would have filled him with delight.
But, whether this be true or false, we can choose the
just turn of the seasons in everything we do of our
own will, and especially in the making of hay. Many
think that hay is best made when the grass is thickest;
and so they delay until it is rank and in flower, and
has already heavily pulled the ground. And there is
another false reason for delay, which is wet weather.
For very few will understand (though it comes year
after year) that we have rain always in South England between the sickle and the scythe, or say just after
the weeks of east wind are over. First we have a
week of sudden warmth, as though the south had come
to see us all; then we have the weeks of east and south-
east wind; and then we have more or less of that rain
of which I spoke, and which always astonishes the
world. Now it is just before, or during, or at the
very end of that rain—but not later—that grass should
be cut for hay. True, upland grass, which is always

thin, should be cut earlier than the grass in the bottoms and along the water meadows; but not even the latest, even in the wettest seasons, should be left (as it is) to flower and even to seed. For what we get when we store our grass is not a harvest of something ripe, but a thing just caught in its prime before maturity: as witness that our corn and straw are best yellow, but our hay is best green. So also Death should be represented with a scythe and Time with a sickle; for Time can take only what is ripe, but Death comes always too soon. In a word, then, it is always much easier to cut grass too late than too early; and I, under that evening and come back to these pleasant fields, looked at the grass and knew that it was time. June was in full advance; it was the beginning of that season when the night has already lost her foothold of the earth and hovers over it, never quite descending, but mixing sunset with the dawn.

Next morning, before it was yet broad day, I awoke, and thought of the mowing. The birds were already chattering in the trees beside my window, all except the nightingale, which had left and flown away to the Weald, where he sings all summer by day as well as by night in the oaks and the hazel spinneys, and especially along the little river Adur, one of the rivers of the Weald. The birds and the thought of the mowing had awakened me, and I went down the stairs and along the stone floors to where I could find a scythe; and when I took it from its nail, I remembered how, fourteen years ago, I had last gone out with my scythe, just so, into the fields at morning. In between that day and this were many things, cities and armies, and a confusion of books, mountains and the desert, and horrible great breadths of sea.

When I got out into the long grass the sun was not yet risen, but there were already many colors in the eastern sky, and I made haste to sharpen my scythe, so that I might get to the cutting before the dew should dry. Some say that it is best to wait till all the dew has risen, so as to get the grass quite dry from the very first. But, though it is an advantage to get the grass quite dry, yet it is not worth while to wait till the dew has risen. For, in the first place, you lose many hours of work (and those the coolest), and next—which is more important—you lose that great ease and thickness in cutting which comes of the dew. So I at once began to sharpen my scythe.

There is an art also in the sharpening of the scythe, and it is worth describing carefully. Your blade must be dry, and that is why you will see men rubbing the scythe-blade with grass before they whet it. Then also your rubber must be quite dry, and on this account it is a good thing to lay it on your coat and keep it there during all your day's mowing. The scythe you stand upright, with the blade pointing away from you, and put your left hand firmly on the back of the blade, grasping it: then you pass the rubber first down one side of the blade-edge and then down the other, beginning near the handle and going on to the point and working quickly and hard. When you first do this you will, perhaps, cut your hand; but it is only at first that such an accident will happen to you.

To tell when the scythe is sharp enough this is the rule. First the stone clangs and grinds against the iron harshly; then it rings musically to one note; then, at last, it purrs as though the iron and stone were exactly suited. When you hear this, your scythe is sharp enough; and I, when I heard it that June dawn, with everything quite silent except the birds, let down the scythe and bent myself to mow.

When one does anything anew, after so many years, one fears very much for one's trick or habit. But all things once learnt are easily recoverable, and I very soon recovered the swing and power of the mower. Mowing well and mowing badly—or rather not mowing at all—are separated by very little; as is also true of writing verse, of playing the fiddle, and of dozens of other things, but of nothing more than of believing. For the bad or young or untaught mower without tradition, the mower Promethean, the mower original and contemptuous of the past, does all these things:

He leaves great crescents of grass uncut. He digs the point of the scythe hard into the ground with a jerk. He loosens the handles and even the fastening of the blade. He twists the blade with his blunders, he blunts the blade, he chips it, dulls it, or breaks it clean off at the tip. If any one is standing by he cuts him in the ankle. He sweeps up into the air wildly, with nothing to resist his stroke. He drags up earth with the grass, which is like making the meadow bleed. But the good mower who does things just as they should be done and have been for a hundred thousand years, falls into none of these fooleries. He goes forward very steadily, his scythe-blade just barely missing the ground, every grass falling; the swish and rhythm of his mowing are always the same.

So great an art can only be learnt by continual practice; but this much is worth writing down, that, as in all good work, to know the thing with which you work is the core of the affair. Good verse is best written on good paper with an easy pen, not with a lump of coal on a whitewashed wall. The pen thinks for you; and so does the scythe mow for you if you treat it honorably and in a manner that makes it recognize its service. The manner is this. You must regard the scythe as a pendulum that swings, not as a knife that cuts. A good mower puts no more strength into his stroke than into his lifting. Again, stand up to your work. The bad mower, eager and full of pain, leans forward and tries to force the scythe through the grass. The good mower, serene and able, stands as nearly straight as the shape of the scythe will let him, and follows up every stroke closely, moving his left foot forward. Then also let every stroke get well away. Mowing is a thing of ample gestures, like drawing a cartoon. Then, again, get yourself into a mechanical and repetitive mood: be thinking of anything at all but your mowing, and be anxious only when there seems some interruption to the monotony of the sound. In this mowing should be like one's prayers—all of a sort and always the same, and so made that you can establish a monotony and work them, as it were, with half your mind: that happier half, the half that does not bother.

In this way, when I had recovered the art after so many years, I went forward over the field, cutting lane after lane through the grass, and bringing out its most secret essences with the sweep of the scythe until the air was full of odors. At the end of every lane I sharpened my scythe and looked back at the work done, and then carried my scythe down again upon my shoulder to begin another. So, long before the bell rang in the chapel above me—that is, long before six o'clock, which is the time for the Angelus—I had many swathes already lying in order parallel like soldiery; and the high grass yet standing, making a great contrast with the shaven part, looked dense and high. **As it** says in the Ballad of Val-ès-Dunes, where—

>   The tall son of the Seven Winds
>   Came riding out of Hither-hythe,

and his horse-hoofs (you will remember) trampled into the press and made a gap in it, and his sword (as you know)

>   was like a scythe
>   In Arcus when the grass is high
>   And all the swathes in order lie,
>   And there's the bailiff standing by
>   A-gathering of the tithe.

So I mowed all that morning, till the houses awoke in the valley, and from some of them rose a little fragrant smoke, and men began to be seen.

I stood still and rested on my scythe to watch the awakening of the village, when I saw coming up to my field a man whom I had known in older times, before I had left the Valley.

He was of that dark silent race upon which all the learned quarrel, but which, by whatever meaningless name it may be called—Iberian, or Celtic, or what you will—is the permanent root of all England, and makes England wealthy and preserves it everywhere, except perhaps in the Fens and in a part of Yorkshire. Everywhere else you will find it active and strong. These people are intensive; their thoughts and their labors

turn inward. It is on account of their presence in
these islands that our gardens are the richest in the
world. They also love low rooms and ample fires and
great warm slopes of thatch. They have, as I believe, an older acquaintance with the English air than
any other of all the strains that make up England.
They hunted in the Weald with stones, and camped in
the pines of the green-sand. They lurked under the
oaks of the upper rivers, and saw the legionaries go up,
up the straight paved road from the sea. They helped
the few pirates to destroy the towns, and mixed with
those pirates and shared the spoils of the Roman villas,
and were glad to see the captains and the priests destroyed. They remain; and no admixture of the
Frisian pirates, or the Breton, or the Angevin and
Norman conquerors, has very much affected their
cunning eyes.

To this race, I say, belonged the man who now approached me. And he said to me, "Mowing?" And I
answered, "Ar." Then he also said "Ar," as in duty
bound; for so we speak to each other in the Stenes of
the Downs.

Next he told me that, as he had nothing to do, he
would lend me a hand; and I thanked him warmly, or,
as we say, "kindly." For it is a good custom of ours
always to treat bargaining as though it were a cour-
teous pastime; and though what he was after was

money, and what I wanted was his labor at the least
pay, yet we both played the comedy that we were free
men, the one granting a grace and the other accepting
it. For the dry bones of commerce, avarice and method
and need, are odious to the Valley; and we cover them
up with a pretty body of fiction and observances. Thus,
when it comes to buying pigs, the buyer does not begin
to decry the pig and the vendor to praise it, as is the
custom with lesser men; but tradition makes them do
business in this fashion:—

First the buyer will go up to the seller when he sees
him in his own steading, and, looking at the pig with
admiration, the buyer will say that rain may or may
not fall, or that we shall have snow or thunder, according to the time of the year. Then the seller, looking
critically at the pig, will agree that the weather is as
his friend maintains. There is no haste at all; great
leisure marks the dignity of their exchange. And the
next step is, that the buyer says: "That's a fine pig
you have there, Mr. ——" (giving the seller's name).
"Ar, powerful fine pig." Then the seller, saying also
"Mr." (for twin brothers rocked in one cradle give
each other ceremonious observance here), the seller, I
say, admits, as though with reluctance, the strength
and beauty of the pig, and falls into deep thought.
Then the buyer says, as though moved by a great
desire, that he is ready to give so much for the pig,

naming half the proper price, or a little less. Then the seller remains in silence for some moments; and at last begins to shake his head slowly, till he says: "I don't be thinking of selling the pig, anyways." He will also add that a party only Wednesday offered him so much for the pig—and he names about double the proper price. Thus all ritual is duly accomplished; and the solemn act is entered upon with reverence and in a spirit of truth. For when the buyer uses this phrase: "I'll tell you what I *will* do," and offers within half a crown of the pig's value, the seller replies that he can refuse him nothing, and names half a crown above its value; the difference is split, the pig is sold, and in the quiet soul of each runs the peace of something accomplished.

Thus do we buy a pig or land or labor or malt or lime, always with elaboration and set forms; and many a London man has paid double and more for his violence and his greedy haste and very unchivalrous higgling. As happened with the land at Underwaltham, which the mortgagees had begged and implored the estate to take at twelve hundred and had privately offered to all the world at a thousand, but which a sharp direct man, of the kind that makes great fortunes, a man in a motor-car, a man in a fur coat, a man of few words, bought for two thousand three hundred before my very eyes, protesting that they might take his offer or leave it; and all because he did not begin by praising the land.

Well then, this man I spoke of offered to help me, and he went to get his scythe. But I went into this house and brought out a gallon jar of small ale for him and for me; for the sun was now very warm, and small ale goes well with mowing. When we had drunk some of this ale in mugs called "I see you," we took each a swathe, he a little behind me because he was the better mower; and so for many hours we swung, one before the other, mowing and mowing at the tall grass of the field. And the sun rose to noon and we were still at our mowing; and we ate food, but only for a little while, and we took again to our mowing. And at last there was nothing left but a small square of grass, standing like a square of linesmen who keep their formation, tall and unbroken, with all the dead lying around them when the battle is over and done.

Then for some little time I rested after all those hours; and the man and I talked together, and a long way off we heard in another field the musical sharpening of a scythe.

The sunlight slanted powdered and mellow over the breadth of the valley; for day was nearing its end. I went to fetch rakes from the steading; and when I had come back the last of the grass had fallen, and all the field lay flat and smooth, with the very green short grass in lanes between the dead and yellow swathes.

These swathes we raked into cocks to keep them from the dew against our return at daybreak; and we made the cocks as tall and steep as we could, for in that shape they best keep off the dew, and it is easier also to spread them after the sun has risen. Then we raked up every straggling blade, till the whole field was a clean floor for the tedding and the carrying of the hay next morning. The grass we had mown was but a little over two acres; for that is all the pasture on my little tiny farm.

When we had done all this, there fell upon us the beneficent and deliberate evening; so that as we sat a little while together near the rakes, we saw the valley more solemn and dim around us, and all the trees and hedgerows quite still, and held by a complete silence. Then I paid my companion his wage, and bade him a good night, till we should meet in the same place before sunrise.

He went off with a slow and steady progress, as all our peasants do, making their walking a part of the easy but continual labor of their lives. But I sat on, watching the light creep around towards the north and change, and the waning moon coming up as though by stealth behind the woods of No Man's Land.

THE STUDENT LIFE

By WILLIAM OSLER

Sir William Osler, one of the best-loved and most influential teachers of his time, was born in Canada in 1849. He began his education in Toronto and at McGill University, Montreal, where he served as professor of medicine, 1874-84. Wherever he worked his gifted and unique personality was a center of inspiration—at the University of Pennsylvania, 1884-89; at Johns Hopkins, 1889-1904. In 1904 he went to Oxford as Regius Professor of Medicine; he died in England in 1919.

Only our medical friends have a right to speak of the great doctor's place in their own world; but one would like to see his honorable place as a man of letters more generally understood. His generous wisdom and infectious enthusiasm are delightfully expressed in his collected writings. No lover of the essay can afford to overlook *Æquanimitas and Other Addresses, An Alabama Student and Other Biographical Essays, Science and Immortality* and *Counsels and Ideals*, this last an anthology collected from his professional papers by one of his pupils. He stands in the honorable line of those great masters who have found their highest usefulness as kindly counselors of the young. His lucid and exquisite prose, with its extraordinary wealth of quotation from the literature of all ages, and his unfailing humor and tenderness, put him in the first rank of didactic essayists. One could get a liberal education in literature merely by following up all his quotations and references. He was more deeply versed in the classics than many professors of Greek and Latin; the whole music of English poetry seemed to be current in his blood. His essay on Keats, taken with Kipling's wonderful story *Via Wireless*, tells the student more about that poet than many a volume of biography. When was biography more delightfully written than in his volume *An Alabama Student?*

Walt Whitman said, when Dr. Osler attended him years ago, "Osler believes in the gospel of encouragement—of putting the best construction on things—the best foot forward. He's a fine fellow and a wise one, I guess." The great doctor's gospel of encouragement is indeed a happy companion for the midnight reader. Rich in every gentle quality that makes life endeared, his books are the most sagacious and helpful of modern writings for the young student. As one who has found them an unfailing delight, I venture to hope that our medical confrères may not be the only readers to enjoy their vivacity and charm.

EXCEPT it be a lover, no one is more interesting as an object of study than a student. Shakespeare might have made him a fourth in his immortal group. The lunatic with his fixed idea, the poet with his fine frenzy, the lover with his frantic idolatry, and the student aflame with the desire for knowledge are of "imagination all compact." To an absorbing passion, a whole-souled devotion, must be joined an enduring energy, if the student is to become a devotee of the gray-eyed goddess to whose law his services are bound. Like the quest of the Holy Grail, the quest of Minerva is not for all. For the one, the pure life; for the other, what Milton calls "a strong propensity of nature." Here again the student often resembles the poet—he is born, not made. While the resultant of two molding forces, the accidental, external conditions, and the hidden germinal energies, which produce in each one of us national, family, and individual traits, the true student possesses in some measure a divine spark which sets at naught their laws. Like the Snark, he defies definition, but there are three unmistakable signs by which you may recognize the genuine article from a Boojum—an absorbing desire to know the truth, an unswerving steadfastness in its pursuit, and an open, honest heart, free from suspicion, guile, and jealousy.

At the outset do not be worried about this big question—Truth. It is a very simple matter if each one of

you starts with the desire to get as much as possible.
No human being is constituted to know the truth, the
whole truth, and nothing but the truth; and even the
best of men must be content with fragments, with
partial glimpses, never the full fruition. In this un-
satisfied quest the attitude of mind, the desire, the
thirst—a thirst that from the soul must rise!—the
fervent longing, are the be-all and the end-all. What
is the student but a lover courting a fickle mistress who
ever eludes his grasp? In this very elusiveness is
brought out his second great characteristic—steadfastness of purpose. Unless from the start the limitations
incident to our frail human faculties are frankly accepted, nothing but disappointment awaits you. The
truth is the best you can get with your best endeavor,
the best that the best men accept—with this you must
learn to be satisfied, retaining at the same time with
due humility an earnest desire for an ever larger portion. Only by keeping the mind plastic and receptive
does the student escape perdition. It is not, as Charles
Lamb remarks, that some people do not know what to
do with truth when it is offered to them, but the tragic
fate is to reach, after years of patient search, a condition of mind-blindness in which the truth is not recognized, though it stares you in the face. This can never
happen to a man who has followed step by step the
growth of a truth, and who knows the painful phases

of its evolution. It is one of the great tragedies of life that every truth has to struggle to acceptance against honest but mind-blind students. Harvey knew his contemporaries well, and for twelve successive years demonstrated the circulation of the blood before daring to publish the facts on which the truth was based.*

Only steadfastness of purpose and humility enable the student to shift his position to meet the new conditions in which new truths are born, or old ones modified beyond recognition. And, thirdly, the honest heart will keep him in touch with his fellow students, and furnish that sense of comradeship without which he travels an arid waste alone. I say advisedly an honest heart—the honest head is prone to be cold and stern, given to judgment, not mercy, and not always able to entertain that true charity which, while it thinketh no evil, is anxious to put the best possible interpretation upon the motives of a fellow worker. It will foster, too, an attitude of generous, friendly rivalry untinged by the green peril, jealousy, that is the best preventive of the growth of a bastard scientific spirit, loving seclusion and working in a lock-and-key laboratory, as timorous of light as is a thief.

---

* "These views, as usual, pleased some more, others less; some chid and calumniated me, and laid it to me as a crime that I had dared to depart from the precepts and opinions of all Anatomists."—De Motu Cordis, chap. i.

You have all become brothers in a great society, not apprentices, since that implies a master, and nothing should be further from the attitude of the teacher than much that is meant in that word, used though it be in another sense, particularly by our French brethren in a most delightful way, signifying a bond of intellectual filiation. A fraternal attitude is not easy to cultivate—the chasm between the chair and the bench is difficult to bridge. Two things have helped to put up a cantilever across the gulf. The successful teacher is no longer on a height, pumping knowledge at high pressure into passive receptacles. The new methods have changed all this. He is no longer Sir Oracle, perhaps unconsciously by his very manner antagonizing minds to whose level he cannot possibly descend, but he is a senior student anxious to help his juniors. When a simple, earnest spirit animates a college, there is no appreciable interval between the teacher and the taught—both are in the same class, the one a little more advanced than the other. So animated, the student feels that he has joined a family whose honor is his honor, whose welfare is his own, and whose interests should be his first consideration.

The hardest conviction to get into the mind of a beginner is that the education upon which he is engaged is not a college course, not a medical course, but a life course, for which the work of a few years under teachers is but a preparation. Whether you will falter and fail in the race or whether you will be faithful to the end depends on the training before the start, and on your staying powers, points upon which I need not enlarge. You can all become good students, a few may become great students, and now and again one of you will be found who does easily and well what others cannot do at all, or very badly, which is John Ferriar's excellent definition of a genius.

In the hurry and bustle of a business world, which is the life of this continent, it is not easy to train first-class students. Under present conditions it is hard to get the needful seclusion, on which account it is that our educational market is so full of wayside fruit. I have always been much impressed by the advice of St. Chrysostom: "Depart from the highway and transplant thyself in some enclosed ground, for it is hard for a tree which stands by the wayside to keep her fruit till it be ripe." The dilettante is abroad in the land, the man who is always venturing on tasks for which he is imperfectly equipped, a habit of mind fostered by the multiplicity of subjects in the curriculum: and while many things are studied, few are studied thoroughly. Men will not take time to get to the heart of a matter. After all, concentration is the price the modern student pays for success. Thoroughness is the most difficult habit to acquire, but it is the pearl of great price, worth all the worry and trouble of the search. The dilettante lives an easy, butterfly life, knowing nothing of the toil and labor with which the treasures of knowledge are dug out of the past, or wrung by patient research in the laboratories. Take, for example, the early history of this country—how easy for the student of the one type to get a smattering, even a fairly full acquaintance with the events of the French and Spanish settlements. Put an original document before him, and it might as well be Arabic. What we need is the other type, the man who knows the records, who, with a broad outlook and drilled in what may be called the embryology of history, has yet a powerful vision for the minutiæ of life. It is these kitchen and backstair men who are to be encouraged, the men who know the subject in hand in all possible relationships. Concentration has its drawbacks. It is possible to become so absorbed in the problem of the "enclitic $\delta\varepsilon$," or the structure of the flagella of the Trichomonas, or of the toes of the prehistoric horse, that the student loses the sense of proportion in his work, and even wastes a lifetime in researches which are valueless because not in touch with current knowledge. You remember poor Casaubon, in "Middlemarch," whose painful scholarship was lost on this account. The best preventive to this is to get denationalized early. The true student is a citizen of the world,

the allegiance of whose soul, at any rate, is too precious to be restricted to a single country. The great
minds, the great works transcend all limitations of
time, of language, and of race, and the scholar can
never feel initiated into the company of the elect until
he can approach all of life's problems from the cosmopolitan standpoint. I care not in what subject he may
work, the full knowledge cannot be reached without
drawing on supplies from lands other than his own—
French, English, German, American, Japanese, Russian, Italian—there must be no discrimination by the
loyal student who should willingly draw from any and
every source with an open mind and a stern resolve to
render unto all their dues. I care not on what stream of
knowledge he may embark, follow up its course, and
the rivulets that feed it flow from many lands. If the
work is to be effective he must keep in touch with
scholars in other countries. How often has it happened that years of precious time have been given to a
problem already solved or shown to be insoluble, because of the ignorance of what had been done elsewhere. And it is not only book knowledge and journal knowledge, but a knowledge of men that is needed.
The student will, if possible, see the men in other lands.
Travel not only widens the vision and gives certainties
in place of vague surmises, but the personal contact
with foreign workers enables him to appreciate better

the failings or successes in his own line of work, perhaps to look with more charitable eyes on the work of some brother whose limitations and opportunities have been more restricted than his own. Or, in contact with a mastermind, he may take fire, and the glow of the enthusiasm may be the inspiration of his life. Concentration must then be associated with large views on the relation of the problem, and a knowledge of its status elsewhere; otherwise it may land him in the slough of a specialism so narrow that it has depth and no breadth, or he may be led to make what he believes to be important discoveries, but which have long been current coin in other lands. It is sad to think that the day of the great polymathic student is at an end; that we may, perhaps, never again see a Scaliger, a Haller, or a Humboldt—men who took the whole field of knowledge for their domain and viewed it as from a pinnacle. And yet a great specializing generalist may arise, who can tell? Some twentieth-century Aristotle may be now tugging at his bottle, as little dreaming as are his parents or his friends of a conquest of the mind, beside which the wonderful victories of the Stagirite will look pale. The value of a really great student to the country is equal to half a dozen grain elevators or a new transcontinental railway. He is a commodity singularly fickle and variable, and not to be grown to order. So far as his advent is concerned there is no telling when or where he may arise. The conditions seem to be present even under the most unlikely externals. Some of the greatest students this country has produced have come from small villages and country places. It is impossible to predict from a study of the environment, which a "strong propensity of nature," to quote Milton's phrase again, will easily bend or break.

The student must be allowed full freedom in his work, undisturbed by the utilitarian spirit of the Philistine, who cries, Cui bono? and distrusts pure science. The present remarkable position in applied science and in industrial trades of all sorts has been made possible by men who did pioneer work in chemistry, in physics, in biology, and in physiology, without a thought in their researches of any practical application. The members of this higher group of productive students are rarely understood by the common spirits, who appreciate as little their unselfish devotion as their unworldly neglect of the practical side of the problems.

Everywhere now the medical student is welcomed as an honored member of the guild. There was a time, I confess, and it is within the memory of some of us, when, like Falstaff, he was given to "taverns and sack and wine and metheglins, and to drinkings and swearings and starings, pribbles and prabbles"; but all that has changed with the curriculum, and the "Meds" now roar you as gently as the "Theologs." On account of the peculiar character of the subject-matter of your studies, what I have said upon the general life and mental attitude of the student applies with tenfold force to you. Man, with all his mental and bodily anomalies and diseases—the machine in order, the machine in disorder, and the business yours to put it to rights. Through all the phases of its career this most complicated mechanism of this wonderful world will be the subject of our study and of your care—the naked, new-born infant, the artless child, the lad and the lassie just aware of the tree of knowledge overhead, the strong man in the pride of life, the woman with the benediction of maternity on her brow, and the aged, peaceful in the contemplation of the past. Almost everything has been renewed in the science and in the art of medicine, but all through the long centuries there has been no variableness or shadow of change in the essential features of the life which is our contemplation and our care. The sick love-child of Israel's sweet singer, the plague-stricken hopes of the great Athenian statesman, Elpenor, bereft of his beloved Artemidora, and "Tully's daughter mourned so tenderly," are not of any age or any race—they are here with us to-day, with the Hamlets, the Ophelias, and the Lears. Amid an eternal heritage of sorrow and suffering our work is laid, and this eternal note of sadness would be insupportable if the daily tragedies were not relieved by the spectacle of the heroism and devotion displayed by the actors. Nothing will sustain you more potently than the power to recognize in your humdrum routine, as perhaps it may be thought, the true poetry of life—the poetry of the commonplace, of the ordinary man, of the plain, toilworn woman, with their loves and their joys, their sorrows and their griefs. The comedy, too, of life will be spread before you, and nobody laughs more often than the doctor at the pranks Puck plays upon the Titanias and the Bottoms among his patients. The humorous side is really almost as frequently turned towards him as the tragic. Lift up one hand to heaven and thank your stars if they have given you the proper sense to enable you to appreciate the inconceivably droll situations in which we catch our fellow creatures. Unhappily, this is one of the free gifts of the gods, unevenly distributed, not bestowed on all, or on all in equal portions. In undue measure it is not without risk, and in any case in the doctor it is better appreciated by the eye than expressed on the tongue. Hilarity and good humor, a breezy cheerfulness, a nature "sloping toward the southern side," as Lowell has it, help enormously both in the study and in the practice of medicine. To many of a somber and sour disposition it is hard to maintain good spirits amid the trials and tribulations of the day, and yet it is an unpardonable mistake to go about among patients with a long face.

Divide your attentions equally between books and men. The strength of the student of books is to sit still—two or three hours at a stretch—eating the heart out of a subject with pencil and notebook in hand, determined to master the details and intricacies, focussing all your energies on its difficulties. Get accustomed to test all sorts of book problems and statements for yourself, and take as little as possible on trust. The Hunterian "Do not think, but try" attitude of mind is the important one to cultivate. The question came up one day, when discussing the grooves left on the nails after fever, how long it took for the nail to grow out, from root to edge. A majority of the class had no further interest; a few looked it up in books; two men marked their nails at the root with nitrate of silver, and a few months later had positive knowledge on the subject. They showed the proper spirit. The little points that come up in your reading try to test for yourselves. With one fundamental difficulty many of you will have to contend from the outset—a lack of proper preparation for really hard study. No one can have watched successive groups of young men pass through the special schools without profoundly regretting the haphazard, fragmentary character of their preliminary education. It does seem too bad that we cannot have a student in his eighteenth year sufficiently grounded in the humanities and in the sciences preliminary to medicine—but this is an educational problem upon which only a Milton or a Locke could discourse with profit. With pertinacity you can overcome the preliminary defects and once thoroughly interested, the work in books becomes a pastime. A serious drawback in the student life is the self-consciousness, bred of too close devotion to books. A man gets shy, "dysopic," as old Timothy Bright calls it, and shuns the looks of men, and blushes like a girl.

The strength of a student of men is to travel—to study men, their habits, character, mode of life, their behavior under varied conditions, their vices, virtues, and peculiarities. Begin with a careful observation of your fellow students and of your teachers; then, every patient you see is a lesson in much more than the malady from which he suffers. Mix as much as you possibly can with the outside world, and learn its ways. Cultivated systematically, the student societies, the students' union, the gymnasium, and the outside social circle will enable you to conquer the diffidence so apt to go with bookishness and which may prove a very serious drawback in after-life. I cannot too strongly impress upon the earnest and attentive men among you the necessity of overcoming this unfortunate failing in your student days. It is not easy for every one to reach a happy medium, and the distinction between a proper self-confidence and "cheek," particularly in junior students, is not always to be made. The latter is met with chiefly among the student pilgrims who, in traveling down the Delectable Mountains, have gone astray and have passed to the left hand, where lieth the country of Conceit, the country in which you remember the brisk lad Ignorance met Christian.

I wish we could encourage on this continent among our best students the habit of wandering. I do not know that we are quite prepared for it, as there is still great diversity in the curricula, even among the leading schools, but it is undoubtedly a great advantage to study under different teachers, as the mental horizon is widened and the sympathies enlarged. The practice would do much to lessen that narrow "I am of Paul and I am of Apollos" spirit which is hostile to the best interests of the profession.

There is much that I would like to say on the question of work, but I can spare only a few moments for a word or two. Who will venture to settle upon so simple a matter as the best time for work? One will tell us there is no best time; all are equally good; and truly, all times are the same to a man whose soul is absorbed in some great problem. The other day I asked Edward Martin, the well-known story-writer, what time he found best for work. "Not in the evening, and never between meals!" was his answer, which may appeal to some of my hearers. One works best at night; another, in the morning; a majority of the students of the past favor the latter. Erasmus, the great exemplar, says, "Never work at night; it dulls the brain and hurts the health." One day, going with George Ross through Bedlam, Dr. Savage, at that time the physician in charge, remarked upon two great groups of patients—those who were depressed in the morning and those who were cheerful, and he suggested that the spirits rose and fell with the bodily temperature—those with very low morning temperatures were depressed, and vice versa. This, I believe, expresses a truth which may explain the extraordinary difference in the habits of students in this matter of the time at which the best work can be done. Outside of the asylum there are also the two great types, the student-lark who loves to see the sun rise, who comes to breakfast with a cheerful morning face, never so "fit" as at 6 A. M. We all know the type. What a contrast to the student-owl with his saturnine morning face, thoroughly unhappy, cheated by the wretched breakfast bell of the two best hours of the day for sleep, no appetite, and permeated with an unspeakable hostility to his vis-à-vis, whose morning garrulity and good humor are equally offensive. Only gradually, as the day wears on and his temperature rises, does he become endurable to himself and to others. But see him really awake at 10 P. M. while our blithe lark is in hopeless coma over his books, from which it is hard to rouse him sufficiently to get his boots off for bed, our lean owl-friend, Saturn no longer in the ascendant, with bright eyes and cheery face, is ready for four hours of anything you wish—deep study, or

Heart affluence in discoursive talk,

and by 2 A. M. he will undertake to unsphere the spirit of Plato. In neither a virtue, in neither a fault we must recognize these two types of students, differently constituted, owing possibly—though I have but little evidence for the belief—to thermal peculiarities.

THE DECLINE OF THE DRAMA

By STEPHEN LEACOCK

Nineteen hundred and ten was an important year. Halley's
comet came along, and some predicted the End of the World.
And Stephen Leacock's first humorous book—*Literary Lapses*—
was published. First *humorous* book, I said, for Mr. Leacock—
who is professor of political economy at McGill University,
Montreal—had published his *Elements of Political Science* in
1906.

It seems to me that I have heard that *Literary Lapses* was
obscurely or privately published in Canada before 1910; that
Mr. John Lane, the famous London publisher, was given a copy
by some one as he got on a steamer to go home to England;
that he read it on the voyage and cabled an offer for it as soon
as he landed. This is very vague in my mind, but it sounds
probable. At any rate, since that time Professor Leacock's humorous volumes have appeared with gratifying regularity—*Nonsense Novels, Behind the Beyond,* etc.; and some more serious
books too, such as *Essays and Literary Studies* and *The Unsolved Riddle of Social Justice.* One of the unsolved riddles
of social injustice is, why should Professor Leacock be so much
more amusing than most people?

We usually think of him as a Canadian, but he was born in
England in 1869.

COMING up home the other night in my car (the
Guy Street car), I heard a man who was hanging onto
a strap say: "The drama is just turning into a bunch
of talk." This set me thinking; and I was glad that it
did, because I am being paid by this paper to think once
a week, and it is wearing. Some days I never think
from morning till night.

This decline of the drama is a thing on which I
feel deeply and bitterly; for I am, or I have been,

something of an actor myself. I have only been in amateur work, I admit, but still I have played some mighty interesting parts. I have acted in Shakespeare as a citizen, I have been a fairy in "A Midsummer Night's Dream," and I was once one end (choice of ends) of a camel in a pantomime. I have had other parts too, such as "A Voice Speaks From Within," or "A Noise Is Heard Without," or a "Bell Rings From Behind," and a lot of things like that. I played as A Noise for seven nights, before crowded houses where people were being turned away from the door; and I have been a Groan and a Sigh and a Tumult, and once I was a "Vision Passes Before the Sleeper."

So when I talk of acting and of the spirit of the Drama, I speak of what I know.

Naturally, too, I was brought into contact, very often into quite intimate personal contact, with some of the greatest actors of the day. I don't say it in any way of boasting, but merely because to those of us who love the stage all dramatic souvenirs are interesting. I remember, for example, that when Wilson Barrett played "The Bat" and had to wear the queer suit with the scales, it was I who put the glue on him.

And I recall a conversation with Sir Henry Irving one night when he said to me, "Fetch me a glass of water, will you?" and I said, "Sir Henry, it is not only a pleasure to get it but it is to me, as a humble devotee

of the art that you have ennobled, a high privilege.
I will go further—" "Do," he said. Henry was like
that, quick, sympathetic, what we call in French
"vibrant."

Forbes Robertson I shall never forget: he owes me
50 cents. And as for Martin Harvey—I simply cannot
call him Sir John, we are such dear old friends—he
never comes to this town without at once calling in my
services to lend a hand in his production. No doubt
everybody knows that splendid play in which he appears, called "The Breed of the Treshams."

There is a torture scene in it, a most gruesome thing.
Harvey, as the hero, has to be tortured, not on the
stage itself, but off the stage in a little room at the
side. You can hear him howling as he is tortured.
Well, it was I who was torturing him. We are so used
to working together that Harvey didn't want to let any-
body do it but me.

So naturally I am a keen friend and student of the
Drama: and I hate to think of it going all to pieces.

The trouble with it is that it is becoming a mere mass
of conversation and reflection: nothing happens in it;
the action is all going out of it and there is nothing
left but thought. When actors begin to think, it is
time for a change. They are not fitted for it.

Now in my day—I mean when I was at the apogee
of my reputation (I think that is the word—it may be

apologee—I forget)—things were very different. What we wanted was action—striking, climatic, catastrophic action, in which things not only happened, but happened suddenly and all in a lump.

And we always took care that the action happened in some place that was worth while, not simply in an ordinary room with ordinary furniture, the way it is in the new drama. The scene was laid in a lighthouse (top story), or in a mad house (at midnight), or in a power house, or a dog house, or a bath house, in short, in some place with a distinct local color and atmosphere.

I remember in the case of the first play I ever wrote (I write plays, too) the manager to whom I submitted it asked me at once, the moment he glanced at it, "Where is the action of this laid?" "It is laid," I answered, "in the main sewer of a great city." "Good, good," he said; "keep it there."

In the case of another play the manager said to me, "What are you doing for atmosphere?" "The opening act," I said, "is in a steam laundry." "Very good," he answered as he turned over the pages, "and have you brought in a condemned cell?" I told him that I had not. "That's rather unfortunate," he said, "because we are especially anxious to bring in a condemned cell. Three of the big theaters have got them this season, and I think we ought to have it in. Can you do it?"

"Yes," I said, "I can, if it's wanted. I'll look through the cast, and no doubt I can find one at least of them that ought to be put to death." "Yes, yes," said the manager enthusiastically, "I am sure you can."

But I think of all the settings that we used, the lighthouse plays were the best. There is something about a lighthouse that you don't get in a modern drawing room. What it is, I don't know; but there's a difference. I always have liked a lighthouse play, and never have enjoyed acting so much, have never thrown myself into acting so deeply, as in a play of that sort.

There is something about a lighthouse—the way you see it in the earlier scenes—with the lantern shining out over the black waters that suggests security, fidelity, faithfulness, to a trust. The stage used generally to be dim in the first part of a lighthouse play, and you could see the huddled figures of the fishermen and their wives on the foreshore pointing out to the sea (the back of the stage).

"See," one cried with his arm extended, "there is lightning in yon sky." (I was the lightning and that my cue for it): "God help all the poor souls at sea to-night!" Then a woman cried, "Look! Look! a boat upon the reef!" And as she said it I had to rush round and work the boat to make it go up and down properly. Then there was more lightning, and some one screamed out, "Look! See! there's a woman in the boat!"

There wasn't really; it was me; but in the darkness it was all the same, and of course the heroine herself couldn't be there yet because she had to be downstairs getting dressed to be drowned. Then they all cried out, "Poor soul! she's doomed," and all the fishermen ran up and down making a noise.

Fishermen in those plays used to get fearfully excited; and what with the excitement and the darkness and the bright beams of the lighthouse falling on the wet oilskins, and the thundering of the sea upon the reef—ah! me, those were plays! That was acting! And to think that there isn't a single streak of lightning in any play on the boards this year!

And then the kind of climax that a play like this used to have! The scene shifted right at the moment of the excitement, and lo! we are in the tower, the top story of the lighthouse, interior scene. All is still and quiet within, with the bright light of the reflectors flooding the little room, and the roar of the storm heard like muffled thunder outside.

The lighthouse keeper trims his lamps. How firm and quiet and rugged he looks. The snows of sixty winters are on his head, but his eye is clear and his grip strong. Hear the howl of the wind as he opens the door and steps forth upon the iron balcony, eighty feet above the water, and peers out upon the storm.

"God pity all the poor souls at sea!" he says. (They

all say that. If you get used to it, and get to like it,
you want to hear it said, no matter how often they
say it.) The waves rage beneath him. (I threw it at
him, really, but the effect was wonderful.)

And then, as he comes in from the storm to the still
room, the climax breaks. A man staggers into the
room in oilskins, drenched, wet, breathless. (They
all staggered in these plays, and in the new drama
they walk, and the effect is feebleness itself.) He
points to the sea. "A boat! A boat upon the reef!
With a woman in it."

And the lighthouse keeper knows that it is his only
daughter—the only one that he has—who is being cast
to death upon the reef. Then comes the dilemma.
They want him for the lifeboat; no one can take it
through the surf but him. You know that because the
other man says so himself.

But if he goes in the boat then the great light will
go out. Untended it cannot live in the storm. And
if it goes out—ah! if it goes out—ask of the angry
waves and the resounding rocks of what to-night's
long toll of death must be without the light!

I wish you could have seen it—you who only see the
drawing-room plays of to-day—the scene when the
lighthouse man draws himself up, calm and resolute,
and says: "My place is here. God's will be done."
And you know that as he says it and turns quietly to

his lamps again, the boat is drifting, at that very moment, to the rocks.

"How did they save her?" My dear sir, if you can ask that question you little understand the drama as it was. Save her? No, of course they didn't save her. What we wanted in the Old Drama was reality and force, no matter how wild and tragic it might be. They did not save her. They found her the next day, in the concluding scene—all that was left of her when she was dashed upon the rocks. Her ribs were broken. Her bottom boards had been smashed in, her gunwale was gone—in short, she was a wreck.

The girl? Oh, yes, certainly they saved the girl. That kind of thing was always taken care of. You see just as the lighthouse man said "God's will be done," his eye fell on a long coil of rope, hanging there. Providential, wasn't it? But then we were not ashamed to use Providence in the Old Drama. So he made a noose in it and threw it over the balcony and hauled the girl up on it. I used to hook her on to it every night.

A rotten play? Oh, I am sure it must have been. But, somehow, those of us who were brought up on that sort of thing, still sigh for it.

AMERICA AND THE ENGLISH TRADITION

By HARRY MORGAN AYRES

This admirable summary of Anglo-American history first appeared (February, 1920) as an editorial in the *Weekly Review*. It seemed to me then, and still does, as a model in that form of writing, perfect in lucidity, temperance and good sense. Mr. Ayres is a member of the faculty of Columbia University (Department of English) and also one of the editors of the *Weekly Review*. Beowulf, Chaucer, Shakespeare and Seneca seem to be his favorite hobbies.

To sum up the gist of Anglo-American relations in half a dozen pages, as Mr. Ayres does here, is surely a remarkable achievement.

THE recently established chair in the history, literature, and institutions of the United States which is to be shared among the several universities of Great Britain, is quite different from the exchange professorships of sometimes unhappy memory. It is not at all the idea to carry over one of our professors each year and indoctrinate him with the true culture at its source. The occupant of the chair will be, if the announced intention is carried out, quite as often British as American, and quite as likely a public man as a professor. The chief object is to bring to England a better knowledge of the United States, and a purpose more laudable can scarcely be imagined. Peace and prosperity will endure in the world in some very precise relation to the extent to which England succeeds in understanding us.

It is not an illusion to suppose that our understanding of the British is on the whole better than theirs of us. The British Empire is a large and comparatively simple fact, now conspicuously before the world for a long time. The United States was, in British eyes, until recently, a comparatively insignificant fact, yet vastly more complicated than they imagined. Each, of course, perfectly knew the faults of the other, assessed with an unerring cousinly eye. The American bragged in a nasal whine, the Briton patronized in a throaty burble. Whoever among the struggling nations of the world might win, England saw to it that she never lost; your Yankee was content with the more ignoble triumphs of merchandising, willing to cheapen life if he could only add to his dollars. But the excellence of English political institutions and methods, the charm of English life, the tremendous power of the Empire for promoting freedom and civilization in the world, these are things which Americans have long recognized and in a way understood. Anything like an equivalent British appreciation of America in the large seems confined to a very few honorable exceptions among them. Admiration for Niagara, which is half British anyway, or enthusiasm for the "Wild West"—

your better-class Englishman always thrills to the
frontier—is no step at all toward rightly appreciat-
ing America.

To no inconsiderable extent this is America's own
fault. She does not present to the world a record
that is easily read. It is obvious, for instance—and
so obvious that it is not often enough stated—that
America has and will continue to have a fundamen-
tally English civilization. English law is the basis of
her law. English speech is her speech, and if with a
difference, it is a difference that the philologist, all
things considered, finds amazingly small. English
literature is her literature—Chaucer and Shakespeare
hers because her blood then coursed indistinguishably
through the English heart they knew so well; Milton,
Dryden, and the Queen Anne men hers, because she
was still a part of England; the later men hers by
virtue of affectionate acquaintanceship and a generous and not inconsiderable rivalry. English history,
in short, is her history. The struggles of the thirteenth century through which law and parliament came
into being, the struggles of the seventeenth century
through which law and parliament came to rule, are
America's struggles upon which she can look back
with the satisfaction that some things that have been
done in the world need never be undone or done over
again, whatever the room for improvement may still

be. Americans, no less than British, recognize that independence was largely an accidental result of a war which sprang out of a false theory of economics, but whose conclusion carried with it a lesson in the management of empire which subsequent history shows the British to have learned thoroughly and for the benefit of all concerned. American independence, however, once established, pointed a way to democratic freedom which England hastened to follow. This we know. And yet—

And yet we allow these obvious and fundamental considerations to become marvelously obscured. We allow England's failure to solve an insoluble Irish problem to arouse in us an attitude of mind possibly excusable in some Irishmen, but wholly inexcusable in any American. We allow a sentimental regard for some immigrant from Eastern Europe, who comes to us with a philosophy born of conditions that in English-speaking lands ceased to be centuries ago, to make us pretend to see in him the true expression of America's traditional ideals. We allow ourselves to be far too easy with the phrase, "He is not pro-German, he is merely anti-British." Why are they anti-British? Why should they be permitted to make it falsely appear that recognition of the English basis of America involves approval of everything that England in her history may or may not have done? Why should they be allowed to pretend that disapproval of some particular act of England justifies repudiation of most of the things by virtue of which we are what we are? America from the first has been part of the great English experiment—great because it is capable of learning from experience.

The world has put a big investment in blood and treasure, and all that they imply, into the education of England. It is satisfied—the world's response to Germany's insolent challenge is the proof of it—that its pains have been well bestowed. England is more nearly fit than any other nation to wield the power that is hers. That is not to deny the peculiar virtues of other nations; indeed, these virtues have largely contributed to the result. Italy has educated her; France has educated her; we have done something; and Germany. In result, she is not perfect—the English would perhaps least of all assert that—but she has learned a great deal and held herself steady while she learned it. It is a bigger job than the world cares to undertake to teach any other nation so much. Nor would it be at all likely to succeed so well. For what England has to offer the world in return is not simply her institutions; it is not merely a formula for the effective discharge of police duty throughout the world;

it is the English freeman, whether he hail from Canada, Australia, Africa, or the uttermost isles of the sea.

A most adaptable fellow, this freeman, doing all sorts of work everywhere, and with tremendous powers of assimilation. Consider him in his origins. He began by assimilating fully his own weight in Danes, while remaining an English freeman. He then perforce accepted a Norman king, as he had accepted a Danish one, hoping, as always, that the king would not trouble him too much. But when Norman William, who was very ill-informed about the breed, killed off most of his natural leaders and harried the rest into villeiny, how did he manage in a small matter of two hundred years or so to make an English gentleman not only of himself but of all the rag-tag of adventurers who had come over with William and since? How did he contrive, out of a band of exiles fleeing from an Egypt of ecclesiastical tyranny, broken younger sons, artisans out of a job, speculators, bondmen, Swedes, Dutchmen, and what not, to make America? Is he one likely to lose his bearings when in his America the age-old problem again heaves in view? This is a job he has been working at pretty successfully for more than a thousand years. Grant him a moment to realize himself afresh in the face of it. Don't expect him to stop and give a coherent explana-

tion of what he is doing. He wouldn't be the **true**
son of the English tradition that he is if he could do
that. Perhaps the occupants of the new chair can
do something of the sort for him.

THE RUSSIAN QUARTER

By Thomas Burke

Thomas Burke, a young newspaper man in London, came into quick recognition with his first book, *Nights in Town* (published in America as *Nights in London*) in 1915. His first really popular success, however, was *Limehouse Nights*, less satisfactory to those who had read the first book, as it was largely a repetition of the same material in fiction form. (In fact, Mr. Burke holds what must be almost a record among authors by having worked over nearly the identical substance in four different versions—as essays and sketches, in *Nights in Town;* as short stories, in *Limehouse Nights;* as a novel, in *Twinkletoes;* as poetry, in *The Song Book of Quong Lee of Limehouse.*)

Mr. Burke has specialized on London, and with great ability. In the Limehouse series his colorings seem just a little too consciously vivid, his roguishness a little too studied, to be quite satisfying. *The Outer Circle*, a volume of rambles in the London suburbs, is to me more truly a work of art.

I HAD known the quarter for many years before it interested me. It was not until I was prowling around on a Fleet Street assignment that I learned to hate it. A murder had been committed over a café in Lupin Street; a popular murder, fruity, cleverly done, and with a sex interest. Of course every newspaper and agency developed a virtuous anxiety to track the culprit, and all resources were directed to that end. Journalism is perhaps the only profession in which so fine a public spirit may be found. So it was that the North Country paper of which I was a hanger-on flung every available man into the fighting line, and

the editor told me that I might, in place of the casual
paragraphs for the London Letter, do something good
on the Vassiloff murder.

It was a night of cold rain, and the pavements were
dashed with smears of light from the shop windows.
Through the streaming streets my hansom leaped; and
as I looked from the window, and noted the despond-
ent biliousness of Bethnal Green, I realized that the
grass withereth, the flower fadeth.

I dismissed the cab at Brick Lane, and, continuing
the tradition which had been instilled into me by my
predecessor on the London Letter, I turned into one
of the hostelries and had a vodka to keep the cold out.
Little Russia was shutting up. The old shawled
women, who sit at every corner with huge baskets of
black bread and sweet cakes, were departing beneath
umbrellas. The stalls of Osborn Street, usually dressed
with foreign-looking confectionery, were also retir-
ing. Indeed, everybody seemed to be slinking away,
and as I sipped my vodka, and felt it burn me with
raw fire, I cursed news editors and all publics which
desired to read about murders. I was perfectly sure
that I shouldn't do the least good; so I had another,
and gazed through the kaleidoscopic window, rushing
with rain, at the cheerful world that held me.

Oh, so sad it is, this quarter! By day the streets
are a depression, with their frowzy doss-houses and

their vapor-baths. Gray and sickly is the light. Gray and sickly, too, are the leering shops, and gray and sickly are the people and the children. Everything has followed the grass and the flowers. Childhood has no place; so above the roofs you may see the surly points of a Council School. Such games as happen are played but listlessly, and each little face is smirched. The gaunt warehouses hardly support their lopping heads, and the low, beetling, gabled houses of the alleys seem for ever to brood on nights of bitter adventure. Fit objects for contempt by day they may be, but when night creeps upon London, the hideous darkness that can almost be touched, then their faces become very powers of terror, and the cautious soul, wandered from the comfort of the main streets, walks and walks in a frenzy, seeking outlet and finding none. Sometimes a hoarse laugh will break sharp on his ear. Then he runs.

Well, I finished my second, and then sauntered out. As I was passing a cruel-looking passage, a girl stepped forward. She looked at me. I looked at her. She had the haunting melancholy of Russia in her face, but her voice was as the voice of Cockaigne. For she spoke and said:—

"Funny-looking little guy, ain't you?"

I suppose I was. So I smiled and said: "We are as God made us, old girl."

She giggled. . . .

I said I felt sure I should do no good on the Vassil-off murder. I didn't. For just then two of her friends came out of the court, each with a boy. It was apparent that she had no boy. I had no idea what the occasion might be, but the other four marched ahead, crying, "Come on!" And, surprised, yet knowing of no good reason for being surprised, I felt the girl's arm slip into mine, and we joined the main column. . . .

That is one of London's greatest charms : it is always ready to toss you little encounters of this sort, if you are out for them.

Across the road we went, through mire and puddle, and down a long, winding court. At about midway our friends disappeared, and, suddenly drawn to the right, I was pushed from behind up a steep, fusty stair. Then I knew where we were going. We were going to the tenements where most of the Russians meet of an evening. The atmosphere in these places is a little more cheerful than that of the cafés—if you can imagine a Russian ever rising to cheerfulness. Most of the girls lodge over the milliners' shops, and thither their friends resort. Every establishment here has a piano, for music, with them, is a somber passion rather than a diversion. You will not hear comic opera, but if you want to climb the lost heights of melody, stand in Bell Yard, and listen to a piano, lost in the high glooms, wailing the heart of Chopin, or Rubinstein or Glazounoff through the fingers of pale, moist girls, while the ghost of Peter the Painter parades the naphtha'd highways.

At the top of the stair I was pushed into a dark, fusty room, and guided to a low, fusty sofa or bed. Then some one struck a match, and a lamp was lit and set on the mantelshelf. It flung a soft, caressing radiance on its shabby home, and on its mistress, and on the other girls and boys. The boys were tough youngsters of the district, evidently very much at home, smoking Russian cigarettes and settling themselves on the bed in a manner that seemed curiously continental in Cockney toughs. I doubt if you would have loved the girls at that moment; and yet . . . you know . . . their black or brassy hair, their untidiness, and the cotton blouses half-dropped from their tumultuous breasts . . .

The girl who had collared me disappeared for a moment, and then brought a tray of Russian tea. "Help 'selves, boys!" We did so, and, watching the others, I discovered that it was the correct thing to lemon the ladies' tea for them and stir it well and light their cigarettes. I did so for Katarina—that was her name —while she watched me with little truant locks of hair running everywhere, and a slow, alluring smile that seemed to hold all the agony and mystery of the steppes.

The room, on which the wallpaper hung in dank strips, contained a full-sized bed and a chair bedstead, a washstand, a samovar, a potpourri of a carpet, and certain mysteries of feminine toilet. A rickety three-legged table stood by the window, and Katarina's robes hung in a dainty riot of frill and color behind the door, which only shut when you thrust a peg of wood through a wired catch.

One of the boys sprawled himself, in clumsy luxury, on the bed, and his girl arranged herself at his side, and when she was settled her hair tumbled in a shower of hairpins, and everybody laughed like children. The other girl went to the piano, and her boy squatted on the floor at her feet.

She began to play. . . . You would not understand, I suppose, the intellectual emotion of the situation. It is more than curious to sit in these rooms, in the filthiest spot in London, and listen to Moszkowsky, Tchaikowsky, and Sibelius, played by a factory girl. It is . . . something indefinable. I had visited similar places in Stepney before, but then I had not had a couple of vodkas, and I had not been taken in tow by an unknown girl. They play and play, while tea and cigarettes, and sometimes vodka or whisky, go round; and as the room gets warmer, so does one's sense of smell get sharper; so do the pale faces get moister; and so does one long more and more for a breath of cold air from the Ural Mountains. The best you can do is to ascend to the flat roof, and take a deep breath of Spitalfields ozone. Then back to the room for more tea and more music.

Sanya played. . . . Despite the unventilated room, the greasy appointments, and other details that would have turned the stomach of Kensington, that girl at the piano, her dress cunningly disarranged, playing, as no one would have dreamed she could play, the finer in- tensities of Wieniawski and Moussorgsky, shook all sense of responsibility from me. The burdens of life vanished. News editors and their assignments be damned. Enjoy yourself, was what the cold, insid- ious music said. Take your moments when the fates send them; that was life's best lesson. Snatch the joy of the fleeting moment. Why ponder on time and tears?

Devilish little fingers they were, Sanya's. Her technique was not perhaps all that it might have been; she might not have won the Gold Medal of our white- shirted academies, but she had enough temperament to make half a dozen Bechstein Hall virtuosi. From valse to nocturne, from sonata to prelude, her fancy ran. With crashing chords she dropped from "L'Au- tomne Bacchanale" to the Nocturne in E flat; scarcely

murmured of that, then tripped elvishly into Moszkowsky's Waltz, and from that she dropped to a song
of Tchaikowsky, almost heartbreaking in its childish
beauty, and then to the lecherous music of the second
act of "Tristan." Mazurka, polonaise, and nocturne
wailed in the stuffy chamber; her little hands lit up
the enchanted gloom of the place with bright thrills,
until the bed and the dingy surroundings faded into
phantoms and left only two stark souls in colloquy:
Katarina's and mine.

Katarina had settled, I forget how, on the sofa, and
was reclining very comfortably with her head on my
shoulder and both arms about me. We did not talk.
No questions passed as to why we had picked one
another up. There we were, warmed with vodka and
tea, at eleven o'clock at night, five stories above the
clamorous world, while her friend shook the silly souls
out of us. With the shy boldness of my native country, I stretched a hand and inclosed her fingers. She
smiled; a curious smile that no other girl in London
could have given; not a flushed smile, or a startled
smile, or a satisfied smile, or a coy smile; but a smile
of companionship, which seemed to have realized the
tragedy of our living. So it was that she had, by
slow stages, reached her comfortable position, for as
my hand wandered from finger to wrist, from wrist to
soft, rounded arm, and so inclosed her neck, she slipped

and buried me in an avalanche of flaming, scented tresses.

Sanya at the piano shot a glance over her shoulder, a very sad-gay glance; she laughed, curiously, I almost said foreignly. I felt somehow as though I had been taken complete possession of by these people. I hardly belonged to myself. Fleet Street was but a street of dream. I seemed now to be awake and in an adorable captivity.

With a final volley of chords, the pianist slid from the chair, and sat by her boy on the carpet, smoothing his face with tobacco-stained fingers, and languishing, while her thick, over-ripe lips took his kisses as a baby bird takes food from its mother.

We talked—all of us—in jerks and snatches. Then the oil in the lamp began to give out, and the room grew dim. Some one said: "Play something!" And some one said: "Too tired!" The girl reclining on the bed grew snappy. She did not lean for caresses. She seemed morose, preoccupied, almost impatient. Twice she snapped up her boy on a casual remark. I believe I talked vodka'd nonsense. . . .

But suddenly there came a whisper of soft feet on the landing, and a secret tap at the door. Some one opened it, and slipped out. One heard the lazy hum of voices in busy conversation. Then silence; and some one entered the room and shut the door. One of the boys asked, casually, "What's up?" His question was not answered, but the girl who had gone to the door snapped something in a sharp tone which might have been either Russian or Yiddish. Katarina loosened herself from me, and sat up. The girl on the bed sat up. The three of them spat angry phrases about, I called over to one of the boys: "What's the joke? Anything wrong?" and received a reply: "Owshdiknow? I ain't a ruddy Russian, am I?"

Katarina suddenly drew back her flaming face. "Here," she said, "you better go."

"Go?"

"Yes—fathead! Go's what I said."

"But—" I began, looking and feeling like a flabbergasted cat.

"Don't I speak plain? Go!"

I suppose a man never feels a finer idiot than when a woman tells him she doesn't want him. If he ever does, it is when a woman tells him that she loves him. Katarina had given me the bullet, and, of course, I felt a fool; but I derived some consolation from the fact that the other boys were being told off. Clearly, big things were in the air, about to happen. Something, evidently, had already happened. I wondered. . . . Then I sat down on the sofa, and flatly told Katarina that I was not going unless I had a reason.

"Oh," she said, blithely, "ain't you? This is my room, ain't it? I brought you here, and you stay here just as long as I choose, and no longer. Who d'you think you are, saying you won't go? This is my room. I let you come here for a drink, and you just got to go when I say. See?"

I was about to make a second stand, when again there came a stealthy tap at the door, and the whispering of slippered feet. Sanya glided to the door, opened it, and disappeared. In a moment she came back, and called, " 'Rina!" Katarina slipped from my embrace, went to the door, and disappeared too. One girl and three boys remained—in silence.

Next moment Katarina reappeared, and said something to Sanya. Sanya pulled her boy by the arm, and went out. The other girl pushed her boy at the neck and literally threw him out. Katarina came over to me, and said: "Go, little fool!"

I said: "Shan't unless I know what the game is."

She stood over me; glared; searched for words to meet the occasion; found none. She gestured. I sat as rigid as an immobile comedian. Finally, she flung her arms, and swept away. At the door she turned; "Blasted little fool! He'll do us both in if y'ain't careful. You don't know him. Both of us he'll have. Serveyeh right."

She disappeared. I was alone. I heard the *sup-sup* of her slippered feet down the stair.

I got up, and moved to the door. I heard nothing. I stood by the window, my thoughts dancing a rag-time. I wondered what to do, and how, and whether. I wondered what was up exactly. I wondered . . . well, I just wondered. My thoughts got into a tangle, sank, and swam, and sank again. Then there was a sudden struggle and spurt from the lamp, and it went black out. From a room across the landing a clock ticked menacingly. I saw, by the thin light from the window, the smoke of a discarded cigarette curling up and up to the ceiling like a snake.

I went again to the door, peered down the steep stair and over the crazy balustrade. Nobody was about; no voices. I slipped swiftly down the five flights, met nobody. I stood in the slobbered vestibule. From afar I heard the sluck of the waters against the staples of the wharves, and the wicked hoot of the tugs.

It was then that a sudden nameless fear seized me; it was that simple terror that comes from nothing but ourselves. I am not usually afraid of any man or thing. I am normally nervous, and there are three or four things that have power to terrify me. But I am not, I think, afraid. At that moment, however, I was afraid of everything: of the room I had left, of the house, of the people, of the inviting lights of the warehouses and the threatening shoals of the alleys.

I stood a moment longer.   Then I raced into Brick Lane, and out into the brilliance of Commercial Street.

A WORD FOR AUTUMN

By A. A. MILNE

This is the sort of urbane pleasantry in which British essayists
are prolific and graceful. Alan Alexander Milne was born in
1882, went to Trinity College, Cambridge; was editor of *The
Granta* (the leading undergraduate publication at Cambridge at
that time); and plunged into the great whirlpool of London
journalism. He was on the staff of *Punch,* 1906-14. He has now
collected several volumes of charming essays, and has had considerable success as a playwright: his comedy, *Mr. Pim Passes
By,* recently played a prosperous run in New York. "A Word
for Autumn" is from his volume *Not That It Matters.*

LAST night the waiter put the celery on with the
cheese, and I knew that summer was indeed dead.
Other signs of autumn there may be—the reddening
leaf, the chill in the early-morning air, the misty evenings—but none of these comes home to me so truly.
There may be cool mornings in July; in a year of
drought the leaves may change before their time; it is
only with the first celery that summer is over.

I knew all along that it would not last. Even in
April I was saying that winter would soon be here.
Yet somehow it had begun to seem possible lately that
a miracle might happen, that summer might drift on
and on through the months—a final upheaval to crown
a wonderful year. The celery settled that. Last night
with the celery autumn came into its own.

There is a crispness about celery that is of the essence of October. It is as fresh and clean as a rainy day after a spell of heat. It crackles pleasantly in the mouth. Moreover it is excellent, I am told, for the complexion. One is always hearing of things which are good for the complexion, but there is no doubt that celery stands high on the list. After the burns and freckles of summer one is in need of something. How good that celery should be there at one's elbow.

A week ago—("A little more cheese, waiter")—a week ago I grieved for the dying summer. I wondered how I could possibly bear the waiting—the eight long months till May. In vain to comfort myself with the thought that I could get through more work in the winter undistracted by thoughts of cricket grounds and country houses. In vain, equally, to tell myself that I could stay in bed later in the mornings. Even the thought of after-breakfast pipes in front of the fire left me cold. But now, suddenly, I am reconciled to autumn. I see quite clearly that all good things must come to an end. The summer has been splendid, but it has lasted long enough. This morning I welcomed the chill in the air; this morning I viewed the falling leaves with cheerfulness; and this morning I said to myself, "Why, of course, I'll have celery for lunch." ("More bread, waiter.")

"Season of mists and mellow fruitfulness," said

Keats, not actually picking out celery in so many words, but plainly including it in the general blessings of the autumn. Yet what an opportunity he missed by not concentrating on that precious root. Apples, grapes, nuts, and vegetable marrows he mentions specially—and how poor a selection! For apples and grapes are not typical of any month, so ubiquitous are they, vegetable marrows are vegetables *pour rire* and have no place in any serious consideration of the seasons, while as for nuts, have we not a national song which asserts distinctly, "Here we go gathering nuts in May"? Season of mists and mellow celery, then let it be. A pat of butter underneath the bough, a wedge of cheese, a loaf of bread and—Thou.

How delicate are the tender shoots unfolded layer by layer. Of what a whiteness is the last baby one of all, of what a sweetness his flavor. It is well that this should be the last rite of the meal—*finis coronat opus*—so that we may go straight on to the business of the pipe. Celery demands a pipe rather than a cigar, and it can be eaten better in an inn or a London tavern than in the home. Yes, and it should be eaten alone, for it is the only food which one really wants to hear oneself eat. Besides, in company one may have to consider the wants of others. Celery is not a thing to share with any man. Alone in your country inn you may call for the celery; but if you are wise you will see that no other traveler wanders into the room. Take warning from one who has learnt a lesson. One day I lunched alone at an inn, finishing with cheese and celery. Another traveler came in and lunched too. We did not speak—I was busy with my celery. From the other end of the table he reached across for the cheese. That was all right! it was the public cheese. But he also reached across for the celery—my private celery for which I owed. Foolishly—you know how one does—I had left the sweetest and crispest shoots till the last, tantalizing myself pleasantly with the thought of them. Horror! to see them snatched from me by a stranger. He realized later what he had done and apologized, but of what good is an apology in such circumstances? Yet at least the tragedy was not without its value. Now one remembers to lock the door.

Yes, I can face the winter with calm. I suppose I had forgotten what it was really like. I had been thinking of the winter as a horrid wet, dreary time fit only for professional football. Now I can see other things—crisp and sparkling days, long pleasant evenings, cheery fires. Good work shall be done this winter. Life shall be lived well. The end of the summer is not the end of the world. Here's to October—and, waiter, some more celery.

"A CLERGYMAN"

By MAX BEERBOHM

Max Beerbohm, I dare say (and I believe it has been said before), is the most subtly gifted English essayist since Charles Lamb. It is not surprising that he has (now for many years) been referred to as "the incomparable Max," for what other contemporary has never once missed fire, never failed to achieve perfection in the field of his choice? Whether in caricature, short story, fable, parody, or essay, he has always been consummate in grace, tact, insouciant airy precision. I hope you will not miss "No. 2 The Pines" (in *And Even Now,* from which this selection also comes), a reminiscence of his first visit to Swinburne in 1899. That beautiful (there is no other word) essay shows an even ampler range of Mr. Beerbohm's powers: a tenderness and lovely grace that remind one, almost against belief, that the gay youth of the '90's now mellows deliciously with the end of the fifth decade. He was so enormously old in 1896, when he published his first book and called it his *Works;* he seems much younger now: he is having his first childhood.

This portrait of the unfortunate cleric annihilated by Dr. Johnson is a triumphant example of the skill with which a perfect artist can manœuver a trifle, carved like an ivory trinket; in such hands, subtlety never becomes mere tenuity.

Max Beerbohm was born in London in 1872; studied at Charterhouse School and Merton College, Oxford; and was a brilliant figure in the *Savoy* and *Yellow Book* circles by the time he was twenty-four. His genius is that of the essay in its purest distillation: a clear cross-section of life as seen through the lens of self; the pure culture (in the biological sense) of observing personality.

I have often wondered how it came about (though the matter is wholly nonpertinent) that Mr. Beerbohm married an American lady—quite a habit with English essayists, by the way: Hilaire Belloc and Bertrand Russell did likewise. *Who's Who* says she was from Memphis, which adds lustre to that admirable city.

He now lives in Italy.

FRAGMENTARY, pale, momentary; almost nothing; glimpsed and gone; as it were, a faint human hand thrust up, never to reappear, from beneath the rolling

177

waters of Time, he forever haunts my memory and
solicits my weak imagination. Nothing is told of him
but that once, abruptly, he asked a question, and received an answer.

This was on the afternoon of April 7th, 1778, at
Streatham, in the well-appointed house of Mr. Thrale.
Johnson, on the morning of that day, had entertained
Boswell at breakfast in Bolt Court, and invited him to
dine at Thrale Hall. The two took coach and arrived
early. It seems that Sir John Pringle had asked Boswell to ask Johnson "what were the best English
sermons for style." In the interval before dinner,
accordingly, Boswell reeled off the names of several
divines whose prose might or might not win commen-
dation. "Atterbury?" he suggested. "JOHNSON: Yes,
Sir, one of the best. BOSWELL: Tillotson? JOHNSON:
Why, not now. I should not advise any one to imitate Tillotson's style; though I don't know; I should
be cautious of censuring anything that has been ap-
plauded by so many suffrages.—South is one of the
best, if you except his peculiarities, and his violence,
and sometimes coarseness of language.—Seed has a
very fine style; but he is not very theological. Jortin's
sermons are very elegant. Sherlock's style, too, is
very elegant, though he has not made it his principal
study.—And you may add Smalridge. BOSWELL: I

ike Ogden's Sermons on Prayer very much, both for
neatness of style and subtility of reasoning. JOHNSON:
should like to read all that Ogden has written.
BOSWELL: What I want to know is, what sermons
afford the best specimen of English pulpit eloquence."
JOHNSON: We have no sermons addressed to the passions, that are good for anything; if you mean that
kind of eloquence. A CLERGYMAN, whose name I do
not recollect: Were not Dodd's sermons addressed
to the passions? JOHNSON: They were nothing, Sir,
be they addressed to what they may."

The suddenness of it! Bang!—and the rabbit that
had popped from its burrow was no more.

I know not which is the more startling—the début
of the unfortunate clergyman, or the instantaneousness
of his end. Why hadn't Boswell told us there was a
clergyman present? Well, we may be sure that so
careful and acute an artist had some good reason.
And I suppose the clergyman was left to take us una-
wares because just so did he take the company. Had
we been told he was there, we might have expected
that sooner or later he would join in the conversation.
He would have had a place in our minds. We may
assume that in the minds of the company around
Johnson he had no place. He sat forgotten, overlooked; so that his self-assertion startled every one

just as on Boswell's page it startles us. In Johnson's massive and magnetic presence only some very
remarkable man, such as Mr. Burke, was sharply distinguishable from the rest. Others might, if they
had something in them, stand out slightly. This unfortunate clergyman may have had something in him,
but I judge that he lacked the gift of seeming as if he
had. That deficiency, however, does not account for
the horrid fate that befell him. One of Johnson's
strongest and most inveterate feelings was his ven-
eration for the Cloth. To any one in Holy Orders
he habitually listened with a grace and charming deference. To-day, moreover, he was in excellent good
humor. He was at the Thrales', where he so loved
to be; the day was fine; a fine dinner was in close
prospect; and he had had what he always declared
to be the sum of human felicity—a ride in a coach.
Nor was there in the question put by the clergyman
anything likely to enrage him. Dodd was one whom
Johnson had befriended in adversity; and it had always been agreed that Dodd in his pulpit was very
emotional. What drew the blasting flash must have
been not the question itself, but the manner in which
it was asked. And I think we can guess what that
manner was.

Say the words aloud: "Were not Dodd's sermons
addressed to the passions?" They are words which,

if you have any dramatic and histrionic sense, *cannot* be said except in a high, thin voice.

You may, from sheer perversity, utter them in a rich and sonorous baritone or bass. But if you do so, they sound utterly unnatural. To make them carry the conviction of human utterance, you have no choice: you must pipe them.

Remember, now, Johnson was very deaf. Even the people whom he knew well, the people to whose voices he was accustomed, had to address him very loudly. It is probable that this unregarded, young, shy clergyman, when at length he suddenly mustered courage to 'cut in,' let his high, thin voice soar *too* high, insomuch that it was a kind of scream. On no other hypothesis can we account for the ferocity with which Johnson turned and rended him. Johnson didn't, we may be sure, mean to be cruel. The old lion, startled, just struck out blindly. But the force of paw and claws was not the less lethal. We have endless testimony to the strength of Johnson's voice; and the very cadence of those words, "They were nothing, Sir, be they addressed to what they may," convinces me that the old lion's jaws never gave forth a louder roar. Boswell does not record that there was any further conversation before the announcement of dinner. Perhaps the whole company had been temporarily deafened. But I am not bothering about them. My heart goes out to the poor dear clergyman exclusively.

I said a moment ago that he was young and shy; and I admit that I slipped those epithets in without having justified them to you by due process of induction. Your quick mind will have already supplied what I omitted. A man with a high, thin voice, and without power to impress any one with a sense of his importance, a man so null in effect that even the retentive mind of Boswell did not retain his very name, would assuredly not be a self-confident man. Even if he were not naturally shy, social courage would soon have been sapped in him, and would in time have been destroyed, by experience. That he had not yet given himself up as a bad job, that he still had faint wild hopes, is proved by the fact that he did snatch the opportunity for asking that question. He must, accordingly, have been young. Was he the curate of the neighboring church? I think so. It would account for his having been invited. I see him as he sits there listening to the great Doctor's pronouncement on Atterbury and those others. He sits on the edge of a chair in the background. He has colorless eyes, fixed earnestly, and a face almost as pale as the clerical bands beneath his somewhat receding chin. His forehead is high and narrow, his hair mouse-colored. His hands are clasped tight before

him, the knuckles standing out sharply. This con-
striction does not mean that he is steeling himself to
speak. He has no positive intention of speaking.
Very much, nevertheless, is he wishing in the back of
his mind that he could say something—something
whereat the great Doctor would turn on him and say,
after a pause for thought, "Why, yes, Sir. That is
most justly observed" or "Sir, this has never occurred
to me. I thank you"—thereby fixing the observer forever high in the esteem of all. And now in a flash the
chance presents itself. "We have," shouts Johnson,
"no sermons addressed to the passions, that are good
for anything." I see the curate's frame quiver with
sudden impulse, and his mouth fly open, and—no, I
can't bear it, I shut my eyes and ears. But audible,
even so, is something shrill, followed by something
thunderous.

Presently I reopen my eyes. The crimson has not
yet faded from that young face yonder, and slowly
down either cheek falls a glistening tear. Shades of
Atterbury and Tillotson! Such weakness shames the
Established Church. What would Jortin and Smalridge have said?—what Seed and South? And, by
the way, who *were* they, these worthies? It is a solemn
thought that so little is conveyed to us by names which
to the palæo-Georgians conveyed so much. We dis-
cern a dim, composite picture of a big man in a big

wig and a billowing black gown, with a big congregation beneath him. But we are not anxious to hear what he is saying. We know it is all very elegant. We know it will be printed and be bound in finely-tooled full calf, and no palæo-Georgian gentleman's library will be complete without it. Literate people in those days were comparatively few; but, bating that, one may say that sermons were as much in request as novels are to-day. I wonder, will mankind continue to be capricious? It is a very solemn thought indeed that no more than a hundred-and-fifty years hence the novelists of our time, with all their moral and political and sociological outlook and influence, will perhaps shine as indistinctly as do those old preachers, with all their elegance, now. "Yes, Sir," some great pundit may be telling a disciple at this moment, "Wells is one of the best. Galsworthy is one of the best, if you except his concern for delicacy of style. Mrs. Ward has a very firm grasp of problems, but is not very creational.—Caine's books are very edifying. I should like to read all that Caine has written. Miss Corelli, too, is very edifying.—And you may add Upton Sinclair." "What I want to know," says the disciple, "is, what English novels may be selected as specially enthralling." The pundit answers: "We have no novels addressed to the passions that are good for anything, if you mean that kind of enthralment."

And here some poor wretch (whose name the disciple will not remember) inquires: "Are not Mrs. Glyn's novels addressed to the passions?" and is in due form annihilated. Can it be that a time will come when readers of this passage in our pundit's Life will take more interest in the poor nameless wretch than in all the bearers of those great names put together, being no more able or anxious to discriminate between (say) Mrs. Ward and Mr. Sinclair than we are to set Ogden above Sherlock, or Sherlock above Ogden? It seems impossible. But we must remember that things are not always what they seem.

Every man illustrious in his day, however much he may be gratified by his fame, looks with an eager eye to posterity for a continuance of past favors, and would even live the remainder of his life in obscurity if by so doing he could insure that future generations would preserve a correct attitude towards him forever. This is very natural and human, but, like so many very natural and human things, very silly. Tillotson and the rest need not, after all, be pitied for our neglect of them. They either know nothing about it, or are above such terrene trifles. Let us keep our pity for the seething mass of divines who were not elegantly verbose, and had no fun or glory while they lasted. And let us keep a specially large portion for one whose lot was so much worse than merely undistinguished.

If that nameless curate had not been at the Thrales'
that day, or, being there, had kept the silence that so
well became him, his life would have been drab enough,
in all conscience. But at any rate an unpromising
career would not have been nipped in the bud. And
that is what in fact happened, I'm sure of it. A robust
man might have rallied under the blow. Not so our
friend. Those who knew him in infancy had not expected that he would be reared. Better for him had
they been right. It is well to grow up and be or-
dained, but not if you are delicate and very sensitive,
and shall happen to annoy the greatest, the most
stentorian and roughest of contemporary personages.
"A Clergyman" never held up his head or smiled
again after the brief encounter recorded for us by
Boswell. He sank into a rapid decline. Before the
next blossoming of Thrale Hall's almond trees he was
no more. I like to think that he died forgiving Dr.
Johnson.

SAMUEL BUTLER: DIOGENES OF THE VICTORIANS

By STUART P. SHERMAN

Professor Sherman's cold compress, applied to the Butler cult, caused much suffering in some regions, where it was said to be more than a cooling bandage—in fact, a wet blanket. In the general rough-and-tumble among critical standards during recent years, Mr. Sherman is one of those who have dealt some swinging blows in favor of the Victorians and the literary Old Guard —which was often square but rarely hollow.

Stuart Pratt Sherman, born in Iowa in 1881, graduated from Williams in 1903, has been since 1911 professor of English at the University of Illinois. His own account of his adventures, written without intended publication, is worth consideration. He says:

"My life hasn't been quite as dryly 'academic,' nor as simply 'middle-Western,' as the record indicates. For example: I lived in Los Angeles from my 5th to my 13th year, and then went on a seven months' adventure in gold mining in the Black Cañon of Arizona, where I had some experience with drouth in the desert, etc. That is not 'literary.'

"Recently, I've been thinking I might write a little paper about some college friends at Williams. I was in college with Harry James Smith (author of *Mrs. Bumpstead Lee*), Max Eastman, and 'Go-to-Hell' Whittlesey. As editor of the *Williams Monthly* I have accepted and rejected manuscripts of both the two latter, and have reminiscences of their literary youth.

"Then I spent a summer in the *Post* and *Nation* in 1908, which is a pleasant chapter to remember; another summer teaching at Columbia; this past summer teaching at the University of California. My favorite recreations are climbing little mountains, chopping wood, and canoeing on Lake Michigan.

"This summer I have been picking out a place to die in—or rather looking over the sites offered in California. I lean towards the high Sierras, up above the Yosemite Valley.

"My ambition in life is to retire—perhaps at the age of seventy—and write only for amusement. When I can abandon the task of improving my contemporaries, I hope to become a popular author."

.Professor Sherman, you will note, is almost an exact contemporary of H. L. Mencken, with whom he has crossed swords
in more than one spirited encounter; and Sherman is likely to
give as good as he takes in such scuffles, or even rather better.
It is high time that his critical sagacity and powerful reasoning
were better known in the market-place.

UNTIL I met the Butlerians I used to think that the
religious spirit in our times was very precious, there
was so little of it. I thought one should hold one's
breath before it as before the flicker of one's last
match on a cold night in the woods. "What if it
should go out?" I said; but my apprehension was
groundless. It can never go out. The religious spirit
is indestructible and constant in quantity like the sum
of universal energy in which matches and suns are alike
but momentary sparkles and phases. This great truth
I learned of the Butlerians: Though the forms and
objects of religious belief wax old as a garment and
are changed, faith, which is, after all, the precious
thing, endures forever. Destroy a man's faith in God
and he will worship humanity; destroy his faith in
humanity and he will worship science; destroy his
faith in science and he will worship himself; destroy
his faith in himself and he will worship Samuel Butler.

What makes the Butlerian cult so impressive is, of
course, that Butler, poor dear, as the English say, was
the least worshipful of men. He was not even—till
his posthumous disciples made him so—a person of
any particular importance. One writing a private

memorandum of his death might have produced something like this: Samuel Butler was an unsociable,
burry, crotchety, obstinate old bachelor, a dilettante
in art and science, an unsuccessful author, a witty
cynic of inquisitive temper and, comprehensively speaking, the unregarded Diogenes of the Victorians. Son
of a clergyman and grandson of a bishop, born in 1835,
educated at Cambridge, he began to prepare for ordina-
tion. But, as we are told, because of scruples regard-
ing infant baptism he abandoned the prospect of holy
orders and in 1859 sailed for New Zealand, where with
capital supplied by his father he engaged in sheep-
farming for five years. In 1864, returning to England
with £8,000, he established himself for life at Clifford's
Inn, London. He devoted some years to painting,
adored Handel and dabbled in music, made occasional
trips to Sicily and Italy, and wrote a dozen books,
which generally fell dead from the press, on religion,
literature, art and scientific theory. "Erewhon," however, a Utopian romance published in 1872, had by
1899 sold between three and four thousand copies.
Butler made few friends and apparently never married. He died in 1902. His last words were: "Have
you brought the cheque book, Alfred?" His body was
cremated and the ashes were buried in a garden by
his biographer and his man-servant, with nothing to
mark the spot.

Butler's indifference to the disposal of his earthly part betokens no contempt for fame. Denied contemporary renown, he had firmly set his heart on immortality, and quietly, persistently, cannily provided for it. If he could not go down to posterity by the suffrage of his countrymen, he would go down by the shrewd use of his cheque book; he would buy his way in. He bought the publication of most of the books produced in his lifetime. He diligently prepared manuscripts for posthumous publication and accumulated and arranged great masses of materials for a biographer. He insured an interest in his literary remains by bequeathing them and all his copyrights to his literary executor, R. A. Streatfeild. He purchased an interest in a biographer by persuading Henry Festing Jones, a feckless lawyer of Butlerian proclivities, to abandon the law and become his musical and literary companion. In return for these services Mr. Jones received between 1887 and 1900 an allowance of £200 a year, and at Butler's death a bequest of £500, the musical copyrights and the manifest responsibility and privilege of assisting Streatfeild with the propagation of Butler's fame, together with their own, in the next generation.

These good and faithful servants performed their duties with exemplary zeal and astuteness. In 1903, the year following the Master's death, Streatfeild published "The Way of All Flesh," a book packed with satirical wit, the first since "Erewhon" which was capable of walking off on its own legs and exciting general curiosity about its author—curiosity intensified by the announcement that the novel had been written between 1872 and 1884. In the wake of this sensation there began the systematic annual relaunching of old works, with fresh introductions and memoirs and a piecemeal feeding out of other literary remains, culminating in 1917 with the publication of "The Note-Books," a skilful collection and condensation of the whole of Butler's intellectual life. Meanwhile, in 1908, the Erewhon dinner had been instituted. In spite of mild deprecation, this feast, with its two toasts to his Majesty and to the memory of Samuel Butler, assumed from the outset the aspect of a solemn sacrament of believers. Among these was conspicuous on the second occasion Mr. George Bernard Shaw, not quite certain, perhaps, whether he had come to give or to receive honor, whether he was himself to be regarded as the beloved disciple or rather as the one for whom Butler, preaching in the Victorian wilderness, had prepared the way with "free and future-piercing suggestions."

By 1914 Streatfeild was able to declare that no fragment of Butler's was too insignificant to publish. In 1915 and 1916 appeared extensive critical studies by

Gilbert Cannan and John F. Harris. In 1919 at last arrives Henry Festing Jones with the authoritative memoir in two enormous volumes with portraits, documents, sumptuous index, elaborate bibliography and a pious accounting to the public for the original manuscripts, which have been deposited like sacred relics at St. John's College, the Bodleian, the British Museum, the Library of Congress and at various shrines in Italy and Sicily. Here are materials for a fresh consideration of the man in relation to his work.

The unconverted will say that such a monument to such a man is absurdly disproportionate. But Butler is now more than a man. He is a spiritual ancestor, leader of a movement, moulder of young minds, founder of a faith. His monument is designed not merely to preserve his memory but to mark as well the present importance of the Butlerian sect. The memoir appears to have been written primarily for them. The faithful will no doubt find it delicious; and I, though an outsider, got through it without fatigue and with a kind of perverse pleasure in its perversity.

It is very instructive, but it by no means simplifies its puzzling and complex subject. Mr. Jones is not of the biographers who look into the heart of a man, reduce him to a formula and recreate him in accordance with it. He works from the outside, inward, and gradually achieves life and reality by an immense ac-

cumulation of objective detail, without ever plucking
out, or even plucking at, the heart of the mystery.
What was the man's "master passion" and his master
faculty? Butler himself did not know; consequently
he could not always distinguish his wisdom from his
folly. He was an ironist entangled in his own net and
an egotist bitten with self-distrust, concealing his
wounds in self-assertion and his hesitancies in an external aggressiveness. Mr. Jones pierces the shell here
and there, but never removes it. Considering his opportunities, he is sparing in composed studies of his
subject based on his own direct observation; and, with
all his ingenuousness and his shocking but illuminating
indiscretions, he is frequently silent as a tomb where
he must certainly possess information for which every
reader will inquire, particularly those readers who do
not, like the Butlerians, accept Samuel Butler as the
happy reincarnation of moderation, common sense and
fearless honesty.

The whole case of the Georgians against the Victorians might be fought out over his life and works;
and indeed there has already been many a skirmish in
that quarter. For, of course, neither Streatfeild nor
Mr. Jones is ultimately responsible for his revival.
Ultimately Butler's vogue is due to the fact that he is a
friend of the Georgian revolution against idealism in
the very citadel of the enemy; the extraordinary ac-

claim with which he is now received is his reward
for having long ago prepared to betray the Victorians
into the hands of a ruthless posterity. He was a traitor
to his own times, and therefore it follows that he was
a man profoundly disillusioned. The question which
we may all reasonably raise with regard to a traitor
whom we have received within our lines is whether he
will make us a good citizen. We should like to know
pretty thoroughly how he fell out with his countrymen
—whether through defects in his own temper and
character or through a clear-eyed and righteous indignation with the incorrigible viciousness of their manners and institutions. We should like to know what
vision of reformation succeeded his disillusion. Hitherto the Georgians have been more eloquent in their
disillusions than in their visions, and have inclined
to welcome Butler as a dissolving agent without much
inspecting his solution.

The Butlerians admire Butler for his withering attack on family life, notably in "The Way of All Flesh";
and many a studious literary man with a talkative wife
and eight romping children would, of course, admit
an occasional flash of romantic envy for Butler's bachelor apartments. Mr. Jones tells us that Theobald and
Christina Pontifex, whose nakedness Butler uncovers,
were drawn without exaggeration from his own father
and mother. His work on them is a masterpiece of

pitiless satire. Butler appears to have hated his father, despised his mother and loathed his sisters in all truth and sincerity. He nursed his vindictive and contemptuous feelings towards them all through his life; he studied these feelings, made notes on them, jested out of them, lived in them, reduced them to a philosophy of domestic antipathy.

He was far more learned than any other English author in the psychology of impiety. When he heard some one say, "Two are better than one," he exclaimed, "Yes, but the man who said that did not know my sisters." When he was forty-eight years old he wrote to a friend that his father was in poor health and not likely to recover; "but may hang on for months or go off with the N. E. winds which we are sure to have later on." In the same letter he writes that he is going to strike out forty weak pages in "Erewhon" and stick in forty stronger ones on the "trial of a middle-aged man 'for not having lost his father at a suitable age.'" His father's one unpardonable offense was not dying early and so enlarging his son's income. If this had been a jest, it would have been a little coarse for a deathbed. But Mr. Jones, who appears to think it very amusing, proves clearly enough that it was not a jest, but an obsession, and a horrid obsession it was. Now a man who attacks the family because his father does not die as promptly as could be desired is not likely to propose a happy substitute: his mood is not reconstructive, funny though it may be in two old boys of fifty, like Butler and Jones, living along like spoiled children on allowances, Butler from his father, Jones from his mother.

The Butlerians admire Butler for his brilliant attack on "romantic" relations between the sexes. Before the advent of Shaw he poured poison on the roots of that imaginative love in which all normal men and maidens walk at least once in a lifetime as in a rosy cloud shot through with golden lights.

His portraits show a man of vigorous physique, capable of passion, a face distinctly virile, rather harshly bearded, with broad masculine eyebrows. Was he ever in love? If not, why was he not? Elementary questions which his biographer after a thousand pages leaves unanswered. Mr. Jones asserts that both Overton and Ernest in "The Way of All Flesh" are in the main accurately autobiographical, and he furnishes much evidence for the point. He remarks a divergence in this fact, that Butler, unlike his hero, was never in prison. Did Butler, like his hero, have children and farm them out? The point is of some interest in the case of a man who is helping us to destroy the conventional family.

Mr. Jones leaves quite in the dark his relations with such women as the late Queen Victoria would not

have approved, relations which J. B. Yeats has, however, publicly discussed. Mr. Jones is ordinarily cynical enough, candid enough, as we shall see. He takes
pains to tell us that his own grandfather was never
married. He does not hesitate to acknowledge abundance of moral ugliness in his subject. Why this access
of Victorian reticence at a point where plain-speaking
is the order of the day and the special pride of contemporary Erewhonians? Why did a young man of
Butler's tastes leave the church and go into exile in
New Zealand for five years? Could a more resolute
biographer perhaps find a more "realistic" explanation than difficulties over infant baptism? Mr. Shaw
told his publisher that Butler was "a shy old bird."
In some respects he was also a sly old bird.

Among the "future-piercing suggestions" extolled
by Mr. Shaw we may be sure that the author of "Man
and Superman" was pleased to acknowledge Butler's
prediscovery that woman is the pursuer. This idea
we may now trace quite definitely to his relations with
Miss Savage, a witty, sensible, presumably virtuous
woman of about his own age, living in a club in London, who urged hm to write fiction, read all his manuscripts, knitted him socks, reviewed his books in
women's magazines and corresponded with him for
years till she died, without his knowledge, in hospital
from cancer. Her letters are Mr. Jones' mainstay in

his first volume and she is, except Butler himself, altogether his most interesting personality. Mr. Jones says that being unable to find any one who could authorize him to use her letters, he publishes them on his own responsibility. But he adds, "I cannot imagine that any relation of hers who may read her letters will experience any feelings other than pride and delight." This lady, he tells us, was the original of Alethea Pontifex. But he marks a difference. Alethea was handsome. Miss Savage, he says, was short, fat, had hip disease, and "that kind of dowdiness which I used to associate with ladies who had been at school with my mother." Butler became persuaded that Miss Savage loved him; this bored him; and the correspondence would lapse till he felt the need of her cheery friendship again. On one occasion she wrote to him, "I wish that you did not know wrong from right." Mr. Jones believes that she was alluding to his scrupulousness in matters of business. Butler himself construed the words as an overture to which he was indisposed to respond. The debate on this point and the pretty uncertainty in which it is left can surely arouse in Miss Savage's relations no other feelings than "pride and delight."

This brings us to the Butlerian substitute for the chivalry which used to be practised by those who bore what the Victorians called "the grand old name of

gentleman." In his later years, after the death of Miss
Savage, in periods of loneliness, depression and ill-
health, Butler made notes on his correspondence re-
proaching himself for his ill-treatment of her. "He
also," says his biographer, "tried to express his re-
morse" in two sonnets from which I extract some lines:

She was too kind, wooed too persistently,
Wrote moving letters to me day by day;

Hard though I tried to love I tried in vain,
For she was plain and lame and fat and short,
Forty and overkind.

'Tis said that if a woman woo, no man
    Should leave her till she have prevailed; and, true,
A man will yield for pity if he can,
    But if the flesh rebel what can he do?
        I could not; hence I grieve my whole life long
        The wrong I did in that I did no wrong.

In these Butlerian times one who should speak of
"good taste" would incur the risk of being called a prig.
Good taste is no longer "in." Yet even now, in the
face of these sonnets, may not one exclaim, Heaven
preserve us from the remorseful moments of a Butlerian Adonis of fifty!

The descendants of eminent Victorians may well be thankful that their fathers had no intimate relations with Butler. There is a familiar story of Whistler, that when some one praised his latest portrait as equal to Velasquez, he snapped back, "Yes, but why lug in Velasquez?" Butler, with similar aversion for rivals, but without Whistler's extempore wit, slowly excogitated his killing sallies and entered them in his notebooks or sent them in a letter to Miss Savage, preserving a copy for the delectation of the next age: "I do not see how I can well call Mr. Darwin the Pecksniff of Science, though this is exactly what he is; but I think I may call Lord Bacon the Pecksniff of his age and then, a little later, say that Mr. Darwin is the Bacon of the Victorian Era." To this he adds another note reminding himself to call "Tennyson the Darwin of Poetry, and Darwin the Tennyson of Science." I can recall but one work of a contemporary mentioned favorably in the biography; perhaps there are two. The staple of his comment runs about as follows: "Middlemarch" is a "longwinded piece of studied brag"; of "John Inglesant," "I seldom was more displeased with any book"; of "Aurora Leigh," "I dislike it very much, but I liked it better than Mrs. Browning, or Mr., either"; of Rossetti, "I dislike his face and his manner and his work, and I hate his poetry and his friends"; of George Meredith, "No wonder if his work repels me that mine should repel him"; "all I remember is that I disliked and distrusted Morley"; of Gladstone, "Who was it said that he was 'a good man in the very worst sense of the words'?" The homicidal spirit here exhibited may be fairly related to his anxiety for the death of his father.

It was on the whole characteristic of Victorian free-thinkers to attack Christianity with reverence and discrimination in an attempt to preserve its substance while removing obstacles to the acceptance of its substance. Butler was Voltairean. When he did not attack mischievously like a gamin, he attacked vindictively like an Italian laborer whose sweetheart has been false to him. I have seen it stated that he was a broad churchman and a communicant; and Mr. Jones produces a letter from a clergyman testifying to his "saintliness." But this must be some of Mr. Jones's fun. From Gibbon, read on the voyage to New Zealand, Butler imbibed, he says, in a letter of 1861, "a calm and philosophic spirit of impartial and critical investigation." In 1862 he writes: "For the present I renounce Christianity altogether. You say people must have something to believe in. I can only say that I have not found my digestion impeded since I left off believing in what does not appear to be supported by sufficient evidence." When in 1865 he printed his "Evidence for the Resurrection of Jesus

Christ," the manner of his attack was impish; and so was the gleeful exchange of notes between him and Miss Savage over the way the orthodox swallowed the bait. In his notebook he wrote: "Mead is the lowest of the intoxicants, just as Church is the lowest of the dissipations, and carraway seed the lowest of the condiments." He went to church once in 1883 to please a friend and was asked whether it had not bored him as inconsistent with his principles. "I said that, having given up Christianity, I was not going to be hampered by its principles. It was the substance of Christianity, and not its accessories of external worship, that I had objected to . . . so I went to church out of pure cussedness." Finally, in a note of 1889: "There will be no comfortable and safe development of our social arrangements—I mean we shall not get infanticide, and the permission of suicide, nor cheap and easy divorce—till Jesus Christ's ghost has been laid; and the best way to lay it is to be a moderate churchman."

Robert Burns was a free-thinker, but he wrote the "Cotter's Saturday Night"; Renan was a free-thinker, but he buried his God in purple; Matthew Arnold was a free-thinker, but he gave new life to the religious poetry of the Bible; Henry Adams believed only in mathematical physics, but he wrote of Mont St. Michel and Chartres with chivalrous and almost Catholic tenderness for the Virgin: for in all these diverse men there was reverence for what men have adored as their highest. There was respect for a tomb, even for the tomb of a God. Butler, having transferred his faith to the Bank of England, diverted himself like a street Arab with a slingshot by peppering the church windows. He established manners for the contemporary Butlerian who, coming down to breakfast on Christmas morning, exclaims with a pleased smile, "Well, this is the birthday of the hook-nosed Nazarene!"

Butler's moral note is rather attractive to young and middle-aged persons: "We have all sinned and come short of the glory of making ourselves as comfortable as we easily might have done." His ethics is founded realistically on physiology and economics; for "goodness is naught unless it tends towards old age and sufficiency of means." Pleasure, dressed like a quiet man of the world, is the best teacher: "The devil, when he dresses himself in angels' clothes, can only be detected by experts of exceptional skill, and so often does he adopt this disguise that it is hardly safe to be seen talking to an angel at all, and prudent people will follow after pleasure as a more homely but more respectable and on the whole more trustworthy guide." There we have something of the tone of our genial Franklin; but Butler is a Franklin without a single impulse of Franklin's wide benevolence and practical beneficence, a Franklin shorn of the spirit of his greatness, namely, his immensely intelligent social consciousness.

Having disposed of Christianity, orthodox and otherwise, and having reduced the morality of "enlightened selfishness" to its lowest terms, Butler turned in the same spirit to the destruction of orthodox Victorian science. We are less concerned for the moment with his substance than with his character and manner as scientific controversialist. "If I cannot," he wrote, "and I know I cannot, get the literary and scientific bigwigs to give me a shilling, I can, and I know I can, heave bricks into the middle of them." Though such professional training as he had was for the church and for painting, he seems never to have doubted that his mother wit was sufficient equipment, supplemented by reading in the British Museum, for the overthrow of men like Darwin, Wallace and Huxley, who from boyhood had given their lives to collecting, studying and experimenting with scientific data. "I am quite ready to admit," he records, "that I am in a conspiracy of one against men of science in general." Having felt himself covertly slighted in a book for which Darwin was responsible, he vindictively assailed, not merely the work, but also the character of Darwin and his friends, who, naturally inferring that he was an unscrupulous "bounder" seeking notoriety, generally ignored him.

His first "contribution" to evolutionary theory had been a humorous skit, written in New Zealand, on the evolution of machines, suggested by "The Origin of Species," and later included in "Erewhon." To support this whimsy he found it useful to revive the abandoned "argument from design"; and mother wit, still working whimsically, leaped to the conception that the organs of our bodies are machines. Thereupon he commenced serious scientific speculator, and produced "Life and Habit," 1878; "Evolution Old and New," 1879; "Unconscious Memory," 1880; and "Luck or Cunning," 1886. The germ of all his speculations, contained in his first volume, is the notion of "the oneness of personality existing between parents and offspring up to the time that the offspring leaves the parent's body"; thence develops his theory that the offspring "unconsciously" remembers what happened to the parents; and thence his theory that a vitalistic purposeful cunning, as opposed to the Darwinian chance, is the significant factor in evolution. His theory has something in common with current philosophical speculation, and it is in part, as I understand, a kind of adumbration, a shrewd guess, at the present attitude of cytologists. It has thus entitled Butler to half a dozen footnotes in a centenary volume on Darwin; but it hardly justifies his transference of Darwin's laurels to Buffon, Lamarck, Erasmus Darwin and himself; nor does it justify his reiterated contention that Darwin was a plagiarist, a fraud, a Pecksniff and a liar. He swelled the ephemeral body of scientific speculation; but his contribution to the verified body of science was negligible, and the injuries that he inflicted upon the scientific spirit were considerable.

For their symptomatic value, we must glance at Butler's sallies into some other fields. He held as an educational principle that it is hardly worth while to study any subject till one is ready to use it. When in his fifties he wished to write music, he took up for the first time the study of counterpoint. Mr. Garnett having inquired what subject Butler and Jones would take up when they had finished "Narcissus," Butler said that they "might write an oratorio on some sacred subject"; and when Garnett asked whether they had anything in particular in mind, he replied that they were thinking of "The Woman Taken in Adultery." In the same decade he cheerfully applied for the Slade professorship of art at Cambridge; and he took credit for the rediscovery of a lost school of sculpture.

At the age of fifty-five he brushed up his Greek, which he "had not wholly forgotten," and read the "Odyssey" for the purposes of his oratorio, "Ulysses." When he got to Circe it suddenly flashed upon him that he was reading the work of a young woman! Thereupon he produced his book, "The Authoress of the Odyssey," with portrait of the authoress, Nausicaa, identification of her birthplace in Sicily, which pleased the Sicilians, and an account of the way in which she wrote her poem. It was the most startling literary discovery since Delia Bacon burst into the silent sea on which Colonel Fabyan of the biliteral cypher is the latest navigator. That the classical scholars laughed at or ignored him did not shake his belief that the work was as important as anything he had done. "Perhaps it was," he would have remarked, if any one else had written it. "I am a prose man," he wrote to Robert Bridges, "and, except Homer and Shakespeare"—he should have added Nausicaa—"I have read absolutely nothing of English poetry and *very little* of English prose." His inacquaintance with English poetry, however, did not embarrass him, when, two years after bringing out his Sicilian authoress, he cleared up the mysteries of Shakespeare's sonnets. Nor did it prevent his dismissing the skeptical Dr. Furnivall, after a discussion at an A. B. C. shop, as a poor old incompetent. "Nothing," said Alethea Pontifex, speaking for her creator, "is well done nor worth doing unless, take it all round, it has come pretty easily." The poor old doctor, like the Greek scholars and the professional men of science, had blunted his wits by too much research.

Butler maintained that every man's work is a portrait of himself, and in his own case the features stand out ruggedly enough. Why should any one see in this infatuated pursuer of paradox a reincarnation of the pagan wisdom? In his small personal affairs he shows a certain old-maidish tidiness and the prudence of an experienced old bachelor, who manages his little pleasures without scandal. But in his intellectual life what vestige do we find of the Greek or even of the Roman sobriety, poise and decorum? In one respect Butler was conservative: he respected the established political and economic order. But he respected it only because it enabled him, without bestirring himself about his bread and butter, to sit quietly in his rooms at Clifford's Inn and invent attacks on every other form of orthodoxy. With a desire to be conspicuous only surpassed by his desire to be original he worked out the central Butlerian principle; videlicet: The fact that all the best qualified judges agree that a thing is true and valuable establishes an overwhelming presumption that it is valueless and false. With his feet firmly planted on this grand radical maxim he employed his lively wit with lawyer-like ingenuity to make out a case against family life, of which he was incapable; against imaginative love, of which he was ignorant; against chivalry, otherwise the conventions of gentlemen, which he had but imperfectly learned; against Victorian men of letters, whom, by his own account, he had never read;

against altruistic morality and the substance of Christianity, which were repugnant to his selfishness and other vices; against Victorian men of science, whose researches he had never imitated; and against Elizabethan and classical scholarship, which he took up in an odd moment as one plays a game of solitaire before going to bed.   To his disciples he could not bequeath his cleverness; but he left them his recipe for originality, his manners and his assurance, which has been gathering compound interest ever since.   In the original manuscript of "Alps and Sanctuaries" he consigned "Raffaele, along with Socrates, Virgil [the last two displaced later by Plato and Dante], Marcus Aurelius Antoninus, Goethe, Beethoven, and *another,* to limbo as the Seven Humbugs of Christiandom."   Who was the unnamed seventh?

BED-BOOKS AND NIGHT-LIGHTS

By H. M. TOMLINSON

I shall not forget with what a thrill of delight I came upon H. M. Tomlinson's *Old Junk,* the volume of essays from which this is borrowed. One feels, in stumbling upon such a book, much as some happy and astounded readers must have felt in 1878 when *An Inland Voyage* came out. It makes one wonder, submitting one's self to the moving music and magic of that prose, so simple and yet so subtle in its flavor, whether poetry is not, after all, an inferior and more mechanic form. "The cool element of prose," that perfect phrase of Milton's, comes back to mind. How direct and satisfying a passage to the mind Mr. Tomlinson's paragraphs have. How they build and cumulate, how the sentences shift, turn and move in delicate loops and ridges under the blowing wind of thought, like the sand of the dunes that he describes in one essay. And through it all, as intangible but as real and beautifying as moonlight, there is the pervading brightness of a particular way of looking at the world, something for which we have no catchword, the illumination of a spirit at once humorous, melancholy, shrewd, lovely and humane. Somehow, when one is caught in the web of that exquisite, considered prose, the awkward symbols of speech seem transparent; we come close to a man's mind.

In Mr. Tomlinson's three books—*The Sea and the Jungle* (1912), *Old Junk* (1920) and *London River* (1921) is revealed one of the most sincere and perfect workmen in contemporary prose.

H. M. Tomlinson was born in 1873; among his early memories he records: "I was an office boy and a clerk among London's ships, in the last days of the clippers. And I am forced to recall some of the things—such as bookkeeping in a jam factory and stoking on a tramp steamer." He joined the staff of the London *Morning Leader* in 1904; which was later merged with the *Daily News,* and to this journal he was attached for several years. During the War he was a correspondent in France; at the danger of incurring his anger (should he see this) I quote Mr. S. K. Ratcliffe on this phase of his work:—"One who was the friend of all, a sweet and fine spirit moving untouched amid the ruin and terror, expressing itself everywhere with perfect simplicity, and at times with a shattering candor."

In 1917 he became associate editor of the London *Nation,* where, if you are interested, you may find his initials almost weekly.

THE rain flashed across the midnight window with a myriad feet. There was a groan in outer darkness, the voice of all nameless dreads. The nervous candle-flame shuddered by my bedside. The groaning rose to a shriek, and the little flame jumped in a panic, and nearly left its white column. Out of the corners of the room swarmed the released shadows. Black specters danced in ecstasy over my bed. I love fresh air, but I cannot allow it to slay the shining and delicate body of my little friend the candle-flame, the comrade who ventures with me into the solitudes beyond midnight. I shut the window.

They talk of the candle-power of an electric bulb. What do they mean? It cannot have the faintest glimmer of the real power of my candle. It would be as right to express, in the same inverted and foolish comparison, the worth of "those delicate sisters, the Pleiades." That pinch of star dust, the Pleiades, exquisitely remote in deepest night, in the profound where light all but fails, has not the power of a sulphur match; yet, still apprehensive to the mind though tremulous on the limit of vision, and sometimes even vanishing, it brings into distinction those distant and difficult hints—hidden far behind all our verified thoughts—which we rarely properly view. I should like to know of any great arc-lamp which could do that. So the star-like candle for me. No other light follows so intimately an author's most ghostly suggestion. We sit, the candle and I, in the midst of the shades we are conquering, and sometimes look up from the lucent page to contemplate the dark hosts of the enemy with a smile before they overwhelm us; as they will, of course. Like me, the candle is mortal; it will burn out.

As the bed-book itself should be a sort of night-light, to assist its illumination, coarse lamps are useless. They would douse the book. The light for such a book must accord with it. It must be, like the book, a limited, personal, mellow, and companionable glow; the solitary taper beside the only worshiper in a sanctuary. That is why nothing can compare with the intimacy of candle-light for a bed-book. It is a living heart, bright and warm in central night, burning for us alone, holding the gaunt and towering shadows at bay. There the monstrous specters stand in our midnight room, the advance guard of the darkness of the world, held off by our valiant little glim, but ready to flood instantly and founder us in original gloom.

The wind moans without; ancient evils are at large and wandering in torment. The rain shrieks across the window. For a moment, for just a moment, the sentinel candle is shaken, and burns blue with terror. The shadows leap out instantly. The little flame recovers, and merely looks at its foe the darkness, and back to its own place goes the old enemy of light and man. The candle for me, tiny, mortal, warm, and brave, a golden lily on a silver stem!

"Almost any book does for a bed-book," a woman once said to me. I nearly replied in a hurry that almost any woman would do for a wife; but that is not the way to bring people to conviction of sin. Her idea was that the bed-book is soporific, and for that reason she even advocated the reading of political speeches. That would be a dissolute act. Certainly you would go to sleep; but in what a frame of mind! You would enter into sleep with your eyes shut. It would be like dying, not only unshriven, but in the act of guilt.

What book shall it shine upon? Think of Plato, or Dante, or Tolstoy, or a Blue Book for such an occasion! I cannot. They will not do—they are no good to me. I am not writing about you. I know those men I have named are transcendent, the greater lights. But I am bound to confess at times they bore me. Though their feet are clay and on earth, just as ours, their stellar brows are sometimes dim in remote clouds. For my part, they are too big for bed-fellows. I cannot see myself, carrying my feeble and restricted glim, following (in pajamas) the statuesque figure of the Florentine where it stalks, aloof in its garb of austere pity, the sonorous deeps of Hades. Hades!

Not for me; not after midnight! Let those go who like it.

As for the Russian, vast and disquieting, I refuse to leave all, including the blankets and the pillow, to follow him into the gelid tranquillity of the upper air, where even the colors are prismatic spicules of ice, to brood upon the erratic orbit of the poor mud-ball below called earth. I know it is my world also; but I cannot help that. It is too late, after a busy day, and at that hour, to begin overtime on fashioning a new and better planet out of cosmic dust. By breakfast-time, nothing useful would have been accomplished. We should all be where we were the night before. The job is far too long, once the pillow is nicely set.

For the truth is, there are times when we are too weary to remain attentive and thankful under the improving eye, kindly but severe, of the seers. There are times when we do not wish to be any better than we are. We do not wish to be elevated and improved. At midnight, away with such books! As for the literary pundits, the high priests of the Temple of Letters, it is interesting and helpful occasionally for an acolyte to swinge them a good hard one with an incense-burner, and cut and run, for a change, to something outside the rubrics. Midnight is the time when one can recall, with ribald delight, the names of all the Great Works which every gentleman ought to have read, but which some of us have not. For there is almost as much clotted nonsense written about literature as there is about theology.

There are few books which go with midnight, solitude, and a candle. It is much easier to say what does not please us then than what is exactly right. The book must be, anyhow, something benedictory by a sinning fellow-man. Cleverness would be repellent at such an hour. Cleverness, anyhow, is the level of mediocrity to-day; we are all too infernally clever. The first witty and perverse paradox blows out the candle. Only the sick in mind crave cleverness, as a morbid body turns to drink. The late candle throws its beams a great distance; and its rays make transparent much that seemed massy and important. The mind at rest beside that light, when the house is asleep, and the consequential affairs of the urgent world have diminished to their right proportions because we see them distantly from another and a more tranquil place in the heavens where duty, honor, witty arguments, controversial logic on great questions, appear such as will leave hardly a trace of fossil in the indurated mud which presently will cover them—the mind then certainly smiles at cleverness.

For though at that hour the body may be dog-tired, the mind is white and lucid, like that of a man from whom a fever has abated. It is bare of illusions. It has a sharp focus, small and starlike, as a clear and lonely flame left burning by the altar of a shrine from which all have gone but one. A book which approaches that light in the privacy of that place must come, as it were, with honest and open pages.

I like Heine then, though. His mockery of the grave and great, in those sentences which are as brave as pennants in a breeze, is comfortable and sedative. One's own secret and awkward convictions, never expressed because not lawful and because it is hard to get words to bear them lightly, seem then to be heard aloud in the mild, easy, and confident diction of an immortal whose voice has the blitheness of one who has watched, amused and irreverent, the high gods in eager and secret debate on the best way to keep the gilt and trappings on the body of the evil they have created.

That first-rate explorer, Gulliver, is also fine in the light of the intimate candle. Have you read lately again his Voyage to the Houyhnhnms? Try it alone again in quiet. Swift knew all about our contemporary troubles. He has got it all down. Why was he called a misanthrope? Reading that last voyage of Gulliver in the select intimacy of midnight I am forced to wonder, not at Swift's hatred of mankind, not at his satire of his fellows, not at the strange and terrible nature of this genius who thought that much of us, but how it is that after such a wise and sorrowful revealing of the things we insist on doing, and our reasons for doing them, and what happens after we have done them, men do not change. It does seem impossible that society could remain unaltered, after the surprise its appearance should have caused it as it saw its face in that ruthless mirror. We point instead to the fact that Swift lost his mind in the end. Well, that is not a matter for surprise.

Such books, and France's "Isle of Penguins," are not disturbing as bed-books. They resolve one's agitated and outraged soul, relieving it with some free expression for the accusing and questioning thoughts engendered by the day's affairs. But they do not rest immediately to hand in the book-shelf by the bed. They depend on the kind of day one has had. Sterne is closer. One would rather be transported as far as possible from all the disturbances of earth's envelope of clouds, and "Tristram Shandy" is sure to be found in the sun.

But best of all books for midnight are travel books. Once I was lost every night for months with Doughty in the "Arabia Deserta." He is a craggy author. A long course of the ordinary facile stuff, such as one gets in the Press every day, thinking it is English, sends one thoughtless and headlong among the bitter herbs and stark boulders of Doughty's burning and spacious expanse; only to get bewildered, and the shins broken,

and a great fatigue at first, in a strange land of fierce
sun, hunger, glittering spar, ancient plutonic rock, and
very Adam himself. But once you are acclimatized,
and know the language—it takes time—there is no
more London after dark, till, a wanderer returned from
a forgotten land, you emerge from the interior of
Arabia on the Red Sea coast again, feeling as though
you had lost touch with the world you used to know.
And if that doesn't mean good writing I know of no
other test.

Because once there was a father whose habit it was
to read with his boys nightly some chapters of the
Bible—and cordially they hated that habit of his—I
have that Book too; though I fear I have it for no
reason that he, the rigid old faithful, would be pleased
to hear about. He thought of the future when he
read the Bible; I read it for the past. The familiar
names, the familiar rhythm of its words, its wonderful well-remembered stories of things long past—like
that of Esther, one of the best in English—the eloquent anger of the prophets for the people then who
looked as though they were alive, but were really dead
at heart, all is solace and home to me. And now I
think of it, it is our home and solace that we want in
a bed-book.

THE PRECEPT OF PEACE

By LOUISE IMOGEN GUINEY

Louise Imogen Guiney (1861-1920), one of the rarest poets and most delicately poised essayists this country has reared, has been hitherto scantily appreciated by the omnipotent General Reader. Her dainty spoor is perhaps too lightly trodden upon earth to be followed by the throng. And yet one has faith in the imperishability of such a star-dust track. This lovely and profound "Precept of Peace" is peculiarly characteristic of her, and reminds one of the humorous tranquillity with which she faced the complete failure (financially speaking) of almost all her books. There was a certain sadness in learning, when the news of her death came, that many of our present-day critical Sanhedrim had never even become aware of her name.

There is no space, in this brief note, to do justice to her. The student will refer to the newly published memoir by her friend, Alice Brown.

She was born in Boston in 1861, daughter of General Patrick Guiney who fought in the Civil War. From 1894-97 she was postmistress in Auburndale, Mass. Her later years were spent in England, mostly at Oxford: the Bodleian Library was a candle and she the ecstatic moth.

A CERTAIN sort of voluntary abstraction is the oldest and choicest of social attitudes. In France, where all esthetic discoveries are made, it was crowned long ago: la sainte indifférence is, or may be, a cult, and le saint indifférent an articled practitioner. For the Gallic mind, brought up at the knee of a consistent paradox, has found that not to appear concerned about a desired good is the only method to possess it; full happiness is given, in other words, to the very man who will never sue for it. This is a secret neat as that of the Sphinx: to "go softly" among events, yet domineer them. Without fear: not because we are brave, but because we are exempt; we bear so charmed a life that not even Baldur's mistletoe can touch us to harm us. Without solicitude: for the essential thing is trained, falcon-like, to light from above upon our wrists, and it has become with us an automatic motion to open the hand, and drop what appertains to us no longer. Be it renown or a new hat, the shorter stick of celery, or

> "The friends to whom we had no natural right,
> The homes that were not destined to be ours,"

it is all one: let it fall away! since only so, by depletions, can we buy serenity and a blithe mien. It is diverting to study, at the feet of Antisthenes and of Socrates his master, how many indispensables man can live without; or how many he can gather together, make over into luxuries, and so abrogate them. Thoreau somewhere expresses himself as full of divine pity for the "mover," who on May-Day clouds city streets with his melancholy household caravans: fatal impedimenta for an immortal. No: furniture is clearly a superstition. "I have little, I want nothing; all my treasure is in Minerva's tower." Not that the novice may not accumulate. Rather, let him collect beetles and Venetian interrogation-marks; if so be that he may distinguish what is truly extrinsic to him, and bestow these toys, eventually, on the children of Satan who clamor at the monastery gate. Of all his store, unconsciously increased, he can always part with sixteen-seventeenths, by way of concession to his individuality, and think the subtraction so much concealing marble chipped from the heroic figure of himself. He would be a donor from the beginning; before he can be seen to own, he will disencumber, and divide. Strange and fearful is his discovery, amid the bric-a-brac of the world, that this knowledge, or this material benefit, is for him alone. He would fain beg off from the acquisition, and shake the touch of the tangible from his imperious wings. It is not enough to cease to strive for personal favor; your true indifférent is Early Franciscan: caring not to have, he fears to hold. Things useful need never become to him things desirable. Towards all commonly-accounted sinecures, he bears the coldest front in Nature, like a magician walking a maze, and scornful of its flower-bordered detentions. "I enjoy life," says Seneca, "because I am ready to leave it." Meanwhile, they who act with too jealous respect for their morrow of civilized comfort, reap only indigestion, and crow's-foot traceries for their deluded eye-corners.

Now nothing is farther from le saint indifférent than

cheap indifferentism, so-called: the sickness of sopho-
mores. His business is to hide, not to display, his lack
of interest in fripperies. It is not he who looks languid,
and twiddles his thumbs for sick misplacedness, like
Achilles among girls. On the contrary, he is a smiling
industrious elf, monstrous attentive to the canons of
polite society. In relation to others, he shows what
passes for animation and enthusiasm; for at all times
his character is founded on control of these qualities,
not on the absence of them. It flatters his sense of
superiority that he may thus pull wool about the ears
of joint and several. He has so strong a will that it
can be crossed and counter-crossed, as by himself, so
by a dozen outsiders, without a break in his apparent
phlegm. He has gone through volition, and come out
at the other side of it; everything with him is a specific
act: he has no habits. Le saint indifférent is a dramatic
wight: he loves to refuse your proffered six per cent,
when, by a little haggling, he may obtain three-and-a-
half. For so he gets away with his own mental proc-
esses virgin: it is inconceivable to you that, being sane,
he should so comport himself. Amiable, perhaps, only
by painful propulsions and sore vigilance, let him appear the mere inheritor of easy good-nature.. Unselfish
out of sheer pride, and ever eager to claim the slippery
side of the pavement, or the end cut of the roast (on
the secret ground, be it understood, that he is not as

Capuan men, who wince at trifles), let him have his
ironic reward in passing for one whose physical con-
noisseurship is yet in the raw. That sympathy which
his rule forbids his devoting to the usual objects, he
expends, with some bravado, upon their opposites; for
he would fain seem a decent partizan of some sort,
not what he is, a bivalve intelligence, Tros Tyriusque.
He is known here and there, for instance, as valorous
in talk; yet he is by nature a solitary, and, for the
most part, somewhat less communicative than

> "The wind that sings to himself as he makes stride,
> Lonely and terrible, on the Andean height."

Imagining nothing idler than words in the face of
grave events, he condoles and congratulates with the
genteelest air in the world. In short, while there is
anything expected of him, while there are spectators
to be fooled, the stratagems of the fellow prove inexhaustible. It is only when he is quite alone that he
drops his jaw, and stretches his legs; then heigho!
arises like a smoke, and envelopes him becomingly, the
beautiful native well-bred torpidity of the gods, of
poetic boredom, of "the Oxford manner."

"How weary, stale, flat, and unprofitable!" sighed
Hamlet of this mortal outlook. As it came from him
in the beginning, that plaint, in its sincerity, can come

only from the man of culture, who feels about him vast mental spaces and depths, and to whom the face of creation is but comparative and symbolic. Nor will he breathe it in the common ear, where it may woo misapprehensions, and breed ignorant rebellion. The unlettered must ever love or hate what is nearest him, and, for lack of perspective, think his own fist the size of the sun. The social prizes, which, with mellowed observers, rank as twelfth or thirteenth in order of desirability, such as wealth and a foothold in affairs, seem to him first and sole; and to them he clings like a barnacle. But to our indifférent, nothing is so vulgar as close suction. He will never tighten his fingers on loaned opportunity; he is a gentleman, the hero of the habitually relaxed grasp. A light unprejudiced hold on his profits strikes him as decent and comely, though his true artistic pleasure is still in "fallings from us, vanishings." It costs him little to loose and to forego, to unlace his tentacles, and from the many who push hard behind, to retire, as it were, on a never-guessed-at competency, "richer than untempted kings." He would not be a life-prisoner, in ever so charming a bower. While the tranquil Sabine Farm is his delight, well he knows that on the dark trail ahead of him, even Sabine Farms are not sequacious. Thus he learns betimes to play the guest under his own cedars, and, with disciplinary intent, goes often from them; and, hearing his heart-strings snap the third night he is away, rejoices that he is again a freedman. Where his foot is planted (though it root not anywhere), he calls that spot home. No Unitarian in locality, it follows that he is the best of travelers, tangential merely, and pleased with each new vista of the human Past. He sometimes wishes his understanding less, that he might itch deliciously with a prejudice. With cosmic congruities, great and general forces, he keeps, all along, a tacit understanding, such as one has with beloved relatives at a distance; and his finger, airily inserted in his outer pocket, is really upon the pulse of eternity. His vocation, however, is to bury himself in the minor and immediate task; and from his intent manner, he gets confounded, promptly and permanently, with the victims of commercial ambition.

The true use of the much-praised Lucius Cary, Viscount Falkland, has hardly been apprehended: he is simply the patron saint of indifférents. From first to last, almost alone in that discordant time, he seems to have heard far-off resolving harmonies, and to have been rapt away with foreknowledge. Battle, to which all knights were bred, was penitential to him. It was but a childish means: and to what end? He meanwhile—and no man carried his will in better abeyance to the scheme of the universe—wanted no diligence in camp or council. Cares sat handsomely on him who

cared not at all, who won small comfort from the
cause which his conscience finally espoused. He
labored to be a doer, to stand well with observers; and
none save his intimate friends read his agitation and
profound weariness. "I am so much taken notice of,"
he writes, "for an impatient desire for peace, that it
is necessary I should likewise make it appear how it is
not out of fear for the utmost hazard of war." And
so, driven from the ardor he had to the simulation of
the ardor he lacked, loyally daring, a sacrifice to one of
two transient opinions, and inly impartial as a star,
Lord Falkland fell: the young never-to-be-forgotten
martyr of Newburg field. The imminent deed he
made a work of art; and the station of the moment the only post of honor. Life and death may be
all one to such a man: but he will at least take the
noblest pains to discriminate between Tweedledum and
Tweedledee, if he has to write a book about the varia-
tions of their antennæ. And like the Carolian exemplar is the disciple. The indifférent is a good thinker,
or a good fighter. He is no "immartial minion," as
dear old Chapman suffers Hector to call Tydides.
Nevertheless, his sign-manual is content with humble
and stagnant conditions. Talk of scaling the Hima-
layas of life affects him, very palpably, as "tall talk."
He deals not with things, but with the impressions and
analogies of things. The material counts for nothing

with him: he has moulted it away. Not so sure of the identity of the higher course of action as he is of his consecrating dispositions, he feels that he may make heaven again, out of sundries, as he goes. Shall not a beggarly duty, discharged with perfect temper, land him in "the out-courts of Glory," quite as successfully as a grand Sunday-school excursion to front the cruel Paynim foe? He thinks so. Experts have thought so before him. Francis Drake, with the national alarum instant in his ears, desired first to win at bowls, on the Devon sward, "and afterwards to settle with the Don." No one will claim a buccaneering hero for an indifférent, however. The Jesuit novices were ball-playing almost at that very time, three hundred years ago, when some too speculative companion, figuring the end of the world in a few moments (with just leisure enough, between, to be shriven in chapel, according to his own thrifty mind), asked Louis of Gonzaga how he, on his part, should employ the precious interval. "I should go on with the game," said the most innocent and most ascetic youth among them. But to cite the behavior of any of the saints is to step over the playful line allotted. Indifference of the mundane brand is not to be confounded with their detachment, which is emancipation wrought in the soul, and the ineffable efflorescence of the Christian spirit. Like most supernatural virtues, it has a laic shadow; the counsel to abstain, and to be unsolicitous, is one not only of perfection, but also of polity. A very little nonadhesion to common affairs, a little reserve of unconcern, and the gay spirit of sacrifice, provide the moral immunity which is the only real estate. The indifférent believes in storms: since tales of shipwreck encompass him. But once among his own kind, he wonders that folk should be circumvented by merely extraneous powers! His favorite catch, woven in among escaped dangers, rises through the roughest weather, and daunts it:

> "Now strike your sailes, ye jolly mariners,
> For we be come into a quiet rode."

No slave to any vicissitude, his imagination is, on the contrary, the cheerful obstinate tyrant of all that is. He lives, as Keats once said of himself, "in a thousand worlds," withdrawing at will from one to another, often curtailing his circumference to enlarge his liberty. His universe is a universe of balls, like those which the cunning Oriental carvers make out of ivory; each entire surface perforated with the same delicate pattern, each moving prettily and inextricably within the other, and all but the outer one impossible to handle. In some such innermost asylum the right sort of dare-devil sits smiling, while men rage or weep.

ON LYING AWAKE AT NIGHT

By STEWART EDWARD WHITE

This is from *The Forest*—one of Stewart Edward White's many delightful volumes. A very large public has enjoyed Mr. White's writings—many of his readers, perhaps, without accurately realizing how extraordinarily good they are.

Mr. White was born in Grand Rapids, Michigan, 1873; studied at the University of Michigan; has hunted big game in Africa; served as major of field artillery, 1917-18; and is a Fellow of the Royal Geographical Society. His first book, *The Westerners*, was published in 1901, since when they have followed regularly.

"Who hath lain alone to hear the wild goose cry?"

ABOUT once in so often you are due to lie awake at night. Why this is so I have never been able to discover. It apparently comes from no predisposing uneasiness of indigestion, no rashness in the matter of too much tea or tobacco, no excitation of unusual incident or stimulating conversation. In fact, you turn in with the expectation of rather a good night's rest. Almost at once the little noises of the forest grow larger, blend in the hollow bigness of the first drowse; your thoughts drift idly back and forth between reality and dream; when—*snap!*—you are broad awake!

Perhaps the reservoir of your vital forces is full to the overflow of a little waste; or perhaps, more subtly, the great Mother insists thus that you enter the temple of her larger mysteries.

For, unlike mere insomnia, lying awake at night in the woods is pleasant. The eager, nervous straining for sleep gives way to a delicious indifference. You do not care. Your mind is cradled in an exquisite poppy-suspension of judgment and of thought. Impressions slip vaguely into your consciousness and as vaguely out again. Sometimes they stand stark and naked for your inspection; sometimes they lose themselves in the mist of half-sleep. Always they lay soft velvet fingers on the drowsy imagination, so that in their caressing you feel the vaster spaces from which they have come. Peaceful-brooding your faculties receive. Hearing, sight, smell—all are preternaturally keen to whatever of sound and sight and woods perfume is abroad through the night; and yet at the same time active appreciation dozes, so these things lie on it sweet and cloying like fallen rose-leaves.

In such circumstance you will hear what the *voyageurs* call the voices of the rapids. Many people never hear them at all. They speak very soft and low and distinct beneath the steady roar and dashing, beneath even the lesser tinklings and gurglings whose quality superimposes them over the louder sounds. They are like the tear-forms swimming across the field of vision, which disappear so quickly when you concentrate your

sight to look at them, and which reappear so magically
when again your gaze turns vacant. In the stillness of
your hazy half-consciousness they speak; when you
bend your attention to listen, they are gone, and only
the tumults and the tinklings remain.

But in the moments of their audibility they are very
distinct. Just as often an odor will wake all a vanished memory, so these voices, by the force of a large
impressionism, suggest whole scenes. Far off are the
cling-clang-cling of chimes and the swell-and-fall murmur of a multitude *en fête,* so that subtly you feel the
gray old town, with its walls, the crowded market-
place, the decent peasant crowd, the booths, the mellow
church building with its bells, the warm, dust-moted
sun. Or, in the pauses between the swish-dash-dash-
ings of the waters, sound faint and clear voices singing
intermittently, calls, distant notes of laughter, as
though many canoes were working against the current
—only the flotilla never gets any nearer, nor the voices
louder. The *voyageurs* call these mist people the
Huntsmen; and look frightened. To each is his vision,
according to his experience. The nations of the earth
whisper to their exiled sons through the voices of the
rapids. Curiously enough, by all reports, they suggest
always peaceful scenes—a harvest-field, a street fair, a
Sunday morning in a cathedral town, careless travelers
—never the turmoils and struggles. Perhaps this is

the great Mother's compensation in a harsh mode of life.

Nothing is more fantastically unreal to tell about, nothing more concretely real to experience, than this undernote of the quick water. And when you do lie awake at night, it is always making its unobtrusive appeal. Gradually its hypnotic spell works. The distant chimes ring louder and nearer as you cross the borderland of sleep. And then outside the tent some little woods noise snaps the thread. An owl hoots, a whippoorwill cries, a twig cracks beneath the cautious prowl of some night creature—at once the yellow sunlit French meadows puff away—you are staring at the blurred image of the moon spraying through the texture of your tent.

The voices of the rapids have dropped into the background, as have the dashing noises of the stream. Through the forest is a great silence, but no stillness at all. The whippoorwill swings down and up the short curve of his regular song; over and over an owl says his rapid *whoo, whoo, whoo*. These, with the ceaseless dash of the rapids, are the web on which the night traces her more delicate embroideries of the unexpected. Distant crashes, single and impressive; stealthy footsteps near at hand; the subdued scratching of claws; a faint *sniff! sniff! sniff!* of inquiry; the sudden clear tin-horn *ko-ko-ko-óh* of the little owl; the mournful, long-drawn-out cry of the loon, instinct with the spirit of loneliness; the ethereal call-note of the birds of passage high in the air; a *patter, patter, patter,* among the dead leaves, immediately stilled; and then at the last, from the thicket close at hand, the beautiful silver purity of the white-throated sparrow—the nightingale of the North—trembling with the ecstasy of beauty, as though a shimmering moonbeam had turned to sound; and all the while the blurred figure of the moon mounting to the ridge-line of your tent— these things combine subtly, until at last the great Silence of which they are a part overarches the night and draws you forth to contemplation.

No beverage is more grateful than the cup of spring water you drink at such a time; no moment more refreshing than that in which you look about you at the darkened forest. You have cast from you with the warm blanket the drowsiness of dreams. A coolness, physical and spiritual, bathes you from head to foot. All your senses are keyed to the last vibrations. You hear the littler night prowlers; you glimpse the greater. A faint, searching woods perfume of dampness greets your nostrils. And somehow, mysteriously, in a manner not to be understood, the forces of the world seem in suspense, as though a touch might crystallize infinite possibilities into infinite power and motion. But the touch lacks. The forces hover on the edge of action, unheeding the little noises. In all humbleness and awe, you are a dweller of the Silent Places.

At such a time you will meet with adventures. One night we put fourteen inquisitive porcupines out of camp. Near McGregor's Bay I discovered in the large grass park of my camp-site nine deer, cropping the herbage like so many beautiful ghosts. A friend tells me of a fawn that every night used to sleep outside his tent and within a foot of his head, probably by way of protection against wolves. Its mother had in all likelihood been killed. The instant my friend moved toward the tent opening the little creature would disappear, and it was always gone by earliest daylight. Nocturnal bears in search of pork are not uncommon. But even though your interest meets nothing but the bats and the woods shadows and the stars, that few moments of the sleeping world forces is a psychical experience to be gained in no other way. You cannot know the night by sitting up; she will sit up with you. Only by coming into her presence from the borders of sleep can you meet her face to face in her intimate mood.

The night wind from the river, or from the open spaces of the wilds, chills you after a time. You begin to think of your blankets. In a few moments you roll yourself in their soft wool. Instantly it is morning.

And, strange to say, you have not to pay by going

through the day unrefreshed. You may feel like turning in at eight instead of nine, and you may fall asleep with unusual promptitude, but your journey will begin clear-headedly, proceed springily, and end with much in reserve. No languor, no dull headache, no exhaustion, follows your experience. For this once your two hours of sleep have been as effective as nine.

A WOODLAND VALENTINE

By Marian Storm

Marian Storm was born in Stormville, N. Y., and educated at Penn Hall, Chambersburg, Pa., and at Smith College. She did editorial and free-lance work in New York after graduation, and later went to Washington to become private secretary to the Argentine Ambassador. Since 1918 she has been connected with the New York *Evening Post*.

This essay comes from *Minstrel Weather,* a series of open-air vignettes which circle the zodiac with the attentive eye of a naturalist and the enchanted ardor of a poet.

FORCES astir in the deepest roots grow restless beneath the lock of frost. Bulbs try the door. February's stillness is charged with a faint anxiety, as if the powers of light, pressing up from the earth's center and streaming down from the stronger sun, had troubled the buried seeds, who strive to answer their liberator, so that the guarding mother must whisper over and over, "Not yet, not yet!" Better to stay behind the frozen gate than to come too early up into realms where the wolves of cold are still aprowl. Wisely the snow places a white hand over eager life unseen, but perceived in February's woods as a swimmer feels the changing moods of water in a lake fed by springs. Only the thick stars, closer and more companionable than in months of foliage, burn alert and serene. In February the Milky Way is revealed

divinely lucent to lonely peoples—herdsmen, moun-
taineers, fishermen, trappers—who are abroad in the
starlight hours of this grave and silent time of year.
It is in the long, frozen nights that the sky has most
red flowers.

February knows the beat of twilight wings. Drifting north again come birds who only pretended to
forsake us—adventurers, not so fond of safety but that
they dare risk finding how snow bunting and pine finch
have plundered the cones of the evergreens, while
chickadees, sparrows, and crows are supervising from
established stations all the more domestic supplies
available, a sparrow often making it possible to annoy
even a duck out of her share of cracked corn. Ranged
along a brown-draped oak branch in the waxing light,
crows show a lordly glistening of feathers. (Sun on a
sweeping wing in flight has the quality of sun on a
ripple.) Where hemlocks gather, deep in somber
woods, the great horned owl has thus soon, perhaps
working amid snows at her task, built a nest wherein
March will find sturdy balls of fluff. The thunderous
love song of her mate sounds through the timber. By
the time the wren has nested these winter babies will
be solemn with the wisdom of their famous race.

There is no season like the end of February for
cleaning out brooks. Hastening yellow waters toss a
dreary wreckage of torn or ashen leaves, twigs, acorn

cups, stranded rafts of bark, and buttonballs from the sycamore, never to come to seed. Standing on one bank or both, according to the sundering flood's ambition, the knight with staff and bold forefinger sets the water princess free. She goes then curtsying and dimpling over the shining gravel, sliding from beneath the ice that roofs her on the uplands down to the softer valleys, where her quickened step will be heard by the frogs in their mansions of mud, and the fish, recluses in rayless pools, will rise to the light she brings.

Down from the frozen mountains, in summer, birds and winds must bear the seed of alpine flowers—lilies that lean against unmelting snows, poppies, bright-colored herbs, and the palely gleaming, fringed beauties that change names with countries. How just and reasonable it would seem to be that flowers which edge the ice in July should consent to bloom in lowlands no colder in February! The pageant of blue, magenta, and scarlet on the austere upper slopes of the Rockies, where nights are bitter to the summer wanderer— why should it not flourish to leeward of a valley barn in months when icicles hang from the eaves in this tamer setting? But no. Mountain tempests are endurable to the silken-petaled. The treacherous lowland winter, with its coaxing suns followed by roaring desolation, is for blooms bred in a different tradition.

The light is clear but hesitant, a delicate wine, by no means the mighty vintage of April. February has no intoxication; the vague eagerness that gives the air a pulse where fields lie voiceless comes from the secret stirring of imprisoned life. Spring and sunrise are forever miracles, but the early hour of the wonder hardly hints the exuberance of its fulfilment. Even the forest dwellers move gravely, thankful for any promise of kindness from the lord of day as he hangs above a sea-gray landscape, but knowing well that their long duress is not yet to end. Deer pathetically haunt the outskirts of farms, gazing upon cattle feeding in winter pasture from the stack, and often, after dark, clearing the fences and robbing the same disheveled storehouse. Not a chipmunk winks from the top rail. The woodchuck, after his single expeditionary effort on Candlemas, which he is obliged to make for mankind's enlightenment, has retired without being seen, in sunshine or shadow, and has not the slightest intention of disturbing himself just yet. Though snowdrops may feel uneasy, he knows too much about the Ides of March! Quietest of all Northern woods creatures, the otter slides from one ice-hung waterfall to the next. The solitary scamperer left is the cottontail, appealing because he is the most pursued and politest of the furry; faithfully trying to give no offense, except when starvation points to winter cabbage, he is none the less fey. So is the mink, though he moves like a phantom.

Mosses, whereon March in coming treads first, show one hue brighter in the swamps. Pussy willows have made a gray dawn in viny caverns where the day's own dawn looks in but faintly, and the flushing of the red willow betrays reveries of a not impossible cowslip upon the bank beneath. The blue jay has mentioned it in the course of his voluble recollections. He is unwilling to prophesy arbutus, but he will just hint that when the leaves in the wood lot show through snow as early as this . . . Once he found a hepatica bud the last day of February . . . Speaking with his old friend, the muskrat, last week . . . And when you can see red pebbles in the creek at five o'clock in the afternoon . . . But it is no use to expect yellow orchids on the west knoll this spring, for some people found them there last year, and after that you might as well . . . Of course cowslips beside red willows are remarkably pretty, just as blue jays in a cedar with blue berries. . . . He is interminable, but then he has seen a great deal of life. And February needs her blue jays' unwearied and conquering faith.

THE ELEMENTS OF POETRY

By George Santayana

George Santayana was born in Madrid in 1863, of Spanish parentage. He graduated from Harvard in 1886, and taught philosophy there, 1889-1911. He lives now, I think, in England. I must be frank: except his poems, I only know his work in that enthralling volume, *Little Essays Drawn from the Writings of George Santayana,* edited by L. Pearsall Smith. Much of it is too esoteric for my grasp, but Mr. Smith's redaction brings the fascination of Santayana's philosophy within the compass of what Tennyson called "a second-rate sensitive mind"; and, if mine is a criterion, such will find it of the highest stimulus. This discourse on poetry seems to me one of the most pregnant utterances on the subject. It is not perfectly appreciated by merely one reading; but even if you have to become a poet to enjoy it fully, that will do yourself least harm.

If poetry in its higher reaches is more philosophical than history, because it presents the memorable types of men and things apart from unmeaning circumstances, so in its primary substance and texture poetry is more philosophical than prose because it is nearer to our immediate experience. Poetry breaks up the trite conceptions designated by current words into the sensuous qualities out of which those conceptions were originally put together. We name what we conceive and believe in, not what we see; things, not images; souls, not voices and silhouettes. This naming, with the whole education of the senses which it accompanies, subserves the uses of life; in order to thread our way through the labyrinth of objects which assault us, we must make a great selection in our sensuous experience; half of what we see and hear we must pass over as insignificant, while we piece out the other half with such an ideal complement as is necessary to turn it into a fixed and well-ordered conception of the world. This labor of perception and understanding, this spelling of the material meaning of experience, is enshrined in our workaday language and ideas; ideas which are literally poetic in the sense that they are "made" (for every conception in an adult mind is a fiction), but which are at the same time prosaic because they are made economically, by abstraction, and for use.

When the child of poetic genius, who has learned this intellectual and utilitarian language in the cradle, goes afield and gathers for himself the aspects of nature, he begins to encumber his mind with the many living impressions which the intellect rejected, and which the language of the intellect can hardly convey; he labors with his nameless burden of perception, and wastes himself in aimless impulses of emotion and reverie, until finally the method of some art offers a vent to his inspiration, or to such part of it as can survive the test of time and the discipline of expression.

The poet retains by nature the innocence of the eye, or recovers it easily; he disintegrates the fictions of common perception into their sensuous elements, gathers these together again into chance groups as the accidents of his environment or the affinities of his temperament may conjoin them; and this wealth of sensation and this freedom of fancy, which make an extraordinary ferment in his ignorant heart, presently bubble over into some kind of utterance.

The fullness and sensuousness of such effusions bring them nearer to our actual perceptions than common discourse could come; yet they may easily seem remote, overloaded, and obscure to those accustomed to think entirely in symbols, and never to be interrupted in the algebraic rapidity of their thinking by a moment's pause and examination of heart, nor ever to plunge for a moment into that torrent of sensation and imagery over which the bridge of prosaic associations habitually carries us safe and dry to some conventional act. How slight that bridge commonly is, how much an affair of trestles and wire, we can hardly conceive until we have trained ourselves to an extreme sharpness of introspection. But psychologists have discovered, what laymen generally will confess, that we hurry by the procession of our mental images as we do by the traffic of the street, intent on business, gladly forgetting the noise and movement of the scene, and looking only for the corner we would turn or the door we would enter. Yet in our alertest moment the depths of the soul are still dreaming; the real world stands

drawn in bare outline against a background of chaos
and unrest. Our logical thoughts dominate experience only as the parallels and meridians make a
checkerboard of the sea. They guide our voyage without controlling the waves, which toss forever in spite
of our ability to ride over them to our chosen ends.
Sanity is a madness put to good uses; waking life is a
dream controlled.

Out of the neglected riches of this dream the poet
fetches his wares. He dips into the chaos that under-
lies the rational shell of the world and brings up some
superfluous image, some emotion dropped by the way
and reattaches it to the present object; he reinstates
things unnecessary, he emphasizes things ignored, he
paints in again into the landscape the tints which the
intellect has allowed to fade from it. If he seems
sometimes to obscure a fact, it is only because he is
restoring an experience. The first element which the
intellect rejects in forming its ideas of things is the
emotion which accompanies the perception; and this
emotion is the first thing the poet restores. He stops
at the image, because he stops to enjoy. He wanders
into the bypaths of association because the bypaths are
delightful. The love of beauty which made him give
measure and cadence to his words, the love of harmony
which made him rhyme them, reappear in his imagination and make him select there also the material that is

itself beautiful, or capable of assuming beautiful forms. The link that binds together the ideas, sometimes so wide apart, which his wit assimilates, is most often the link of emotion; they have in common some element of beauty or of horror.

NOCTURNE

By SIMEON STRUNSKY

Simeon Strunsky is one of the most brilliant and certainly the most modest of American journalists. I regret that I cannot praise him, for at present we both work in the same office, and kinds words uttered in public would cause him to avoid me forever. All that is necessary is for my readers to examine his books and they will say for themselves what I am restrained from hinting. There is a spontaneous play of chaff in Mr. Strunsky's lighter vein which is unsurpassed by any American humorist; his more inward musing is well exemplified by this selection (from *Post-Impressions*, 1914). If you read *Post-Impressions, The Patient Observer, Belshazzar Court, Professor Latimer's Progress* and *Sinbad and His Friends,* you will have made a fair start.

Strunsky was born in Russia in 1879; studied at the Horace Mann High School (New York) and graduated from Columbia University in 1900. He worked on the staff of the New International Encyclopædia in 1900-06, and since then has been on the staff of the New York *Evening Post,* of which he is now editor.

ONCE every three months, with fair regularity, she was brought into the Night Court, found guilty, and fined. She came in between eleven o'clock and midnight, when the traffic of the court is at its heaviest, and it would be an hour, perhaps, before she was called to the bar. When her turn came she would rise from her seat at one end of the prisoners' bench and confront the magistrate.

Her eyes did not reach to the level of the magistrate's desk. A policeman in citizen's clothes would mount the witness stand, take oath with a seriousness

of mien which was surprising, in view of the fre
quency with which he was called upon to repeat the
formula, and testify in an illiterate drone to a definite
infraction of the law of the State, committed in his
presence and with his encouragement. While he spoke
the magistrate would look at the ceiling. When she
was called upon to answer she defended herself with
an obvious lie or two, while the magistrate looked over
her head. He would then condemn her to pay the
sum of ten dollars to the State and let her go.

She came to look forward to her visits at the Night
Court.

The Night Court is no longer a center of general
interest. During the first few months after it was
established, two or three years ago, it was one of the
great sights of a great city. For the newspapers it
was a rich source of human-interest stories. It replaced Chinatown in its appeal to visitors from out-of-
town. It stirred even the languid pulses of the native
inhabitant with its offerings of something new in the
way of "life." The sociologists, sincere and amateur,
crowded the benches and took notes.

To-day the novelty is worn off. The newspapers
long ago abandoned the Night Court, clergymen go to
it rarely for their texts, and the tango has taken its
place. But the sociologists and the casual visitor have

not disappeared. Serious people, anxious for an immediate vision of the pity of life, continue to fill the benches comfortably. No session of the court is without its little group of social investigators, among whom the women are in the majority. Many of them are young women, exceedingly sympathetic, handsomely gowned, and very well taken care of.

As she sat at one end of the prisoners' bench waiting her turn before the magistrate's desk, she would cast a sidelong glance over the railing that separated her from the handsomely gowned, gently bred, sympathetic young women in the audience. She observed with extraordinary admiration and delight those charming faces softened in pity, the graceful bearing, the admirably constructed yet simple coiffures, the elegance of dress, which she compared with the best that the windows in Sixth Avenue could show. She was amazed to find such gowns actually being worn instead of remaining as an unattainable ideal on smiling lay figures in the shop windows.

Occupants of the prisoners' bench are not supposed to stare at the spectators. She had to steal a glance now and then. Her visits to the Night Court had become so much a matter of routine that she would venture a peep over the railing while the case immediately preceding her own was being tried. Once or twice she was surprised by the clerk who called her name. She stood up mechanically and faced the magistrate as Officer Smith, in civilian clothes, mounted the witness stand.

She had no grudge against Officer Smith. She did not visualize him either as a person or as a part of a system. He was merely an incident of her trade. She had neither the training nor the imagination to look behind Officer Smith and see a communal policy which has not the power to suppress, nor the courage to acknowledge, nor the skill to regulate, and so contents itself with sending out full-fed policemen in civilian clothes to work up the evidence that defends society against her kind through the imposition of a ten-dollar fine.

To some of the women on the visitors' benches the cruelty of the process came home: this business of setting a two-hundred-pound policeman in citizen's clothes, backed up by magistrates, clerks, court criers, interpreters, and court attendants, to worrying a ten-dollar fine out of a half-grown woman under an enormous imitation ostrich plume. The professional sociologists were chiefly interested in the money cost of this process to the tax-payer, and they took notes on the proportion of first offenders. Yet the Night Court is a remarkable advance in civilization. Formerly, in addition to her fine, the prisoner would pay a commission to the professional purveyor of bail.

Sometimes, if the magistrate was young or new to
the business, she would be given a chance against
Officer Smith. She would be called to the witness
chair and under oath be allowed to elaborate on the
obvious lies which constituted her usual defense. This
would give her the opportunity, between the magistrate's questions, of sweeping the courtroom with a
full, hungry look for as much as half a minute at a
time. She saw the women in the audience only, and
their clothes. The pity in their eyes did not move her,
because she was not in the least interested in what
they thought, but in how they looked and what they
wore. They were part of a world which she would
read about—she read very little—in the society columns of the Sunday newspaper. They were the
women around whom headlines were written and whose
pictures were printed frequently on the first page.

She could study them with comparative leisure in
the Night Court. Outside in the course of her daily
routine she might catch an occasional glimpse of these
same women, through the windows of a passing taxi,
or in the matinée crowds, or going in and out of the
fashionable shops. But her work took her seldom into
the region of taxicabs and fashionable shops. The
nature of her occupation kept her to furtive corners
and the dark side of streets. Nor was she at such
times in the mood for just appreciation of the beau-

tiful things in life. More than any other walk of life, hers was of an exacting nature, calling for intense powers of concentration both as regards the public and the police. It was different in the Night Court. Here, having nothing to fear and nothing out of the usual to hope for, she might give herself up to the esthetic contemplation of a beautiful world of which, at any other time, she could catch mere fugitive aspects.

Sometimes I wonder why people think that life is only what they see and hear, and not what they read of. Take the Night Court. The visitor really sees nothing and hears nothing that he has not read a thousand times in his newspaper and had it described in greater detail and with better-trained powers of observation than he can bring to bear in person. What new phase of life is revealed by seeing in the body, say, a dozen practitioners of a trade of whom we know there are several tens of thousands in New York? They have been described by the human-interest reporters, analyzed by the statisticians, defended by the social revolutionaries, and explained away by the optimists. For that matter, to the faithful reader of the newspapers, daily and Sunday, what can there be new in this world from the Pyramids by moonlight to the habits of the night prowler? Can the upper classes really acquire for themselves, through slumming parties and visits to the Night Court, anything like the knowledge that books and newspapers can furnish them? Can the lower classes ever hope to obtain that complete view of the Fifth Avenue set which the Sunday columns offer them? And yet there the case stands: only by seeing and hearing for ourselves, however imperfectly, do we get the sense of reality.

That is why our criminal courts are probably our most influential schools of democracy. More than our settlement houses, more than our subsidized dancing-schools for shopgirls, they encourage the get-together process through which one-half the world learns how the other half lives. On either side of the railing of the prisoners' cage is an audience and a stage.

That is why she would look forward to her regular visits at the Night Court. She saw life there.

BEER AND CIDER

By GEORGE SAINTSBURY

How pleasant it is to find the famous Professor Saintsbury—
known to students as the author of histories of the English and
French literatures, the *History of Criticism* and *History of English Prosody*—spending the evening so hospitably in his cellar. I
print this—from his downright delightful *Notes on a Cellar Book*
—as a kind of tantalizing penance. It is a charming example
of how pleasantly a great scholar can unbend on occasion.

George Saintsbury, born in 1845, studied at Merton College,
Oxford, taught school 1868-76, was a journalist in London
1876-95, and held the chair of English Literature at Edinburgh
University, 1895-1915. If you read *Notes on a Cellar Book,* as
you should, you will agree that it is a charmingly light-hearted
causerie for a gentleman to publish at the age of seventy-five.
More than ever one feels that sound liquor, in moderation, is a
preservative of both body and wit.

THERE is no beverage which I have liked "to live
with" more than Beer; but I have never had a cellar
large enough to accommodate much of it, or an establishment numerous enough to justify the accommoda-
tion. In the good days when servants expected beer,
but did not expect to be treated otherwise than as
servants, a cask or two was necessary; and persons
who were "quite" generally took care that the small
beer they drank should be the same as that which they
gave to their domestics, though they might have other
sorts as well. For these better sorts at least the good
old rule was, when you began on one cask always to

have in another. Even Cobbett, whose belief in beer
was the noblest feature in his character, allowed that
it required some keeping. The curious "white ale,"
or lober agol—which, within the memory of man, used
to exist in Devonshire and Cornwall, but which, even
half a century ago, I have vainly sought there—was,
I believe, drunk quite new; but then it was not pure
malt and not hopped at all, but had eggs ("pullet-
sperm in the brewage") and other foreign bodies in it.

I did once drink, at St. David's, ale so new that it
frothed from the cask as creamily as if it had been
bottled: and I wondered whether the famous beer of
Bala, which Borrow found so good at his first visit
and so bad at his second, had been like it.[1]

On the other hand, the very best Bass I ever drank
had had an exactly contrary experience. In the year
1875, when I was resident at Elgin, I and a friend now
dead, the Procurator-Fiscal of the district, devoted the
May "Sacrament holidays," which were then still kept
in those remote parts, to a walking tour up the Find-
horn and across to Loch Ness and Glen Urquhart.
At the Freeburn Inn on the first-named river we

---

[1] This visit (in the early eighties) had another relish. The
inn coffee-room had a copy of Mr. Freeman's book on the adjoin-
ing Cathedral, and this was copiously annotated in a beautiful
and scholarly hand, but in a most virulent spirit. "Why can't
you call things by their plain names?" (in reference to the historian's Macaulayesque periphrases) etc. I have often wondered
who the annotator was.

found some beer of singular excellence: and, asking the damsel who waited on us about it, were informed that a cask of Bass had been put in during the previous October, but, owing to a sudden break in the weather and the departure of all visitors, had never been tapped till our arrival.

Beer of ordinary strength left too long in the cask gets "hard" of course; but no one who deserves to drink it would drink it from anything but the cask if he could help it. Jars are makeshifts, though useful makeshifts: and small beer will not keep in them for much more than a week. Nor are the very small barrels, known by various affectionate diminutives ("pin," etc.) in the country districts, much to be recommended. "We'll drink it in the firkin, my boy!" is the lowest admission in point of volume that should be allowed. Of one such firkin I have a pleasant memory and memorial, though it never reposed in my home cellar. It was just before the present century opened, and some years before we Professors in Scotland had, of our own motion and against considerable opposition, given up half of the old six months' holiday without asking for or receiving a penny more salary. (I have since chuckled at the horror and wrath with which Mr. Smillie and Mr. Thomas would hear of such profligate conduct.) One could therefore move about with fairly long halts: and I had taken from a friend a house at Abingdon for some time. So, though I could not even then drink quite as much beer as I could thirty years earlier a little higher up the Thames, it became necessary to procure a cask. It came—one of Bass's minor mildnesses—affectionately labeled "Mr. George Saintsbury. Full to the bung." I detached the card, and I believe I have it to this day as my choicest (because quite unsolicited) testimonial.

Very strong beer permits itself, of course, to be bottled and kept in bottles: but I rather doubt whether it also is not best from the wood; though it is equally of course, much easier to cellar it and keep it bottled. Its kinds are various and curious. "Scotch ale" is famous, and at its best (I never drank better than Younger's) excellent: but its tendency, I think, is to be too sweet. I once invested in some—not Younger's —which I kept for nearly sixteen years, and which was still treacle at the end. Bass's No. 1 requires no praises. Once when living in the Cambridgeshire village mentioned earlier I had some, bottled in Cambridge itself, of great age and excellence. Indeed, two guests, though both of them were Cambridge men, and should have had what Mr. Lang once called the "robust" habits of that University, fell into one ditch after partaking of it. (I own that the lanes thereabouts are very dark.) In former days, though probably not at present, you could often find rather choice specimens of strong beer produced at small breweries in the country. I remember such even in the Channel Islands. And I suspect the Universities themselves have been subject to "declensions and fallings off." I know that in my undergraduate days at Merton we always had proper beer-glasses, like the old "flute" champagnes, served regularly at cheese-time with a most noble beer called "Archdeacon," which was then actually brewed in the sacristy of the College chapel. I have since—a slight sorrow to season the joy of reinstatement there—been told that it is now obtained from outside.[2] And All Souls is the only other college in which, from actual recent experience, I can imagine the possibility of the exorcism,

Strongbeerum! discede a lay-fratre Petro,
if lay-brother Peter were so silly as to abuse, or play tricks with, the good gift.

---

[2] When I went up this March to help man the last ditch for Greek, I happened to mention "Archdeacon": and my interlocutor told me that he believed no college now brewed within its walls. After the defeat, I thought of the stages of the Decline and Fall of Things: and how a sad but noble ode might be written (by the right man) on the Fates of Greek and Beer at Oxford. He would probably refer in the first strophe to the close of the *Eumenides*; in its antistrophe to Mr. Swinburne's great adaptation thereof in regard to Carlyle and Newman; while the epode and any reduplication of the parts would be occupied by showing how the departing entities were of no equivocal magnificence like the Eumenides themselves; of no flawed perfection (at least as it seemed to their poet) like the two great English writers, but wholly admirable and beneficent—too good for the generation who would banish them, and whom they banished.

I have never had many experiences of real "home-brewed," but two which I had were pleasing. There was much home-brewing in East Anglia at the time I lived there, and I once got the village carpenter to give me some of his own manufacture. It was as good light ale as I ever wish to drink (many times better than the wretched stuff that Dora has foisted on us), and he told me that, counting in every expense for material, cost and wear of plant, etc., it came to about a penny ³ a quart. The other was very different. The late Lord de Tabley—better or at least longer known as Mr. Leicester Warren—once gave a dinner at the Athenæum at which I was present, and had up from his Cheshire cellars some of the old ale for which that county is said to be famous, to make flip after dinner. It was shunned by most of the pusillanimous guests, but not by me, and it was excellent. But I should like to have tried it unflipped.⁴

---

³ This was one of the best illustrations of the old phrase, "a good pennyworth," that I ever knew for certain. I add the two last words because of a mysterious incident of my youth. I and one of my sisters were sitting at a window in a certain seaside place when we heard, both of us distinctly and repeatedly, this mystic street cry: "A bible and a pillow-case for a penny!" I rushed downstairs to secure this bargain, but the crier was now far off, and it was too late.

⁴ By the way, are they still as good for flip at New College, Oxford, as they were in the days when it numbered hardly any undergraduates except scholars, and one scholar of my acquaintance had to himself a set of three rooms and a garden? And is "The Island" at Kennington still famous for the same excellent compound?

I never drank mum, which all know from The Anti-
quary, some from "The Ryme of Sir Lancelot Bogle,"
and some again from the notice which Mr. Gladstone's
love of Scott (may it plead for him!) gave it once in
some Budget debate, I think. It is said to be brewed
of wheat, which is not in its favor (wheat was meant
to be eaten, not drunk) and very bitter, which is.
Nearly all bitter drinks are good. The only time I
ever drank "spruce" beer I did not like it. The come-
liest of black malts is, of course, that noble liquor
called of Guinness. Here at least I think England
cannot match Ireland, for our stouts are, as a rule, too
sweet and "clammy." But there used to be in the
country districts a sort of light porter which was one
of the most refreshing liquids conceivable for hot
weather. I have drunk it in Yorkshire at the foot of
Roseberry Topping, out of big stone bottles like champagne magnums. But that was nearly sixty years ago.
Genuine lager beer is no more to be boycotted than
genuine hock, though, by the way, the best that I ever
drank (it was at the good town of King's Lynn) was
Low not High Dutch in origin. It was so good that
I wrote to the shippers at Rotterdam to see if I could
get some sent to Leith, but the usual difficulties in
establishing connection between wholesale dealers and
individual buyers prevented this. It was, however,
something of a consolation to read the delightful name,

"our top-and-bottom-fermentation beer," in which the manufacturer's letter, in very sound English for the most part, spoke of it. English lager I must say I have never liked; perhaps I have been unlucky in my specimens. And good as Scotch strong beer is, I cannot say that the lighter and medium kinds are very good in Scotland. In fact, in Edinburgh I used to import beer of this kind from Lincolnshire,[5] where there is no mistake about it. My own private opinion is that John Barleycorn, north of Tweed, says: "I am for whisky, and not for ale."

"Cider and perry," says Burton, "are windy drinks"; yet he observes that the inhabitants of certain shires in England (he does not, I am sorry to say, mention Devon) of Normandy in France, and of Guipuzcoa in Spain, "are no whit offended by them." I have never

---

[5] It came from Alford, the chef-lieu, if it cannot be called the capital, of the Tennyson country. I have pleasant associations with the place, quite independent of the beery ones. And it made me, partially at least, alter one of the ideas of my early criticism—that time spent on a poet's local habitations was rather wasted. I have always thought "The Dying Swan" one of its author's greatest things, and one of the champion examples of pure poetry in English literature. But I never fully heard the "eddying song" that "flooded"

> the creeping mosses and clambering weeds,
> And the willow branches hoar and dank,
> And the wavy swell of the soughing reeds,
> And the wave-worn horns of the echoing bank,
> And the silvery marish-flowers that throng
> The desolate creeks and pools among—

till I saw them.

liked perry on the few occasions on which I have tasted it; perhaps because its taste has always reminded me of the smell of some stuff that my nurse used to put on my hair when I was small. But I certainly have been no whit offended by cider, either in divers English shires, including very specially those which Burton does not include, Devon, Dorset, and Somerset, or in Normandy. The Guipuzcoan variety I have, unfortunately, had no opportunity of tasting. Besides, perry seems to me to be an abuse of that excellent creature the pear, whereas cider-apples furnish one of the most cogent arguments to prove that Providence had the production of alcoholic liquors directly in its eye. They are good for nothing else whatever, and they are excellent good for that. I think I like the weak ciders, such as those of the west and the Normandy, better than the stronger ones,[6] and draught cider much better than bottled. That of Norfolk, which has been much commended of late, I have never tasted; but I have had both Western and West-Midland cider in my cellar, often in bottle and once or twice in cask. It is a pity that the liquor—extremely agreeable to the taste, one of the most thirst-quenching to be anywhere found, of no overpowering alcoholic strength as a rule, and almost sovereign for gout—is not to be drunk without

[6] Herefordshire and Worcestershire cider can be very strong and the perry, they say, still stronger.

caution, and sometimes has to be given up altogether
from other medical aspects. Qualified with brandy—
a mixture which was first imparted to me at a road-
side inn by a very amiable Dorsetshire farmer whom
I met while walking from Sherborne to Blandford in
my first Oxford "long"—it is capital: and cider-cup
who knoweth not? If there be any such, let him not
wait longer than to-morrow before establishing knowledge. As for the pure juice of the apple, four gallons
a day per man used to be the harvest allowance in
Somerset when I was a boy. It is refreshing only to
think of it now.

Of mead or metheglin, the third indigenous liquor of
Southern Britain, I know little. Indeed, I should have
known nothing at all of it had it not been that the
parish-clerk and sexton of the Cambridgeshire village
where I lived, and the caretaker of a vinery which I
rented, was a bee-keeper and mead-maker. He gave me
some once. I did not care much for it. It was like a
sweet weak beer, with, of course, the special honey
flavor. But I should imagine that it was susceptible
of a great many different modes of preparation, and
it is obvious, considering what it is made of, that it
could be brewed of almost any strength. Old literary
notices generally speak of it as strong.

A FREE MAN'S WORSHIP

By Bertrand Russell

"A Free Man's Worship" was written in 1902; it was republished by Mr. Russell in 1918 in his volume *Mysticism and Logic*.
It is interesting to note carefully Mr. Russell's views in this
fine essay in connection with the fact that he was imprisoned by
the British Government as a pacifist during the War.

Much of Mr. Russell's writing, in mathematical and philosophical fields, is above the head of the desultory reader; but so
stimulating a paper as this one should not be neglected by the
moderately inquisitive amateur.

Bertrand Russell was born in 1872, studied at Trinity College,
Cambridge, and is widely known as a thinker of uncompromising
liberalism.

To Dr. Faustus in his study Mephistopheles told the
history of the Creation, saying:

"The endless praises of the choirs of angels had begun to grow wearisome; for, after all, did he not deserve their praise? Had he not given them endless joy?
Would it not be more amusing to obtain undeserved
praise, to be worshiped by beings whom he tortured?
He smiled inwardly, and resolved that the great drama
should be performed.

"For countless ages the hot nebula whirled aimlessly
through space. At length it began to take shape, the
central mass threw off planets, the planets cooled, boiling seas and burning mountains heaved and tossed,
from black masses of cloud hot sheets of rain deluged

the barely solid crust. And now the first germ of life grew in the depths of the ocean, and developed rapidly in the fructifying warmth into vast forest trees, huge ferns springing from the damp mould, sea monsters breeding, fighting, devouring, and passing away. And from the monsters, as the play unfolded itself, Man was born, with the power of thought, the knowledge of good and evil, and the cruel thirst for worship. And Man saw that all is passing in this mad, monstrous world, that all is struggling to snatch, at any cost, a few brief moments of life before Death's inexorable decree. And Man said: 'There is a hidden purpose, could we but fathom it, and the purpose is good; for we must reverence something, and in the visible world there is nothing worthy of reverence.' And Man stood aside from the struggle, resolving that God intended harmony to come out of chaos by human efforts. And when he followed the instincts which God had transmitted to him from his ancestry of beasts of prey, he called it Sin, and asked God to forgive him. But he doubted whether he could be justly forgiven, until he invented a divine Plan by which God's wrath was to have been appeased. And seeing the present was bad, he made it yet worse, that thereby the future might be better. And he gave God thanks for the strength that enabled him to forgo even the joys that were possible. And God smiled; and when he saw that Man had become perfect in renunciation and worship, he sent another sun through the sky, which crashed into Man's sun; and all returned again to nebula.

" 'Yes,' he murmured, 'it was a good play; I will have it performed again.' "

Such, in outline, but even more purposeless, more void of meaning, is the world which Science presents for our belief. Amid such a world, if anywhere, our ideals henceforward must find a home. That Man is the product of causes which had no prevision of the end they were achieving; that his origin, his growth, his hopes and fears, his loves and his beliefs, are but the outcome of accidental collocations of atoms; that no fire, no heroism, no intensity of thought and feeling, can preserve an individual life beyond the grave; that all the labors of the ages, all the devotion, all the in- spiration, all the noonday brightness of human genius, are destined to extinction in the vast death of the solar system, and that the whole temple of Man's achieve- ment must inevitably be buried beneath the debris of a universe in ruins—all these things, if not quite beyond dispute, are yet so nearly certain, that no philosophy which rejects them can hope to stand. Only within the scaffolding of these truths, only on the firm founda- tion of unyielding despair, can the soul's habitation henceforth be safely built.

How, in such an alien and inhuman world, can so

powerless a creature as Man preserve his aspirations untarnished? A strange mystery it is that Nature, omnipotent but blind, in the revolutions of her secular hurryings through the abysses of space, has brought forth at last a child, subject still to her power, but gifted with sight, with knowledge of good and evil, with the capacity of judging all the works of his unthinking Mother. In spite of Death, the mark and seal of the parental control, Man is yet free, during his brief years, to examine, to criticize, to know, and in imagination to create. To him alone, in the world with which he is acquainted, this freedom belongs; and in this lies his superiority to the resistless forces that control his outward life.

The savage, like ourselves, feels the oppression of his impotence before the powers of Nature; but having in himself nothing that he respects more than Power, he is willing to prostrate himself before his gods, without inquiring whether they are worthy of his worship. Pathetic and very terrible is the long history of cruelty and torture, of degradation and human sacrifice, endured in the hope of placating the jealous gods: surely, the trembling believer thinks, when what is most precious has been freely given, their lust for blood must be appeased, and more will not be required. The religion of Moloch—as such creeds may be generically called —is in essence the cringing submission of the slave, who dare not, even in his heart, allow the thought that his master deserves no adulation. Since the independence of ideals is not yet acknowledged, Power may be freely worshiped, and receive an unlimited respect, despite its wanton infliction of pain.

But gradually, as morality grows bolder, the claim of the ideal world begins to be felt; and worship, if it is not to cease, must be given to gods of another kind than those created by the savage. Some, though they feel the demands of the ideal, will still consciously reject them, still urging that naked Power is worthy of worship. Such is the attitude inculcated in God's answer to Job out of the whirlwind: the divine power and knowledge are paraded, but of the divine goodness there is no hint. Such also is the attitude of those who, in our own day, base their morality upon the struggle for survival, maintaining that the survivors are necessarily the fittest. But others, not content with an answer so repugnant to the moral sense, will adopt the position which we have become accustomed to regard as specially religious, maintaining that, in some hidden manner, the world of fact is really harmonious with the world of ideals. Thus Man creates God, all-powerful and all-good, the mystic unity of what is and what should be.

But the world of fact, after all, is not good; and, in submitting our judgment to it, there is an element of slavishness from which our thoughts must be purged. For in all things it is well to exalt the dignity of Man, by freeing him as far as possible from the tyranny of non-human Power. When we have realized that Power is largely bad, that man, with his knowledge of good and evil, is but a helpless atom in a world which has no such knowledge, the choice is again presented to us: Shall we worship Force, or shall we worship Goodness? Shall our God exist and be evil, or shall he be recognized as the creation of our own conscience? ✓

The answer to this question is very momentous, and affects profoundly our whole morality. The worship of Force, to which Carlyle and Nietzsche and the creed of Militarism have accustomed us, is the result of failure to maintain our own ideals against a hostile universe: it is itself a prostrate submission to evil, a sacrifice of our best to Moloch. If strength indeed is to be respected, let us respect rather the strength of those who refuse that false "recognition of facts" which fails to recognize that facts are often bad. Let us admit that, in the world we know there are many things that would be better otherwise, and that the ideals to which we do and must adhere are not realized in the realm of matter. Let us preserve our respect for truth, for beauty, for the ideal of perfection which life does not permit us to attain, though none of these things meet with the approval of the unconscious uni-

verse. If Power is bad, as it seems to be, let us reject
it from our hearts. In this lies Man's true freedom:
in determination to worship only the God created by
our own love of the good, to respect only the heaven
which inspires the insight of our best moments. In
action, in desire, we must submit perpetually to the
tyranny of outside forces; but in thought, in aspiration,
we are free, free from our fellowmen, free from the
petty planet on which our bodies impotently crawl, free
even, while we live, from the tyranny of death. Let
us learn, then, that energy of faith which enables us
to live constantly in the vision of the good; and let us
descend, in action, into the world of fact, with that
vision always before us.

When first the opposition of fact and ideal grows
fully visible, a spirit of fiery revolt, of fierce hatred of
the gods, seems necessary to the assertion of freedom.
To defy with Promethean constancy a hostile universe,
to keep its evil always in view, always actively hated,
to refuse no pain that the malice of Power can invent,
appears to be the duty of all who will not bow before
the inevitable. But indignation is still a bondage, for
it compels our thoughts to be occupied with an evil
world; and in the fierceness of desire from which rebellion springs there is a kind of self-assertion which
it is necessary for the wise to overcome. Indignation
is a submission of our thoughts, but not of our desires;

the Stoic freedom in which wisdom consists is found in the submission of our desires, but not of our thoughts. From the submission of our desires springs the virtue of resignation; from the freedom of our thoughts springs the whole world of art and philosophy, and the vision of beauty by which, at last, we half reconquer the reluctant world. But the vision of beauty is possible only to unfettered contemplation, to thoughts not weighted by the load of eager wishes; and thus Freedom comes only to those who no longer ask of life that it shall yield them any of those personal goods that are subject to the mutations of Time.

Although the necessity of renunciation is evidence of the existence of evil, yet Christianity, in preaching it, has shown a wisdom exceeding that of the Promethean philosophy of rebellion. It must be admitted that, of the things we desire, some, though they prove impossible, are yet real goods; others, however, as ardently longed for, do not form part of a fully purified ideal. The belief that what must be renounced is bad, though sometimes false, is far less often false than untamed passion supposes; and the creed of religion, by providing a reason for proving that it is never false, has been the means of purifying our hopes by the discovery of many austere truths.

But there is in resignation a further good element: even real goods, when they are unattainable, ought not to be fretfully desired. To every man comes, sooner or later, the great renunciation. For the young, there is nothing unattainable; a good thing desired with the whole force of a passionate will, and yet impossible, is to them not credible. Yet, by death, by illness, by poverty, or by the voice of duty, we must learn, each one of us, that the world was not made for us, and that, however beautiful may be the things we crave for, Fate may nevertheless forbid them. It is the part of courage, when misfortune comes, to bear without repining the ruin of our hopes, to turn away our thoughts from vain regrets. This degree of submission to Power is not only just and right: it is the very gate of wisdom.

But passive renunciation is not the whole wisdom; for not by renunciation alone can we build a temple for the worship of our own ideals. Haunting foreshadowings of the temple appear in the realm of imagination, in music, in architecture, in the untroubled kingdom of reason, and in the golden sunset magic of lyrics, where beauty shines and glows, remote from the touch of sorrow, remote from the fear of change, remote from the failures and disenchantments of the world of fact. In the contemplation of these things the vision of heaven will shape itself in our hearts, giving at once a touchstone to judge the world about us, and an inspiration by which to fashion to our needs whatever is not incapable of serving as a stone in the sacred temple.

Except for those rare spirits that are born without sin, there is a cavern of darkness to be traversed before that temple can be entered. The gate of the cavern is despair, and its floor is paved with the gravestones of abandoned hopes. There Self must die; there the eagerness, the greed of untamed desire must be slain, for only so can the soul be freed from the empire of Fate. But out of the cavern the Gate of Renunciation leads again to the daylight of wisdom, by whose radiance a new insight, a new joy, a new tenderness, shine forth to gladden the pilgrim's heart.

When, without the bitterness of impotent rebellion, we have learnt both to resign ourselves to the outward rule of Fate and to recognize that the non-human world is unworthy of our worship, it becomes possible at last so to transform and refashion the unconscious universe, so to transmute it in the crucible of imagination, that a new image of shining gold replaces the old idol of clay. In all the multiform facts of the world —in the visual shapes of trees and mountains and clouds, in the events of the life of man, even in the very omnipotence of Death—the insight of creative idealism can find the reflection of a beauty which its own thoughts first made. In this way mind asserts its subtle mastery over the thoughtless forces of Nature. The more evil the material with which it deals, the more thwarting to untrained desire, the greater is its achievement in inducing the reluctant rock to yield up its hidden treasures, the prouder its victory in compelling the opposing forces to swell the pageant of its triumph. Of all the arts, Tragedy is the proudest, the most triumphant; for it builds its shining citadel in the very center of the enemy's country, on the very summit of his highest mountain; from its impregnable watch-towers, his camps and arsenals, his columns and forts, are all revealed; within its walls the free life continues, while the legions of Death and Pain and Despair, and all the servile captains of tyrant Fate, afford the burghers of that dauntless city new spectacles of beauty. Happy those sacred ramparts, thrice happy the dwellers on that all-seeing eminence. Honor to those brave warriors who, through countless ages of warfare, have preserved for us the priceless heritage of liberty, and have kept undefiled by sacrilegious invaders the home of the unsubdued.

But the beauty of Tragedy does but make visible a quality which, in more or less obvious shapes, is present always and everywhere in life. In the spectacle of Death, in the endurance of intolerable pain, and in the irrevocableness of a vanished past, there is a sacredness, an overpowering awe, a feeling of the vastness, the depth, the inexhaustible mystery of existence, in which, as by some strange marriage of pain, the sufferer is bound to the world by bonds of sorrow. In these moments of insight, we lose all eagerness of temporary desire, all struggling and striving for petty ends, all care for the little trivial things that, to a superficial view, make up the common life of day by day; we see, surrounding the narrow raft illumined by the flickering light of human comradeship, the dark ocean on whose rolling waves we toss for a brief hour; from the great night without, a chill blast breaks in upon our refuge; all the loneliness of humanity amid hostile forces is concentrated upon the individual soul, which must struggle alone, with what of courage it can command, against the whole weight of a universe that cares nothing for its hopes and fears. Victory, in this struggle with the powers of darkness, is the true baptism into the glorious company of heroes, the true initiation into the overmastering beauty of human existence. From that awful encounter of the soul with the outer world, renunciation, wisdom, and charity are born; and with their birth a new life begins. To take into the inmost shrine of the soul the irresistible forces whose puppets we seem to be—Death and change, the irrevocableness of the past, and the powerlessness of man before the blind hurry of the universe from vanity to vanity—to feel these things and know them is to conquer them.

This is the reason why the Past has such magical power. The beauty of its motionless and silent pictures is like the enchanted purity of late autumn, when the leaves, though one breath would make them fall, still glow against the sky in golden glory. The Past does not change or strive; like Duncan, after life's fitful fever it sleeps well; what was eager and grasping, what was petty and transitory, has faded away, the things that were beautiful and eternal shine out of it like stars in the night. Its beauty, to a soul not worthy of it, is unendurable; but to a soul which has conquered Fate it is the key of religion.

The life of Man, viewed outwardly, is but a small thing in comparison with the forces of Nature. The slave is doomed to worship Time and Fate and Death, because they are greater than anything he finds in himself, and because all his thoughts are of things which they devour. But, great as they are, to think of them greatly, to feel their passionless splendor, is greater still. And such thought makes us free men; we no longer bow before the inevitable in Oriental subjection, but we absorb it, and make it a part of ourselves. To abandon the struggle for private happiness, to expel all eagerness of temporary desire, to burn with passion for eternal things—this is emancipation, and this is the free man's worship. And this liberation is effected by a contemplation of Fate; for Fate itself is subdued by the mind which leaves nothing to be purged by the purifying fire of Time.

United with his fellow-men by the strongest of all ties, the tie of a common doom, the free man finds that a new vision is with him always, shedding over every daily task the light of love. The life of Man is a long march through the night, surrounded by invisible foes, tortured by weariness and pain, towards a goal that few can hope to reach, and where none may tarry long. One by one, as they march, our comrades vanish from our sight, seized by the silent orders of omnipotent Death. Very brief is the time in which we can help them, in which their happiness or misery is decided. Be it ours to shed sunshine on their path, to lighten their sorrows by the balm of sympathy, to give them the pure joy of a never-tiring affection, to strengthen failing courage, to instil faith in hours of despair. Let us not weigh in grudging scales their merits and demerits, but let us think only of their need—of the sorrows, the difficulties, perhaps the blindnesses, that make the misery of their lives; let us remember that they are fellow-sufferers in the same darkness, actors in the same tragedy with ourselves. And so, when their day is over, when their good and their evil have become eternal by the immortality of the past, be it ours to feel that, where they suffered, where they failed, no deed of ours was the cause; but wherever a spark of the divine fire kindled in their hearts, we were ready with encouragement, with sympathy, with brave words in which high courage glowed.

Brief and powerless is Man's life; on him and all his race the slow, sure doom falls pitiless and dark. Blind to good and evil, reckless of destruction, omnipotent matter rolls on its relentless way; for Man, condemned to-day to lose his dearest, to-morrow himself to pass through the gate of darkness, it remains only to cherish, ere yet the blow falls, the lofty thoughts that ennoble his little day; disdaining the coward terrors of the slave of Fate, to worship at the shrine that his own hands have built; undismayed by the empire of chance, to preserve a mind free from the wanton tyranny that rules his outward life; proudly defiant of the irresistible forces that tolerate, for a moment, his knowledge and his condemnation, to sustain alone, a weary but unyielding Atlas, the world that his own ideals have fashioned despite the trampling march of unconscious power.

SOME HISTORIANS

By PHILIP GUEDALLA

Philip Guedalla, born 1889, is a London barrister and at the present time an Independent Liberal candidate for the House of Commons. He has written excellent light verse and parodies, and a textbook on European history, 1715-1815. His most conspicuous achievement so far is the brilliant volume *Supers and Supermen,* from which my selection is taken.

Supers and Supermen is a collection of historical and political portraits and skits. It is mercilessly and gloriously humorous. Those who can always follow the wit and irony that Guedalla knows how to conceal in a cunningly turned phrase, will find the book a prodigious delight. He has an unerring eye for the absurd; his paradoxes, when pondered, have a way of proving excellent truth. (Truth is sometimes like the furniture in Through the Looking Glass, which could only be reached by resolutely walking away from it.)

Ten years ago Mr. Guedalla was considered the most continuously and insolently brilliant undergraduate of the Oxford of that day. The charm and vigor of his ironical wit have not lessened since his fellow-undergraduates strove to convince themselves that no man could be as clever as "P. G." seemed to be. When Mr. Guedalla "holds the mirror up to Nietzsche" or "gives thanks that Britons never never will be Slavs," or dynasticizes Henry James into three reigns: "James I, James II, and the Old Pretender;" or when he speaks of "the cheerful clatter of Sir James Barrie's cans as he went round with the milk of human kindness," there will be some who will sigh; but there will also (I hope) be many who will forgive the bravado for the quicksilver wit.

IT was Quintillian or Mr. Max Beerbohm who said, "History repeats itself: historians repeat each other." The saying is full of the mellow wisdom of either writer, and stamped with the peculiar veracity of the Silver Age of Roman or British epigram. One might have added, if the aphorist had stayed for an answer,

that history is rather interesting when it repeats itself:
historians are not. In France, which is an enlightened
country enjoying the benefits of the Revolution and a
public examination in rhetoric, historians are expected
to write in a single and classical style of French. The
result is sometimes a rather irritating uniformity; it
is one long Taine that has no turning, and any quotation may be attributed with safety to Guizot, because
la nuit tous les chats sont gris. But in England, which
is a free country, the restrictions natural to ignorant
(and immoral) foreigners are put off by the rough
island race, and history is written in a dialect which
is not curable by education, and cannot (it would
seem) be prevented by injunction.

Historians' English is not a style; it is an industrial disease. The thing is probably scheduled in the
Workmen's Compensation Act, and the publisher may
be required upon notice of the attack to make a suitable payment to the writer's dependants. The workers in this dangerous trade are required to adopt (like
Mahomet's coffin) a detached standpoint—that is, to
write as if they took no interest in the subject. Since
it is not considered good form for a graduate of less
than sixty years' standing to write upon any period that
is either familiar or interesting, this feeling is easily
acquired, and the resulting narrations present the dreary
impartiality of the Recording Angel without that com-

pleteness which is the sole attraction of his style.
Wilde complained of Mr. Hall Caine that he wrote
at the top of his voice; but a modern historian, when
he is really detached, writes like some one talking in
the next room, and few writers have equaled the legal
precision of Coxe's observation that the Turks "sawed
the Archbishop and the Commandant in half, and
committed other grave violations of international
law."

Having purged his mind of all unsteadying interest
in the subject, the young historian should adopt a
moral code of more than Malthusian severity, which
may be learned from any American writer of the last
century upon the Renaissance or the decadence of
Spain. This manner, which is especially necessary in
passages dealing with character, will lend to his work
the grave dignity that is requisite for translation into
Latin prose, that supreme test of an historian's style.
It will be his misfortune to meet upon the byways
of history the oddest and most abnormal persons, and
he should keep by him (unless he wishes to forfeit his
Fellowship) some convenient formula by which he
may indicate at once the enormity of the subject and
the disapproval of the writer. The writings of Lord
Macaulay will furnish him at need with the necessary
facility in lightning characterization. It was the practice of Cicero to label his contemporaries without dis-

tinction as "heavy men," and the characters of history
are easily divisible into "far-seeing statesmen" and
"reckless libertines." It may be objected that although it is sufficient for the purposes of contemporary
caricature to represent Mr. Gladstone as a collar or
Mr. Chamberlain as an eye-glass, it is an inadequate
record for posterity. But it is impossible for a busy
man to write history without formulæ, and after all
sheep are sheep and goats are goats. Lord Macaulay
once wrote of some one, "In private life he was stern,
morose, and inexorable"; he was probably a Dutch-
man. It is a passage which has served as a lasting
model for the historian's treatment of character. I
had always imagined that Cliché was a suburb of Paris,
until I discovered it to be a street in Oxford. Thus,
if the working historian is faced with a period of "de-
plorable excesses," he handles it like a man, and writes
always as if he was illustrated with steel engravings:

The imbecile king now ripened rapidly towards
a crisis. Surrounded by a Court in which the
inanity of the day was rivaled only by the de-
bauchery of the night, he became incapable towards the year 1472 of distinguishing good from
evil, a fact which contributed considerably to the
effectiveness of his foreign policy, but was hardly
calculated to conform with the monastic tradi-

tions of his House. Long nights of drink and
dicing weakened a constitution that was already
undermined, and the council-table, where once
Campo Santa had presided, was disfigured with
the despicable apparatus of Bagatelle. The
burghers of the capital were horrified by the wild
laughter of his madcap courtiers, and when it
was reported in London that Ladislas had played
at Halma the Court of St. James's received his
envoy in the deepest of ceremonial mourning.

That is precisely how it is done. The passage ex-
hibits the benign and contemporary influences of Lord
Macaulay and Mr. Bowdler, and it contains all the
necessary ingredients, except perhaps a "venal Chan-
cellor" and a "greedy mistress." Vice is a subject of
especial interest to historians, who are in most cases
residents in small county towns; and there is un-
bounded truth in the rococo footnote of a writer on
the Renaissance, who said *à propos* of a Pope: "The
disgusting details of his vices smack somewhat of the
morbid historian's lamp." The note itself is a fine
example of that concrete visualization of the subject
which led Macaulay to observe that in consequence of
Frederick's invasion of Silesia "black men fought on
the coast of Coromandel and red men scalped each
other by the Great Lakes of North America."

A less exciting branch of the historian's work is the reproduction of contemporary sayings and speeches. Thus, an obituary should always close on a note of regretful quotation:

> He lived in affluence and died in great pain. "Thus," it was said by the most eloquent of his contemporaries, "thus terminated a career as varied as it was eventful, as strange as it was unique."

But for the longer efforts of sustained eloquence greater art is required. It is no longer usual, as in Thucydides' day, to compose completely new speeches, but it is permissible for the historian to heighten the colors and even to insert those rhetorical questions and complexes of personal pronouns which will render the translation of the passage into Latin prose a work of consuming interest and lasting profit:

> The Duke assembled his companions for the forlorn hope, and addressed them briefly in *oratio obliqua*. "His father," he said, "had always cherished in his heart the idea that he would one day return to his own people. Had he fallen in vain? Was it for nothing that they had dyed with their loyal blood the soil of a hundred battlefields? The past was dead, the future was yet

> to come. Let them remember that great sacrifices were necessary for the attainment of great ends, let them think of their homes and families, and if they had any pity for an exile, an outcast, and an orphan, let them die fighting."

That is the kind of passage that used to send the blood of Dr. Bradley coursing more quickly through his veins. The march of its eloquence, the solemnity of its sentiment, and the rich balance of its pronouns unite to make it a model for all historians: it can be adapted for any period.

It is not possible in a short review to include the special branches of the subject. Such are those efficient modern text-books, in which events are referred to either as "factors" (as if they were a sum) or as "phases" (as if they were the moon). There is also the solemn business of writing economic history, in which the historian may lapse at will into algebra, and anything not otherwise describable may be called "social tissue." A special subject is constituted by the early conquests of Southern and Central America; in these there is a uniform opening for all passages running:

> It was now the middle of October, and the season was drawing to an end. Soon the mountains would be whitened with the snows of winter

and every rivulet swollen to a roaring torrent. Cortez, whose determination only increased with misfortune, decided to delay his march until the inclemency of the season abated. . . . It was now the middle of November, and the season was drawing to an end. . . .

There is, finally, the method of military history. This may be patriotic, technical, or in the manner prophetically indicated by Virgil as *Belloc, horrida Belloc.* The finest exponent of the patriotic style is undoubtedly the Rev. W. H. Fitchett, a distinguished colonial clergyman and historian of the Napoleonic wars. His night-attacks are more nocturnal, and his scaling parties are more heroically scaligerous than those of any other writer. His drummer-boys are the most moving in my limited circle of drummer-boys. One gathers that the Peninsular War was full of pleas-ing incidents of this type:

THE NIGHT ATTACK

It was midnight when Staff-Surgeon Pettigrew showed the flare from the summit of Sombrero. At once the whole plain was alive with the hum of the great assault. The four columns speedily got into position with flares and bugles at the head of each. One made straight for the Watergate, a second for the Bailey-guard, a third for the Porter-house, and the last (led by the saintly Smeathe) for the Tube station. Let us follow the second column on its secret mission through the night, lit by torches and cheered on by the huzzas of a thousand English throats. "—— the ——s," cried Cocker in a voice hoarse with patriotism; at that moment a red-hot shot hurtled over the plain and, ricocheting treacherously from the frozen river, dashed the heroic leader to the ground. Captain Boffskin, of the Buffs, leapt up with the dry coughing howl of the British infantryman. "—— them," he roared, "—— them to ——"; and for the last fifty yards it was neck and neck with the ladders. Our gallant drummer-boys laid to again, but suddenly a shot rang out from the silent ramparts. The 94th Léger were awake. *We were discovered!*

The war of 1870 requires more special treatment. Its histories show no particular characteristic, but its appearance in fiction deserves special attention. There is a standard pattern.

How the Prussians Came to Guitry-le-sec
It was a late afternoon in early September, or an early afternoon in late September—I forget these

things—when I missed the boat express from Kerplouarnec to Pouzy-le-roi and was forced by the time-table to spend three hours at the forgotten hamlet of Guitry-le-sec, in the heart of Dauphiné. It contained besides a quantity of underfed poultry one white church, one white mairie, and nine white houses. An old man with a white beard came towards me up the long white road. "It was on just such an afternoon as this forty years ago," he began, "that . . ."

"Stop!" I said sharply. "I have met you in a previous existence. You are going to say that a solitary Uhlan appeared sharply outlined against the sky behind M. Jules' farm." He nodded feebly.

"The red trousers had left the village half an hour before to look for the hated Prussian in the cafés of the neighboring town. You were alone when the spiked helmets marched in. You can hear their shrieking fifes to this day." He wept quietly.

I went on. "There was an officer with them, a proud, ugly man with a butter-colored mustache. He saw the little Mimi and drove his coarse Suabian hand upward through his Mecklenburger mustache. You dropped on one knee. . . ." But he had fled.

In the first of the three cafés I saw a second old man. "Come in, Monsieur," he said. I waited on the doorstep. "It was on just such an afternoon. . . ." I went on. At the other two cafés two further old men attempted me with the story; I told the last that he was rescued by Zouaves, and walked happily to the station, to read about Vichy Célestins until the train came in from the south.

The Russo-Japanese War is a more original subject and derives its particular flavor from the airy grace with which Sir Ian Hamilton has described it. Like this:

WAO-WAO, *Jan.* 31.—The *rafale* was purring like a *mistral* as I shaved this morning. I wonder where it is; must ask ——. —— is a charming fellow with the face of a Baluchi Kashgai and a voice like a circular saw.

11 :40—It was eleven-forty when I looked at my watch. The shrapnel-bursts look like a plantation of powder-puffs suspended in the sky. Victor says there is a battle going on : capital chap Victor.

2 P. M.—Lunched with an American lady-doctor. How feminine the Americans can be.

7 P. M.—A great day. It was Donkelsdorp over again. Substitute the Tenth Army for the Traffordshire's baggage wagon, swell Honks Spruit into the roaring Wang-ho, elevate Oom Kop into the frowning scarp of Pyjiyama, and you have it. The Staff were obviously gratified when I told them about Donkelsdorp.

The Rooskis came over the crest-line in a huddle of massed battalions, and Gazeka was after them like a rat after a terrier. I knew that his horse-guns had no horses (a rule of the Japanese service to discourage unnecessary changing of ground), but his men bit the trails and dragged them up by their teeth. Slowly the Muscovites peeled off the steaming mountain and took the funicular down the other side.

I wonder what my friend Smuts would make of the Yen-tai coal mine? Well, well.—*"Something accomplished, something done."*

The technical manner is more difficult of acquisition for the beginner, since it involves a knowledge of at least two European languages. It is cardinal rule that all places should be described as *points d'appui,* the simple process of scouting looks far better as *Verschleierung,* and the adjective "strategical" may be used without any meaning in front of any noun.

But the military manner was revolutionized by the war.   Mr. Belloc created a new Land and a new Water.   We know now why the Persian commanders demanded "earth and water" on their entrance into a Greek town; it was the weekly demand of the Great General Staff, as it called for its favorite paper.   Mr. Belloc has woven Baedeker and geometry into a new style: it is the last cry of historians' English, because one was invented by a German and the other by a Greek.

WINTER MIST

By ROBERT PALFREY UTTER

Robert Palfrey Utter was born in 1875, in Olympia, Washington. He graduated from Harvard (I am sorry there are so many Harvard men in this book: I didn't know they were Harvard men until too late) in 1898 and took his Ph.D. there in 1906. After a varied experience, including editorial work on the *Youth's Companion,* reporting on the New York *Evening Post,* ranching in Mexico and graduate study at Harvard, he went to Amherst, 1906-18, as associate professor of English. He was on the faculty of the A. E. F. University at Beaune, France, 1919; and in 1920 became associate professor of English at the University of California.

Mr. Utter has contributed largely to the magazines, and has published *Guide to Good English* (1914), *Every-Day Words and Their Uses* (1916), and *Every-Day Pronunciation* (1918).

Former students of his at Amherst have told me of the lasting stimulus his teaching has given them: that he can beautifully practise what he preaches of the art of writing, this essay shows.

FROM a magazine with a rather cynical cover I learned very recently that for pond skating the proper costume is brown homespun with a fur collar on the jacket, whereas for private rinks one wears a gray herringbone suit and taupe-colored alpine. Oh, barren years that I have been a skater, and no one told me of this! And here's another thing. I was patiently trying to acquire a counter turn under the idle gaze of a hockey player who had no better business till the others arrived than to watch my efforts. "What I don't see about that game," he said at last, "is who wins?" It had never occurred to me to ask. He looked bored, and I remembered that the pictures in the magazine showed the wearers of the careful costumes for rink and pond skating as having rather blank eyes that looked illimitably bored. I have hopes of the "rocker" and the "mohawk"; I might acquire a proper costume for skating on a small river if I could learn what it is; but a bored look—why, even hockey does not bore me, unless I stop to watch it. I don't wonder that those who play it look bored. Even Alexander, who played a more imaginative game than hockey, was bored—poor fellow, he should have taken up fancy skating in his youth; I never heard of a human being who pretended to a complete conquest of it.

I like pond skating best by moonlight. The hollow among the hills will always have a bit of mist about it, let the sky be clear as it may. The moonlight, which seems so lucid and brilliant when you look up, is all pearl and smoke round the pond and the hills. The shore that was like iron under your heel as you came down to the ice is vague, when you look back at it from the center of the pond, as the memory of a dream. The motion is like flying in a dream; you float free and the world floats under you; your velocity is without effort and without accomplishment, for, speed as you may, you leave nothing behind and approach nothing. You look upward. The mist is overhead now;

you see the moon in a "hollow halo" at the bottom of
an "icy crystal cup," and you yourself are in just such
another. The mist, palely opalescent, drives past her
out of nothing into nowhere. Like yourself, she is the
center of a circle of vague limit and vaguer content,
where passes a swift, ceaseless stream of impression through a faintly luminous halo of consciousness.

If by moonlight the mist plays upon the emotions
like faint, bewitching music, in sunlight it is scarcely
less. More often than not when I go for my skating
to our cosy little river, a winding mile from the mill-
dam to the railroad trestle, the hills are clothed in
silver mist which frames them in vignettes with blurred
edges. The tone is that of Japanese paintings on white
silk, their color showing soft and dull through the
frost-powder with which the air is filled. At the mill-
dam the hockey players furiously rage together, but
I heed them not, and in a moment am beyond the first
bend, where their clamor comes softened on the air
like that of a distant convention of politic crows. The
silver powder has fallen on the ice, just enough to
cover earlier tracings and leave me a fresh plate to
etch with grapevines and arabesques. The stream
winds ahead like an unbroken road, striped across
with soft-edged shadows of violet, indigo, and
lavender. On one side it is bordered with leaning

birch, oak, maple, hickory, and occasional groups of hemlocks under which the very air seems tinged with green. On the other, rounded masses of scrub oak and alder roll back from the edge of the ice like clouds of reddish smoke. The river narrows and turns, then spreads into a swamp, where I weave my curves round the straw-colored tussocks. Here, new as the snow is, there are earlier tracks than mine. A crow has traced his parallel hieroglyph, alternate footprints with long dashes where he trailed his middle toe as he lifted his foot and his spur as he brought it down. Under a low shrub that has hospitably scattered its seed is a dainty, close-wrought embroidery of tiny bird feet in irregular curves woven into a circular pattern. A silent glide towards the bank, where among bare twigs little forms flit and swing with low conversational notes, brings me in company with a working crew of pine siskins, methodically rifling seed cones of birch and alder, chattering sotto voce the while. Under a leaning hemlock the writing on the snow tells of a squirrel that dropped from the lowest branch, hopped aimlessly about for a few yards, then went up the bank. Farther on, where the river narrows again, a flutter-headed rabbit crossing at top speed has made a line seemingly as free from frivolous indirection as if it had been defined by all the ponderosities of mathematics. There is no pursuing track;

was it his own shadow he fled, or the shadow of hawk?

The mist now lies along the base of the hills, leaving the upper ridges almost imperceptibly veiled and the rounded tops faintly softened. The snowy slopes are etched with brush and trees so fine and soft that they remind me of Dürer's engravings, the fur of Saint Jerome's lion, the cock's feathers in the coat of arms with the skull. From behind the veil of the southernmost hill comes a faint note as

> From undiscoverable lips that blow
> An immaterial horn.

It is the first far premonition of the noon train; I pause and watch long for the next sign. At last I hear its throbbing, which ceases as it pauses at the flag station under the hill. There the invisible locomotive shoots a column of silver vapor above the surface of the mist, breaking in rounded clouds at the top, looking like nothing so much as the photograph of the explosion of a submarine mine, a titanic outburst of force in static pose, a geyser of atomized water standing like a frosted elm tree. Then quick puffs of dusky smoke, the volley of which does not reach my ear till the train has stuck its black head out of fairyland and become a prosaic reminder of dinner.

High on its narrow trestle it leaps across my little
river and disappears between the sandbanks. Far
behind it the mist is again spreading into its even
layers. Silence is renewed, and I can hear the musical
creaking of four starlings in an apple tree as they
eviscerate a few rotten apples on the upper branches.
I turn and spin down the curves and reaches of the
river without delaying for embroideries or arabesques.
At the mill-dam the hockey game still rages; the players
take no heed of the noon train.

> Let Zal and Rustum bluster as they will,
> Or Hatim call to supper . . .

Their minds and eyes are intent on a battered disk of
hard rubber. I begin to think I have misjudged them
when I consider what effort of imagination must be
involved in the concentration of the faculties on such
an object, transcending the call of hunger and the lure
of beauty. Is it to them as is to the mystic "the great
syllable Om" whereby he attains Nirvana? I cannot
attain it; I can but wonder what the hockey players
win one-half so precious as the stuff they miss.

TRIVIA

By LOGAN PEARSALL SMITH

It would be extravagant to claim that Pearsall Smith's *Trivia*, the remarkable little book from which these miniature essays are extracted, is well known: it is too daintily, fragile and absurd and sophisticated to appeal to a very large public. But it has a cohort of its own devotees and fanatics, and since its publication in 1917 it has become a sort of password in a secret brotherhood or intellectual Suicide Club. I say suicide advisedly, for Mr. Smith's irony is glitteringly edged. Its incision is so keen that the reader is often unaware the razor edge has turned against himself until he perceives the wound to be fatal.

Pearsall Smith was, in a way, one of the Men of the Nineties. But he had Repressions—(an excellent thing to have, brothers. Most of the great literature is founded on judicious repressions). He came of an excellent old intellectual Quaker family down in the Philadelphia region. His father (if we remember rightly) was one of Walt Whitman's staunchest friends in the Camden days. But when the strong wine of the Nineties was foaming in the vats and noggins, Mr. Smith (so we imagine it, at least) was still too close to that "guarded education in morals and manners" that he had had at Haverford College, Pennsylvania (and further tinctured with docility at Harvard and Balliol) to give full rein to his inward gush of hilarious satirics. Like a Strong Silent Man he held in that wellspring of champagne and mercury until many many years later. When it came out (in 1902 he first began to print his *Trivia*, privately; the book was published by Doubleday in 1917) it sparkled all the more tenderly for its long cellarage.

But we must be statistical. Logan Pearsall Smith was born at Melville, N. J., in 1865. As a boy he lived in Philadelphia and Germantown (do you know Germantown? it is a foothill of that mountain range whereof Parnassus and Olivet are twin peaks) and was three years at Haverford in the class of '85. He went to Harvard for a year, then to Balliol College, Oxford, where he took his degree in 1893. Ever since then, eheu, he has lived in England.

STONEHENGE

THEY sit there for ever on the dim horizon of my mind, that Stonehenge circle of elderly disapproving

Faces—Faces of the Uncles and Schoolmasters and
Tutors who frowned on my youth.

In the bright center and sunlight I leap, I caper,
I dance my dance; but when I look up, I see they are
not deceived. For nothing ever placates them, nothing ever moves to a look of approval that ring of bleak,
old, contemptuous Faces.

THE STARS

Battling my way homeward one dark night against
the wind and rain, a sudden gust, stronger than the
others, drove me back into the shelter of a tree. But
soon the Western sky broke open; the illumination of
the Stars poured down from behind the dispersing
clouds.

I was astonished at their brightness, to see how they
filled the night with their soft lustre. So I went my
way accompanied by them; Arcturus followed me, and
becoming entangled in a leafy tree, shone by glimpses,
and then emerged triumphant, Lord of the Western
Sky. Moving along the road in the silence of my own
footsteps, my thoughts were among the Constellations.
I was one of the Princes of the starry Universe; in
me also there was something that was not insignificant
and mean and of no account.

THE SPIDER

What shall I compare it to, this fantastic thing I call my Mind? To a waste-paper basket, to a sieve choked with sediment, or to a barrel full of floating froth and refuse?

No, what it is really most like is a spider's web, insecurely hung on leaves and twigs, quivering in every wind, and sprinkled with dewdrops and dead flies. And at its center, pondering for ever the Problem of Existence, sits motionless the spider-like and uncanny Soul.

L'OISEAU BLEU

What is it, I have more than once asked myself, what is it that I am looking for in my walks about London? Sometimes it seems to me as if I were following a Bird, a bright Bird that sings sweetly as it floats about from one place to another.

When I find myself, however, among persons of middle age and settled principles, see them moving regularly to their offices—what keeps them going? I ask myself. And I feel ashamed of myself and my Bird.

There is though a Philosophic Doctrine—I studied it at College, and I know that many serious people believe it—which maintains that all men, in spite of appearances and pretensions, all live alike for Pleasure. This theory certainly brings portly, respected persons very near to me. Indeed, with a sense of low complicity, I have sometimes watched a Bishop. Was he, too, on the hunt for Pleasure, solemnly pursuing his Bird?

I SEE THE WORLD

"But you go nowhere, see nothing of the world," my cousins said.

Now though I do go sometimes to the parties to which I am now and then invited, I find, as a matter of fact, that I get really much more pleasure by looking in at windows, and have a way of my own of seeing the World. And of summer evenings, when motors hurry through the late twilight, and the great houses take on airs of inscrutable expectation, I go owling out through the dusk; and wandering toward the West, lose my way in unknown streets—an unknown City of revels. And when a door opens and a bediamonded Lady moves to her motor over carpets unrolled by powdered footmen, I can easily think her some great Courtezan, or some half-believed Duchess, hurrying to card-tables and lit candles and strange scenes of joy. I like to see that there are still splendid people on this flat earth; and at dances, standing in the street with the crowd, and stirred by the music, the lights, the rushing sound of voices, I think the Ladies as beautiful as Stars who move up those lanes of light past our rows of vagabond faces; the young men look like Lords in novels; and if (it has once or twice happened) people I know go by me, they strike me as changed and rapt beyond my sphere. And when on hot nights windows are left open, and I can look in at Dinner Parties, as I peer through lace curtains and window-flowers at the silver, the women's shoulders, the shimmer of their jewels, and the divine attitudes of their heads as they lean and listen, I imagine extraordinary intrigues and unheard-of wines and passions.

The Church of England

I have my Anglican moments; and as I sat there that Sunday afternoon, in the Palladian interior of the London Church, and listened to the unexpressive voices chanting the correct service, I felt a comfortable assurance that we were in no danger of being betrayed into any unseemly manifestations of religious fervor. We had not gathered together at that performance to abase ourselves with furious hosannas before any dark Creator of an untamed Universe, no Deity of freaks and miracles and sinister hocus-pocus; but to pay our duty to a highly respected Anglican First Cause—undemonstrative, gentlemanly, and conscientious—whom, without loss of self-respect, we could decorously praise.

Consolation

The other day, depressed on the Underground, I tried to cheer myself by thinking over the joys of our human lot. But there wasn't one of them for which I seemed to care a button—not Wine, nor Friendship, nor Eating, nor Making Love, nor the Consciousness of Virtue. Was it worth while then going up in a lift into a world that had nothing less trite to offer?

Then I thought of reading—the nice and subtle happiness of reading. This was enough, this joy not dulled by Age, this polite and unpunished vice, this selfish, serene, life-long intoxication.

The Kaleidoscope

I find in my mind, in its miscellany of ideas and musings, a curious collection of little landscapes and pictures, shining and fading for no reason. Sometimes they are views in no way remarkable—the corner of a road, a heap of stones, an old gate. But there are many charming pictures too: as I read, between my eyes and book, the Moon sheds down on harvest fields her chill of silver; I see autumnal avenues, with the leaves falling, or swept in heaps; and storms blow among my thoughts, with the rain beating for ever on the fields. Then Winter's upward glare of snow appears; or the pink and delicate green of Spring in the windy sunshine; or cornfields and green waters, and youths bathing in Summer's golden heats.

And as I walk about, certain places haunt me; a cathedral rises above a dark blue foreign town, the color of ivory in the sunset light; now I find myself in a French garden, full of lilacs and bees, and shut-in sunshine, with the Mediterranean lounging and washing outside its walls; now in a little college library, with busts, and the green reflected light of Oxford lawns—and again I hear the bells, reminding me of the familiar Oxford hours.

THE POPLAR

There is a great tree in Sussex, whose cloud of thin foliage floats high in the summer air. The thrush sings in it, and blackbirds, who fill the late, decorative sunshine with a shimmer of golden sound. There the nightingale finds her green cloister; and on those branches sometimes, like a great fruit, hangs the lemon-colored Moon. In the glare of August, when all the world is faint with heat, there is always a breeze in those cool recesses, always a noise, like the noise of water, among its lightly-hung leaves.

But the owner of this Tree lives in London, reading books.

BEYOND LIFE

By JAMES BRANCH CABELL

To my taste, *Beyond Life,* an all-night soliloquy put into the mouth of the author's *alter ego* Charteris, is the most satisfying of Mr. Cabell's books. Its point of view is deftly sharpened, its manner is urbane and charming, without posture or allegorical pseudo-romantics. From this book I have taken the two closing sections, which form a beautiful and significant whole.

James Branch Cabell, born in Richmond, Virginia, in 1879, graduated from William and Mary College in 1898. He had some newspaper experience in Richmond and on the New York *Herald,* and began publishing in 1904. Not until 1915, until Mr. McBride, the New York publisher, and his untiring literary assistant, Mr. Guy Holt (to whom much of Cabell's appreciation is due), began their work, did critics begin to take him at all seriously. Since that time Mr. Cabell's reputation has been enormously enhanced by the idiotic suppression of his novel *Jurgen.* The Cabell cult has been almost too active in zeal, but there can be no doubt of his very real and refreshing imaginative talent.

I ASK of literature precisely those things of which I feel the lack in my own life. I appeal for charity, and implore that literature afford me what I cannot come by in myself. . . .

For I want distinction for that existence which ought to be peculiarly mine, among my innumerable fellows who swarm about earth like ants. Yet which one of us is noticeably, or can be appreciably different, in this throng of human ephemeræ and all their millions and inestimable millions of millions of predecessors and oncoming progeny? And even though one mote may transiently appear exceptional, the distinction of those

who in their heydays are "great" personages—much
as the Emperor of Lilliput overtopped his subjects by
the breadth of Captain Gulliver's nail—must suffer
loss with time, and must dwindle continuously, until
at most the man's recorded name remains here and
there in sundry pedants' libraries. There were how
many dynasties of Pharaohs, each one of whom was
absolute lord of the known world, and is to-day forgotten? Among the countless popes who one by one
were adored as the regent of Heaven upon earth, how
many persons can to-day distinguish? and does not
time breed emperors and czars and presidents as plenti-
ful as blackberries, and as little thought of when their
season is out? For there is no perpetuity in human
endeavor: we strut upon a quicksand: and all that any
man may do for good or ill is presently forgotten,
because it does not matter. I wail to a familiar tune,
of course, in this lament for the evanescence of human
grandeur and the perishable renown of kings. And
indeed to the statement that imperial Cæsar is turned
to clay and Mizraim now cures wounds, and that in
short Queen Anne is dead, we may agree lightly
enough; for it is, after all, a matter of no personal
concern: but how hard it is to concede that the banker
and the rector and the traffic-officer, to whom we more
immediately defer, and we ourselves, and the little gold
heads of our children, may be of no importance, either!

. . . In art it may so happen that the thing which a man makes endures to be misunderstood and gabbled over: yet it is not the man himself. We retain the *Iliad,* but oblivion has swallowed Homer so deep that many question if he ever existed at all. . . . So we pass as a cloud of gnats, where I want to live and be thought of, if only by myself, as a distinguishable entity. And such distinction is impossible in the long progress of suns, whereby in thought to separate the personality of any one man from all others that have lived, becomes a task to stagger Omniscience. . . .

I want my life, the only life of which I am assured, to have symmetry or, in default of that, at least to acquire some clarity. Surely it is not asking very much to wish that my personal conduct be intelligible to me! Yet it is forbidden to know for what purpose this universe was intended, to what end it was set a-going, or why I am here, or even what I had prefer- ably do while here. It vaguely seems to me that I am expected to perform an allotted task, but as to what it is I have no notion. . . . And indeed, what have I done hitherto, in the years behind me? There are some books to show as increment, as something which was not anywhere before I made it, and which even in bulk will replace my buried body, so that my life will be to mankind no loss materially. But the course of my life, when I look back, is as orderless as a trickle of water that is diverted and guided by every pebble and crevice and grass-root it encounters. I seem to have done nothing with pre-meditation, but rather, to have had things done to me. And for all the rest of my life, as I know now, I shall have to shave every morning in order to be ready for no more than this! . . . I have attempted to make the best of my material circumstances always; nor do I see to-day how any widely varying course could have been wiser or even feasible: but material things have nothing to do with that life which moves in me. Why, then, should they direct and heighten and provoke and curb every action of life? It is against the tyranny of matter I would rebel —against life's absolute need of food, and books, and fire, and clothing, and flesh, to touch and to inhabit, lest life perish. . . . No, all that which I do here or refrain from doing lacks clarity, nor can I detect any symmetry anywhere, such as living would assuredly display, I think, if my progress were directed by any particular motive. . . . It is all a muddling through, somehow, without any recognizable goal in view, and there is no explanation of the scuffle tendered or anywhere procurable. It merely seems that to go on living has become with me a habit. . . .

And I want beauty in my life. I have seen beauty in a sunset and in the spring woods and in the eyes of divers women, but now these happy accidents of light and color no longer thrill me. And I want beauty in my life itself, rather than in such chances as befall it. It seems to me that many actions of my life were beautiful, very long ago, when I was young in an evanished world of friendly girls, who were all more lovely than any girl is nowadays. For women now are merely more or less good-looking, and as I know, their looks when at their best have been painstakingly enhanced and edited. . . . But I would like this life which moves and yearns in me, to be able itself to attain to comeliness, though but in transitory performance. The life of a butterfly, for example, is just a graceful gesture: and yet, in that its loveliness is complete and perfectly rounded in itself, I envy this bright flicker through existence. And the nearest I can come to my ideal is punctiliously to pay my bills, be polite to my wife, and contribute to deserving charities: and the program does not seem, somehow, quite adequate. There are my books, I know; and there is beauty "embalmed and treasured up" in many pages of my books, and in the books of other persons, too, which I may read at will: but this desire inborn in me is not to be satiated by making marks upon paper, nor by deciphering them. . . . In short, I am enamored of that flawless beauty of which all poets have perturbedly divined the existence somewhere, and which life as men know it simply does not afford nor anywhere foresee. . . .

And tenderness, too—but does that appear a mawkish thing to desiderate in life? Well, to my finding human beings do not like one another. Indeed, why should they, being rational creatures? All babies have a temporary lien on tenderness, of course: and therefrom children too receive a dwindling income, although on looking back, you will recollect that your childhood was upon the whole a lonesome and much put-upon period. But all grown persons ineffably distrust one another. . . . In courtship, I grant you, there is a passing aberration which often mimics tenderness, sometimes as the result of honest delusion, but more frequently as an ambuscade in the endless struggle between man and woman. Married people are not ever tender with each other, you will notice: if they are mutually civil it is much: and physical contacts apart, their relation is that of a very moderate intimacy. My own wife, at all events, I find an unfailing mystery, a Sphinx whose secrets I assume to be not worth knowing: and, as I am mildly thankful to narrate, she knows very little about me, and evinces as to my affairs no morbid interest. That is not to assert that if I were ill she would not nurse me through any imaginable contagion, nor that if she were drowning I would not plunge in after her, whatever my delinquencies at swimming: what I mean is that, pending such high crises, we tolerate each other amicably, and never think of doing more. . . . And from our blood-kin we grow apart inevitably. Their lives and their interests are no longer the same as ours, and when we meet it is with conscious reservations and much manufactured talk. Besides, they know things about us which we resent. . . . And with the rest of my fellows, I find that convention orders all our dealings, even with children, and we do and say what seems more or less expected. And I know that we distrust one another all the while, and instinctively conceal or misrepresent our actual thoughts and emotions when there is no very apparent need. . . . Personally, I do not like human beings because I am not aware, upon the whole, of any generally distributed qualities which entitle them as a race to admiration and affection. But toward people in books—such as Mrs. Millamant, and Helen of Troy, and Bella Wilfer, and Mélusine, and Beatrix Esmond—I may intelligently overflow with tenderness and caressing words, in part because they deserve it, and in part because I know they will not suspect me of being "queer" or of having ulterior motives. . . .

And I very often wish that I could know the truth about just any one circumstance connected with my life. . . . Is the phantasmagoria of sound and noise and color really passing or is it all an illusion here in my brain? How do you know that you are not dream-

ing me, for instance? In your conceded dreams, I am
sure, you must invent and see and listen to persons
who for the while seem quite as real to you as I do
now. As I do, you observe, I say! and what thing is
it to which I so glibly refer as I? If you will try to
form a notion of yourself, of the sort of a something
that you suspect to inhabit and partially to control
your flesh and blood body, you will encounter a walking bundle of superfluities: and when you mentally
have put aside the extraneous things—your garments
and your members and your body, and your acquired
habits and your appetites and your inherited traits and
your prejudices, and all other appurtenances which
considered separately you recognize to be no integral
part of you,—there seems to remain in those pearl-
colored brain-cells, wherein is your ultimate lair, very
little save a faculty for receiving sensations, of which
you know the larger portion to be illusory. And
surely, to be just a very gullible consciousness provi-
sionally existing among inexplicable mysteries, is not
an enviable plight. And yet this life—to which I cling
tenaciously—comes to no more. Meanwhile I hear
men talk about "the truth"; and they even wager
handsome sums upon their knowledge of it: but I align
myself with "jesting Pilate," and echo the forlorn
query that recorded time has left unanswered. . . .

Then, last of all, I desiderate urbanity. I believe

this is the rarest quality in the world. Indeed, it probably does not exist anywhere. A really urbane person—a mortal open-minded and affable to conviction of his own shortcomings and errors, and unguided in anything by irrational blind prejudices—could not but in a world of men and women be regarded as a monster. We are all of us, as if by instinct, intolerant of that which is unfamiliar: we resent its impudence: and very much the same principle which prompts small boys to jeer at a straw-hat out of season induces their elders to send missionaries to the heathen. The history of the progress of the human race is but the picaresque romance of intolerance, a narrative of how —what is it Milton says?—"truth never came into the world but, like a bastard, to the ignominy of him that brought her forth, till time hath washed and salted the infant, declared her legitimate, and churched the father of his young Minerva." And I, who prattle to you, very candidly confess that I have no patience with other people's ideas unless they coincide with mine: for if the fellow be demonstrably wrong I am fretted by his stupidity, and if his notion seem more nearly right than mine I am infuriated. . . . Yet I wish I could acquire urbanity, very much as I would like to have wings. For in default of it, I cannot even manage to be civil to that piteous thing called human nature, or to view its parasites, whether they be politicians or clergymen or popular authors, with one-half the commiseration which the shifts they are put to, quite certainly, would rouse in the urbane. . . .

So I in point of fact desire of literature, just as you guessed, precisely those things of which I most poignantly and most constantly feel the lack in my own life. And it is that which romance affords her postulants. The philtres of romance are brewed to free us from this unsatisfying life that is calendared by fiscal years, and to contrive a less disastrous elusion of our own personalities than many seek dispersedly in drink and drugs and lust and fanaticism, and sometimes in death. For, beset by his own rationality, the normal man is goaded to evade the strictures of his normal life, upon the incontestable ground that it is a stupid and unlovely routine; and to escape likewise from his own personality, which bores him quite as much as it does his associates. So he hurtles into these very various roads from reality, precisely as a goaded sheep flees without notice of what lies ahead. . . .

And romance tricks him, but not to his harm. For, be it remembered that man alone of animals plays the ape to his dreams. Romance it is undoubtedly who whispers to every man that life is not a blind and aimless business, not all a hopeless waste and confusion; and that his existence is a pageant (appreciatively ob-

served by divine spectators), and that he is strong
and excellent and wise : and to romance he listens, willing and thrice willing to be cheated by the honeyed
fiction. The things of which romance assures him are
very far from true: yet it is solely by believing himself
a creature but little lower than the cherubim that man
has by interminable small degrees become, upon the
whole, distinctly superior to the chimpanzee: so that,
however extravagant may seem these flattering whispers to-day, they were immeasurably more remote
from veracity when men first began to listen to their
sugared susurrus, and steadily the discrepancy lessens.
To-day these things seem quite as preposterous to calm
consideration as did flying yesterday: and so, to the
Gradgrindians, romance appears to discourse foolishly,
and incurs the common fate of prophets : for it is about
to-morrow and about the day after to-morrow, that
romance is talking, by means of parables. And all
the while man plays the ape to fairer and yet fairer
dreams, and practice strengthens him at mimickry. . . .

To what does the whole business tend?—why, how
in heaven's name should I know? We can but be content to note that all goes forward, toward something.
. . . It may be that we are nocturnal creatures per-
turbed by rumors of a dawn which comes inevitably,
as prologue to a day wherein we and our children have
no part whatever. It may be that when our arboreal

propositus descended from his palm-tree and began to walk upright about the earth, his progeny were forthwith committed to a journey in which to-day is only a way-station. Yet I prefer to take it that we are components of an unfinished world, and that we are but as seething atoms which ferment toward its making, if merely because man as he now exists can hardly be the finished product of any Creator whom one could very heartily revere. We are being made into something quite unpredictable, I imagine: and through the purging and the smelting, we are sustained by an instinctive knowledge that we are being made into something better. For this we know, quite incommunicably, and yet as surely as we know that we will to have it thus.

And it is this will that stirs in us to have the creatures of earth and the affairs of earth, not as they are, but "as they ought to be," which we call romance. But when we note how visibly it sways all life we perceive that we are talking about God.

THE FISH REPORTER

By ROBERT CORTES HOLLIDAY

This informal commentary on the picturesque humors of trade journalism is typical of Mr. Holliday's great skill in capturing the actual vibration of urban life. He has something of George Gissing's taste for the actuality of city scenes and characters, with rather more pungent idiosyncrasy in his manner of self-expression. Careful observers of the art of writing will see how much shrewd skill there is in the apparently unstudied manner. One of Mr. Holliday's favorite discussions on the art of writing is a phrase of Booth Tarkington's—"How to get the ink out of it." In other words, how to strip away mere literary and conscious adornment, and to get down to a translucent portraiture of life itself in its actual contour and profile.

We are told that Mr. Holliday, in his native Indianapolis (where he was born in 1880), was a champion bicycle rider at the age of sixteen. That triumph, however, was not permanently satisfying, for he came to New York in 1899 to study art; lived for a while, precariously, as an illustrator; worked for several years as a bookseller in Charles Scribner's retail store, and passed through all sorts of curious jobs on Grub Street, among others book reviewer on the *Tribune* and *Times*. He was editor of *The Bookman* after that magazine was taken over by the George H. Doran Company, and retired to the genteel dignity of "contributing editor" in 1920, to obtain leisure for more writing of his own.

Mr. Holliday has the genuine gift of the personal essay, mellow, fluent, and pleasantly eccentric. His *Walking-Stick Papers, Broome Street Straws, Turns about Town* and *Peeps at People* have that charming rambling humor that descends to him from his masters in this art, Hazlitt and Thackeray. When Mr. Holliday was racking his wits for a title for *Men and Books and Cities* (that odd Borrovian chronicle of his mind, body and digestion on tour across the continent) I suggested *The Odyssey of an Oddity*. He deprecated this; but I still think it would have been a good title, because strictly true.

MEN of genius, blown by the winds of chance, have been, now and then, mariners, bar-keps, schoolmasters, soldiers, politicians, clergymen, and what not. And from these pursuits have they sucked the essence of yarns and in the setting of these activities found a flavor to stir and to charm hearts untold. Now, it is a thousand pities that no man of genius has ever been a fish reporter. Thus has the world lost great literary treasure, as it is highly probable that there is not under the sun any prospect so filled with the scents and colors of story as that presented by the commerce in fish.

Take whale oil. Take the funny old buildings on Front Street, out of paintings, I declare, by Howard Pyle, where the large merchants in whale oil are. Take salt fish. Do you know the oldest salt-fish house in America, down by Coenties Slip? Ah! you should. The ghost of old Long John Silver, I suspect, smokes an occasional pipe in that old place. And many are the times I've seen the slim shade of young Jim Hawkins come running out. Take Labrador cod for export to the Mediterranean lands or to Porto Rico via New York. Take herrings brought to this port from Iceland, from Holland, and from Scotland; mackerel from Ireland, from the Magdalen Islands, and from Cape Breton; crabmeat from Japan; fish-balls from Scandinavia; sardines from Norway and from France; caviar from Russia; shrimp which comes from Florida, Mississippi, and Georgia, or salmon from Alaska, and Puget Sound, and the Columbia River.

Take the obituaries of fishermen. "In his prime, it is said, there was not a better skipper in the Gloucester fishing fleet." Take disasters to schooners, smacks, and trawlers. "The crew were landed, but lost all their belongings." New vessels, sales, etc. "The sealing schooner *Tillie B.,* whose career in the South Seas is well known, is reported to have been sold to a moving-picture firm." Sponges from the Caribbean Sea and the Gulf of Mexico. "To most people, familiar only with the sponges of the shops, the animal as it comes from the sea would be rather unrecognizable." Why, take anything you please! It is such stuff as stories are. And as you eat your fish from the store how little do you reck of the glamor of what you are doing!

However, as it seems to me unlikely that a man of genius will be a fish reporter shortly I will myself do the best I can to paint the tapestry of the scenes of his calling. The advertisement in the newspaper read: "Wanted—Reporter for weekly trade paper." Many called, but I was chosen. Though, doubtless, no man living knew less about fish than I.

The news stands are each like a fair, so laden are they with magazines in bright colors. It would seem almost as if there were a different magazine for every few hundred and seven-tenth person, as the statistics put these .natters. And yet, it seems, there is a vast, a very vast, periodical literature of which we, that is, magazine readers in general, know nothing whatever. There is, for one, that fine, old, standard publication, *Barrel and Box,* devoted to the subjects and the interests of the coopering industry; there is too, *The Dried Fruit Packer and Western Canner,* as alert a magazine as one could wish—in its kind; and from the home of classic American literature comes *The 'New England Tradesman and Grocer.* And so on. At the place alone where we went to press twenty-seven trade journals were printed every week, from one for butchers to one for bankers.

The Fish Industries Gazette—Ah, yes! For some reason not clear (though it is an engaging thing, I think) the word "gazette" is the great word among the titles of trade journals. There are *The Jewellers' Gazette* and *The Women's Wear Gazette* and *The Poulterers' Gazette* (of London), and *The Maritime Gazette* (of Halifax), and other gazettes quite without number. This word "gazette" makes its appeal, too, curiously enough, to those who christen country papers; and trade journals have much of the intimate charm of country papers. The "trade" in each case is a kind of neighborly community, separated in its parts by space, but joined in unity of sympathy. "Per-

sonals" are a vital feature of trade papers. "Walter
Conner, who for some time has conducted a bakery
and fish market at Hudson, N. Y., has removed to
Fort Edward, leaving his brother Ed in charge at the
Hudson place of business."

· *The Fish Industries Gazette,* as I say, was one of
several in its field, in friendly rivalry with *The Oyster
Trade and Fisherman* and *The Pacific Fisheries.* It
comprised two departments: the fresh fish and oyster
department, and myself. I was, as an editorial announcement said at the beginning of my tenure of
office, a "reorganization of our salt, smoked, and
pickled fish department." The delectable, mellow spirit
of the country paper, so removed from the crash and
whirr of metropolitan journalism, rested in this, too,
that upon the *Gazette* I did practically everything on
the paper except the linotyping. Reporter, editorial
writer, exchange editor, make-up man, proof-reader,
correspondent, advertisement solicitor, was I.

As exchange editor, did I read all the papers in the
English language in eager search of fish news. And
while you are about the matter, just find me a finer bit
of literary style evoking the romance of the vast
wastes of the moving sea, in Stevenson, Defoe, anywhere you please, than such a news item as this:
"Capt. Ezra Pound, of the bark *Elnora,* of Salem,
Mass., spoke a lonely vessel in latitude this and longi-

tude that, September 8. She proved to be the whaler *Wanderer*, and her captain said that she had been nine months at sea, that all on board were well, and that he had stocked so many barrels of whale oil."

As exchange editor was it my business to peruse reports from Eastport, Maine, to the effect that one of the worst storms in recent years had destroyed large numbers of the sardine weirs there. To seek fish recipes, of such savory sound as those for "broiled redsnapper," "shrimps bordelaise," and "baked fish croquettes." To follow fishing conditions in the North Sea occasioned by the Great War. To hunt down jokes of piscatory humor. "The man who drinks like a fish does not take kindly to water.—Exchange." To find other "fillers" in the consular reports and elsewhere: "Fish culture in India," "1800 Miles in a Dory," "Chinese Carp for the Philippines," "Americans as Fish Eaters." And, to use a favorite term of trade papers, "etc., etc." Then to "paste up" the winnowed fruits of this beguiling research.

As editorial writer, to discuss the report of the commission recently sent by congress to the Pribilof Islands, Alaska, to report on the condition of our national herd of fur seals; to discuss the official interpretation here of the Government ruling on what constitutes "boneless" codfish; to consider the campaign in Canada to promote there a more popular consumption of fish, and to brightly remark *à propos* of this that "a fish a day keeps the doctor away"; to review the current issue of *The Journal of the Fisheries Society of Japan,* containing leading articles on "Are Fishing Motor Boats Able to Encourage in Our Country" and "Fisherman the Late Mr. H. Yamaguchi Well Known"; to combat the prejudice against dogfish as food, a prejudice like that against eels, in some quarters eyed askance as "calling cousins with the great sea-serpent," as Juvenal says; to call attention to the doom of one of the most picturesque monuments in the story of fish, the passing of the pleasant and celebrated old Trafalgar Hotel at Greenwich, near London, scene of the famous Ministerial white-bait dinners of the days of Pitt; to make a jest on an exciting idea suggested by some medical man that some of the features of a Ritz-Carlton Hotel, that is, baths, be introduced into the fo'c's'les of Grand Banks fishing vessels; to keep an eye on the activities of our Bureau of Fisheries; to hymn a praise to the monumental new Fish Pier at Boston; to glance at conditions at the premier fish market of the world, Billingsgate; to herald the fish display at the Canadian National Exhibition at Toronto, and, indeed, etc., and again etc.

As general editorial roustabout, to find each week a "leader," a translation, say, from *In Allgemeine Fisherei-Zeitung,* or *Economic Circular No. 10,* "Mussels in the Tributaries of the Missouri," or the last biennial report of the Superintendent of Fisheries of Wisconsin, or a scientific paper on "The Porpoise in Captivity" reprinted by permission of *Zoologica,* of the New York Zoölogical Society. To find each week for reprint a poem appropriate in sentiment to the feeling of the paper. One of the "Salt Water Ballads" would do, or John Masefield singing of "the whale's way," or "Down to the white dipping sails"; or Rupert Brooke: "And in that heaven of all their wish, There shall be no more land, say fish"; or a "weather rhyme" about "mackerel skies," when "you're sure to get a fishing day"; or something from the New York *Sun* about "the lobster pots of Maine"; or Oliver Herford, in the *Century,* "To a Goldfish"; or, best of all, an old song of fishing ways of other days.

And to compile from the New York *Journal of Commerce* better poetry than any of this, tables, beautiful tables of "imports into New York": "Oct. 15.— From Bordeaux, 225 cs. cuttlefish bone; Copenhagen, 173 pkgs. fish; Liverpool, 969 bbls. herrings, 10 walrus hides, 2,000 bags salt; La Guayra, 6 cs. fish sounds; Belize, 9 bbls. sponges; Rotterdam, 7 pkgs. seaweed, 9,000 kegs herrings; Barcelona, 235 cs. sardines; Bocas Del Toro, 5 cs. turtle shells; Genoa, 3 boxes corals; Tampico, 2 pkgs. sponges; Halifax, 1 cs. seal skins, 35 bbls. cod liver oil, 215 cs. lobsters, 490 bbls.

codfish; Akureyri, 4,150 bbls. salted herrings," and much more. Beautiful tables of "exports from New York." "To Australia" (cleared Sep. 1); "to Argentina";—Haiti, Jamaica, Guatemala, Scotland, Salvador, Santo Domingo, England, and to places many more. And many other gorgeous tables, too. "Fishing vessels at New York," for one, listing the "trips" brought into this port by the *Stranger,* the *Sarah O'Neal,* the *Nourmahal,* a farrago of charming sounds, and a valuable tale of facts.

As make-up man, of course, so to "dress" the paper that the "markets," Oporto, Trinidad, Porto Rico, Demerara, Havana, would be together; that "Nova Scotia Notes"—"Weather conditions for curing have been more favorable since October set in"—would follow "Halifax Fish Market"—"Last week's arrivals were: Oct. 13, schr. *Hattie Loring,* 960 quintals," etc.—that "Pacific Coast Notes"—"The tug *Tatoosh* will perform the service for the Seattle salmon packers of towing a vessel from Seattle to this port via the Panama Canal"—would follow "Canned Salmon"; that shellfish matter would be in one place; reports of saltfish where such should be; that the weekly tale of the canned fish trade politically embraced the canned fish advertising; and so on and so on.

Finest of all, as reporter, to go where the fish reporter goes. There the sight-seeing cars never find their way; the hurried commuter has not his path, nor knows of these things at all; and there that racy character who, voicing a multitude, declares that he would rather be a lamp post on Broadway than Mayor of St. Louis, goes not for to see. Up lower Greenwich Street the fish reporter goes, along an eerie, dark, and narrow way, beneath a strange, thundering roof, the "L" overhead. He threads his way amid seemingly chaotic, architectural piles of boxes, of barrels, crates, casks, kegs, and bulging bags; roundabout many great fetlocked draught horses, frequently standing or plunging upon the sidewalk, and attached to many huge trucks and wagons; and much of the time in the street he is compelled to go, finding the side walks too congested with the traffic of commerce to admit of his passing there.

You probably eat butter, and eggs, and cheese. Then you would delight in Greenwich Street. You could feast your highly creditable appetite for these excellent things for very nearly a solid mile upon the signs of "wholesale dealers and commission merchants" in them. The letter press, as you might say, of the fish reporter's walk is a noble pæan to the earth's glorious yield for the joyous sustenance of man. For these princely merchants' signs sing of opulent stores of olive oil, of sausages, beans, soups, extracts, and spices, sugar, Spanish, Bermuda, and Havana onions, "fine"

apples, teas, coffee, rice, chocolates, dried fruits and
raisins, and of loaves and of fishes, and of "fish products." Lo! dark and dirty and thundering Greenwich
Street is to-day's translation of the Garden of Eden.

Here is a great house whose sole vocation is the im-
portation of caviar for barter here. Caviar from
over-seas now comes, when it comes at all, mainly by
the way of Archangel, recently put on the map, for
most of us, by the war. The fish reporter is told, however, if it be summer, that there cannot be much doing
in the way of caviar until fall, "when the spoonbill
start coming in." And on he goes to a great saltfish
house, where many men in salt-stained garments are
running about, their arms laden with large flat objects,
of sharp and jagged edge, which resemble dried and
crackling hides of some animal curiously like a huge
fish; and numerous others of "the same" are trundling
round wheelbarrow-like trucks likewise so laden.
Where stacks of these hides stand on their tails against
the walls, and goodness knows how many big boxes
are, containing, as those open show, beautifully soft,
thick, cream-colored slabs, which is fish. And where
still other men, in overalls stained like a painter's
palette, are knocking off the heads of casks and dipping
out of brine still other kinds of fish for inspection.

Here it is said by the head of the house, by the
stove (it is chill weather) in his office like a ship-

master's cabin: "Strong market on foreign mackerel. Mines hinder Norway catch. Advices from abroad report that German resources continue to purchase all available supplies from the Norwegian fishermen. No Irish of any account. Recent shipment sold on the deck at high prices. Fair demand from the Middle West."

So, by stages, on up to turn into North Moore Street, looking down a narrow lane between two long bristling rows of wagons pointed out from the curbs, to the façades of the North River docks at the bottom, with the tops of the buff funnels of ocean liners, and Whistleranean silhouettes of derricks, rising beyond. Hereabout are more importers, exporters, and "producers" of fish, famous in their calling beyond the celebrities of popular publicity. And he that has official entrée may learn, by mounting dusky stairs, half-ladder and half-stair, and by passing through low-ceilinged chambers freighted with many barrels, to the sanctums of the fish lords, what's doing in the foreign herring way, and get the current market quotations, at present sky-high, and hear that the American shore mackerel catch is very fine stock.

Then roundabout, with a step into the broad vista of homely Washington Street, and a turn through Franklin Street, where is the man decorated by the Imperial Japanese Government with a gold medal, if he should care to wear it, for having distinguished himself in the development of commerce in the marine products of Japan, back to Hudson Street. An authentic railroad is one of the spectacular features of Hudson Street.

Here down the middle of the way are endless trains, stopping, starting, crashing, laden to their ears with freight, doubtless all to eat. Tourists should come from very far to view Hudson Street. Here is a spectacle as fascinating, as awe-inspiring, as extraordinary as any in the world. From dawn until darkness falls, hour after hour, along Hudson Street slowly, steadily moves a mighty procession of great trucks. One would not suppose there were so many trucks on the face of the earth. It is a glorious sight, and any man whose soul is not dead should jump with joy to see it. And the thunder of them altogether as they bang over the stones is like the music of the spheres.

There is on Hudson Street a tall handsome building where the fish reporter goes, which should be enjoyed in this way: Up in the lift you go to the top, and then you walk down, smacking your lips. For all the doors in that building are brimming with poetry. And the tune of it goes like this: "Toasted Corn-Flake Co.," "Seaboard Rice," "Chili Products," "Red Bloom Grape Juice Sales Office," "Porto Rico and Singapore Pineapple Co.," "Sunnyland Foodstuffs," "Importers of Fruit Pulps, Pimentos," "Sole Agents U. S. A. Italian Salad Oil," "Raisin Growers," "Log Cabin Syrups," "Jobbers in Beans, Peas," "Chocolate and Cocoa Preparations," "Ohio Evaporated Milk Co.," "Bernese Alps and Holland Condensed Milk Co.," "Brazilian Nuts Co.," "Brokers Pacific Coast Salmon," "California Tuna Co.," and thus on and on.

The fish reporter crosses the street to see the head of the Sardine Trust, who has just thrown the market into excitement by a heavy cut in prices of last year's pack. Thence, pausing to refresh himself by the way at a sign "Agency for Reims Champagne and Moselle Wines—Bordeaux Clarets and Sauternes," over to Broadway to interview the most august persons of all, dealers in fertilizer, "fish scrap." These mighty gentlemen live, when at business, in palatial suites of offices constructed of marble and fine woods and laid with rich rugs. The reporter is relayed into the innermost sanctum by a succession of richly clothed attendants. And he learns, it may be, that fishing in Chesapeake Bay is so poor that some of the "fish factories" may decide to shut down. Acid phosphate, it is said, is ruling at $13 f.o.b. Baltimore.

And so the fish reporter enters upon the last lap of his rounds. Through, perhaps, the narrow, crooked lane of Pine Street he passes, to come out at length upon a scene set for a sea tale. Here would a lad, heir to vast estates in Virginia, be kidnapped and smuggled aboard to be sold a slave in Africa. This is Front Street. A white ship lies at the foot of it. Cranes rise at her side. Tugs, belching smoke, bob beyond. All about are ancient warehouses, redolent of the Thames, with steep roofs and sometimes stairs outside, and with tall shutters, a crescent-shaped hole in each. There is a dealer in weather-vanes. Other things dealt in hereabout are these: chronometers, "nautical instruments," wax gums, cordage and twine, marine paints, cotton wool and waste, turpentine, oils, greases, and rosin. Queer old taverns, public houses, are here, too. Why do not their windows rattle with a "Yo, ho, ho"?

There is an old, old house whose business has been fish oil within the memory of men. And here is another. Next, through Water Street, one comes in search of the last word on salt fish. Now the air is filled with gorgeous smell of roasting coffee. Tea, coffee, sugar, rice, spices, bags and bagging here have their home. And there are haughty bonded warehouses filled with fine liquors. From his white cabin at the top of a venerable structure comes the dean of the saltfish business. "Export trade fair," he says; "good demand from South America."

SOME NONSENSE ABOUT A DOG

By HARRY ESTY DOUNCE

Harry Esty Dounce was born in Syracuse in 1889 and graduated from Hamilton College in 1910. His first job was as a
cub reporter on the journal that newspapermen affectionately
call "the old *Sun*"; the adjective is pronounced as though it
were in italics. He was on the staff of the Syracuse *Herald*,
1912-14; spent a year in New Orleans writing short stories, and
returned in 1916 to the magazine staff of the *Sun*. He was
editor of the *Sun's* book review section, 1919-20; in 1920 he
joined the staff of the New York *Evening Post*.

"My hand will miss the insinuated nose—"
Sir William Watson.

BUT the dog that was written of must have been a
big dog. Nibbie was just a comfortable lapful, once
he had duly turned around and curled up with his nose
in his tail.

This is for people who know about dogs, in particular little mongrels without pedigree or market value.
Other people, no doubt, will find it disgustingly maud-
lin. I would have found it so before Nibbie came.

The day he came was a beautiful bright, cool one in
an August. A touring car brought him. They put
him down on our corner, meaning to lose him, but he
crawled under the car, and they had to prod him out
and throw stones before they could drive on. So that

331

when I came home I found, with his mistress-elect, a sort of potbellied bundle of tarry oakum, caked with mud, panting convulsively still from fright, and showing the whites of uncommonly liquid brown eyes and a pink tongue. There was tennis that evening and he went along—I carried him over the railroad tracks; he gave us no trouble about the balls, but lay huddled under the bench where she sat, and shivered if a man came near him.

That night he got chop bones and she got a sensible homily on the unwisdom of feeding strays, and he was left outdoors. He slept on the mat. The second morning we thought he had gone. The third, he was back, wagging approval of us and intent to stay, which seemed to leave no choice but to take him in. We had fun over names. "Jellywaggles," suggested from next door, was undeniably descriptive. "Rags" fitted, or "Toby" or "Nig"—but they had a colored maid next door; finally we called him "Nibs," and soon his tail would answer to it.

Cleaned up—scrubbed, the insoluble matted locks clipped from his coat, his trampish collar replaced with a new one bearing a license tag—he was far from being unpresentable. A vet. once opined that for a mongrel he was a good dog, that a black cocker mother had thrown her cap over Scottish mills, so to speak. This analysis accounted for him perfectly. Always, depend-

ing on the moment's mood, he was either terrier or
spaniel, the snap and scrap and perk of the one alternat-
ing with the gentle snuggling indolence of the other. ⟋

As terrier he would dig furiously by the hour after
a field mouse; as spaniel he would "read" the breeze
with the best nose among the dog folk of our neighborhood, or follow a trail quite well. I know there was
retrieving blood. A year ago May he caught and
brought me, not doing the least injury, an oriole that
probably had flown against a wire and was struggling
disabled in the grass.

Nibbie was shabby-genteel black, sunburnt as to the
mustache, grizzled as to the raggy fringe on his
haunches. He had a white stock and shirt-frill and a
white fore paw. The brown eyes full of heart were the
best point. His body coat was rough Scottish worsted,
the little black pate was cotton-soft like shoddy, and
the big black ears were genuine spaniel silk. As a
terrier he held them up smartly and carried a plumy
fishhook of a tail; as a spaniel the ears drooped and
the tail swung meekly as if in apology for never having
been clipped. The other day when we had to say
good-by to him each of us cut one silky tuft from an
ear, very much as we had so often when he'd been
among the burdocks in the field where the garden is.

Burrs were by no means Nibbie's only failing. In
flea time it seemed hardly possible that a dog of his size

could sustain his population. We finally found a true
flea bane, but, deserted one day, he was populous again
the next. They don't relish every human; me they did;
I used to storm at him for it, and he used, between
spasms of scratching, to listen admiringly and wag.
We think he supposed his tormentors were winged in-
sects, for he sought refuge in dark clothes-closets
where a flying imp wouldn't logically come.

He was wilful, insisted on landing in laps when their
makers wanted to read. He *would* make advances to
visitors who were polite about him. He *would* get up
on the living-room table, why and how, heaven knows,
finding his opportunity when we were out of the house,
and taking care to be upstairs on a bed—white, grime-
able coverlets preferred—by the time we had the front
door open; I used to slip up to the porch and catch
through a window the diving flourish of his sinful tail.

One of his faults must have been a neurosis really.
He led a hard life before we took him in, as witnessed
the game hind leg that made him sit up side-saddle
fashion, and two such scars on his back as boiling hot
grease might have made. And something especially
cruel had been done to him when asleep, for if you
bent over him napping or in his bed he would half
rouse and growl, and sometimes snap blindly. (We
dreaded exuberant visiting children.) Two or three
experiments I hate to remember now convinced me that

it couldn't be whipped out of him, and once wide awake
he was sure to be perplexedly apologetic.

He was spoiled. That was our doing. We babied
him abominably—he was, for two years, the only subject we had for such malpractice. He had more foolish
names than Wogg, that dog of Mrs. Stevenson's, and
heard more Little Language than Stella ever did, re-
ciprocating by kissing proffered ears in his doggy way.
Once he had brightened up after his arrival, he showed
himself ready to take an ell whenever we gave an inch,
and he was always taking them, and never paying
penalties. He had conscience enough to be sly. I remember the summer evening we stepped outside for
just an instant, and came back to find a curious groove
across the butter, on the dining table, and an ever-so-
innocent Nibbie in a chair in the next room.

While we were at the table he was generally around
it, bulldozing for tid-bits—I fear he had reason to
know that this would work. One fortnight when his
Missie was away he slept on his Old Man's bed (we
had dropped titles of dignity with him by then) and
he rang the welkin hourly, answering far-away dog
friends, and occasionally came north to lollop my face
with tender solicitude, just like the fool nurse in the
story, waking the patient up to ask if he was sleeping
well.

More recently, when a beruffled basket was waiting,

he developed an alarming trick of stealing in there to try it, so I fitted that door with a hook, insuring a crack impervious to dogs. And the other night I had to take the hook, now useless, off; we couldn't stand hearing it jingle. He adopted the junior member on first sight and sniff of him, by the way; would look on beaming as proudly as if he'd hatched him.

The last of his iniquities arose from a valor that lacked its better part, an absurd mixture of Falstaff and bantam rooster. At the critical point he'd back out of a fuss with a dog of his own size. But let a police dog, an Airedale, a St. Bernard, or a big ugly cur appear and Nibbie was all around him, black-guarding him unendurably. It was lucky that the big dogs in our neighborhood were patient. And he never would learn about automobiles. Usually tried to tackle them head on, often stopped cars with merciful drivers. When the car wouldn't stop, luck would save him by a fraction of an inch. I couldn't spank that out of him either. We had really been expecting what finally happened for two years.

That's about all. Too much, I am afraid. A decent fate made it quick the other night, and clean and close at hand, in fact, on the same street corner where once a car had left the small scapegrace for us. We tell ourselves how glad we are it happened as it did, in-stead of an agonal ending such as many of his people

come to. We tell ourselves we couldn't have had him
for ever in any event; that some day, for the junior
member's sake, we shall get another dog. We keep
telling ourselves these things, and talking with animation on other topics. The muzzle, the leash, the drinking dish are hidden, the last muddy paw track swept up,
the nose smudges washed off the favorite front window pane.

But the house is full of a little snoofing, wagging,
loving ghost. I know how the boy Thoreau felt about
a hereafter with dogs barred. I want to think that
somewhere, some time, I will be coming home again,
and that when the door opens Nibbie will be on hand
to caper welcome.

THE FIFTY-FIRST DRAGON

By HEYWOOD BROUN

Heywood Broun, who has risen rapidly through the ranks of
newspaper honor from sporting reporter and war correspondent
to one of the most highly regarded dramatic and literary critics
in the country, is another of these Harvard men, but, as far
as this book is concerned, the last of them. Broun graduated
from Harvard in 1910; was several years on the New York
Tribune, and is now on the *World.*

There is no more substantially gifted newspaper man in his
field; his beautifully spontaneous humor and drollery are coun-
terbalanced by a fine imaginative sensitiveness and a remarkable
power in the fable or allegorical essay, such as the one here
reprinted. His book, *Seeing Things at Night,* is only the first-
fruit of truly splendid possibilities. If I may be allowed to
prophesy, thus hazarding all, I will say that Heywood Broun
is likely, in the next ten or fifteen years, to do as fine work,
both imaginative and critical, as any living American of his era.

OF all the pupils at the knight school Gawaine le
Cœur-Hardy was among the least promising. He was
tall and sturdy, but his instructors soon discovered that
he lacked spirit. He would hide in the woods when
the jousting class was called, although his companions
and members of the faculty sought to appeal to his
better nature by shouting to him to come out and break
his neck like a man. Even when they told him that the
lances were padded, the horses no more than ponies
and the field unusually soft for late autumn, Gawaine
refused to grow enthusiastic. The Headmaster and
the Assistant Professor of Pleasaunce were discussing
the case one spring afternoon and the Assistant Professor could see no remedy but expulsion.

"No," said the Headmaster, as he looked out at the purple hills which ringed the school, "I think I'll train him to slay dragons."

"He might be killed," objected the Assistant Professor.

"So he might," replied the Headmaster brightly, but he added, more soberly, "we must consider the greater good. We are responsible for the formation of this lad's character."

"Are the dragons particularly bad this year?" interrupted the Assistant Professor. This was characteristic. He always seemed restive when the head of the school began to talk ethics and the ideals of the institution.

"I've never known them worse," replied the Headmaster. "Up in the hills to the south last week they killed a number of peasants, two cows and a prize pig. And if this dry spell holds there's no telling when they may start a forest fire simply by breathing around indiscriminately."

"Would any refund on the tuition fee be necessary in case of an accident to young Cœur-Hardy?"

"No," the principal answered, judicially, "that's all covered in the contract. But as a matter of fact he won't be killed. Before I send him up in the hills I'm going to give him a magic word."

"That's a good idea," said the Professor. "Sometimes they work wonders."

From that day on Gawaine specialized in dragons. His course included both theory and practice. In the morning there were long lectures on the history, anatomy, manners and customs of dragons. Gawaine did not distinguish himself in these studies. He had a marvelously versatile gift for forgetting things. In the afternoon he showed to better advantage, for then he would go down to the South Meadow and practise with a battle-ax. In this exercise he was truly impressive, for he had enormous strength as well as speed and grace. He even developed a deceptive display of ferocity. Old alumni say that it was a thrilling sight to see Gawaine charging across the field toward the dummy paper dragon which had been set up for his practice. As he ran he would brandish his ax and shout "A murrain on thee!" or some other vivid bit of campus slang. It never took him more than one stroke to behead the dummy dragon.

Gradually his task was made more difficult. Paper gave way to papier-mâché and finally to wood, but even the toughest of these dummy dragons had no terrors for Gawaine. One sweep of the ax always did the business. There were those who said that when the practice was protracted until dusk and the dragons threw long, fantastic shadows across the meadow

Gawaine did not charge so impetuously nor shout so loudly. It is possible there was malice in this charge. At any rate, the Headmaster decided by the end of June that it was time for the test. Only the night before a dragon had come close to the school grounds and had eaten some of the lettuce from the garden. The faculty decided that Gawaine was ready. They gave him a diploma and a new battle-ax and the Headmaster summoned him to a private conference.

"Sit down," said the Headmaster. "Have a cigarette."

Gawaine hesitated.

"Oh, I know it's against the rules," said the Headmaster. "But after all, you have received your preliminary degree. You are no longer a boy. You are a man. To-morrow you will go out into the world, the great world of achievement."

Gawaine took a cigarette. The Headmaster offered him a match, but he produced one of his own and began to puff away with a dexterity which quite amazed the principal.

"Here you have learned the theories of life," continued the Headmaster, resuming the thread of his discourse, "but after all, life is not a matter of theories. Life is a matter of facts. It calls on the young and the old alike to face these facts, even though they are hard and sometimes unpleasant. Your problem, for example, is to slay dragons."

"They say that those dragons down in the south wood are five hundred feet long," ventured Gawaine, timorously.

"Stuff and nonsense!" said the Headmaster. "The curate saw one last week from the top of Arthur's Hill. The dragon was sunning himself down in the valley. The curate didn't have an opportunity to look at him very long because he felt it was his duty to hurry back to make a report to me. He said the monster, or shall I say, the big lizard?—wasn't an inch over two hundred feet. But the size has nothing at all to do with it. You'll find the big ones even easier than the little ones. They're far slower on their feet and less aggressive, I'm told. Besides, before you go I'm going to equip you in such fashion that you need have no fear of all the dragons in the world."

"I'd like an enchanted cap," said Gawaine.

"What's that?" answered the Headmaster, testily.

"A cap to make me disappear," explained Gawaine.

The Headmaster laughed indulgently. "You mustn't believe all those old wives' stories," he said. "There isn't any such thing. A cap to make you disappear, indeed! What would you do with it? You haven't even appeared yet. Why, my boy, you could walk from here to London, and nobody would so much as look at you. You're nobody. You couldn't be more invisible than that."

Gawaine seemed dangerously close to a relapse into his old habit of whimpering. The Headmaster reassured him: "Don't worry; I'll give you something much better than an enchanted cap. I'm going to give you a magic word. All you have to do is to repeat this magic charm once and no dragon can possibly harm a hair of your head. You can cut off his head at your leisure."

He took a heavy book from the shelf behind his desk and began to run through it. "Sometimes," he said, "the charm is a whole phrase or even a sentence. I might, for instance, give you 'To make the'—No, that might not do. I think a single word would be best for dragons."

"A short word," suggested Gawaine.

"It can't be too short or it wouldn't be potent. There isn't so much hurry as all that. Here's a splendid magic word: 'Rumplesnitz.' Do you think you can learn that?"

Gawaine tried and in an hour or so he seemed to have the word well in hand. Again and again he interrupted the lesson to inquire, "And if I say 'Rumplesnitz' the dragon can't possibly hurt me?" And always the Headmaster replied, "If you only say 'Rumplesnitz,' you are perfectly safe."

Toward morning Gawaine seemed resigned to his career. At daybreak the Headmaster saw him to the edge of the forest and pointed him to the direction in which he should proceed. About a mile away to the southwest a cloud of steam hovered over an open meadow in the woods and the Headmaster assured Gawaine that under the steam he would find a dragon. Gawaine went forward slowly. He wondered whether it would be best to approach the dragon on the run as he did in his practice in the South Meadow or to walk slowly toward him, shouting "Rumplesnitz" all the way.

The problem was decided for him. No sooner had he come to the fringe of the meadow than the dragon spied him and began to charge. It was a large dragon and yet it seemed decidedly aggressive in spite of the Headmaster's statement to the contrary. As the dragon charged it released huge clouds of hissing steam through its nostrils. It was almost as if a gigantic teapot had gone mad. The dragon came forward so fast and Gawaine was so frightened that he had time to say "Rumplesnitz" only once. As he said it, he swung his battle-ax and off popped the head of the dragon. Gawaine had to admit that it was even easier to kill a real dragon than a wooden one if only you said "Rumplesnitz."

Gawaine brought the ears home and a small section

of the tail. His school mates and the faculty made much of him, but the Headmaster wisely kept him from being spoiled by insisting that he go on with his work. Every clear day Gawaine rose at dawn and went out to kill dragons. The Headmaster kept him at home when it rained, because he said the woods were damp and unhealthy at such times and that he didn't want the boy to run needless risks. Few good days passed in which Gawaine failed to get a dragon. On one particularly fortunate day he killed three, a husband and wife and a visiting relative. Gradually he developed a technique. Pupils who sometimes watched him from the hill-tops a long way off said that he often allowed the dragon to come within a few feet before he said "Rumplesnitz." He came to say it with a mocking sneer. Occasionally he did stunts. Once when an excursion party from London was watching him he went into action with his right hand tied behind his back. The dragon's head came off just as easily.

As Gawaine's record of killings mounted higher the Headmaster found it impossible to keep him completely in hand. He fell into the habit of stealing out at night and engaging in long drinking bouts at the village tavern. It was after such a debauch that he rose a little before dawn one fine August morning and started out after his fiftieth dragon. His head was heavy and his mind sluggish. He was heavy in other respects as well, for he had adopted the somewhat vulgar practice of wearing his medals, ribbons and all, when he went out dragon hunting. The decorations began on his chest and ran all the way down to his abdomen. They must have weighed at least eight pounds.

Gawaine found a dragon in the same meadow where he had killed the first one. It was a fair-sized dragon, but evidently an old one. Its face was wrinkled and Gawaine thought he had never seen so hideous a countenance. Much to the lad's disgust, the monster refused to charge and Gawaine was obliged to walk toward him. He whistled as he went. The dragon regarded him hopelessly, but craftily. Of course it had heard of Gawaine. Even when the lad raised his battle-ax the dragon made no move. It knew that there was no salvation in the quickest thrust of the head, for it had been informed that this hunter was protected by an enchantment. It merely waited, hoping something would turn up. Gawaine raised the battle-ax and suddenly lowered it again. He had grown very pale and he trembled violently. The dragon suspected a trick. "What's the matter?" it asked, with false solicitude.

"I've forgotten the magic word," stammered Gawaine.

"What a pity," said the dragon. "So that was the

secret. It doesn't seem quite sporting to me, all this magic stuff, you know. Not cricket, as we used to say when I was a little dragon; but after all, that's a matter of opinion."

Gawaine was so helpless with terror that the dragon's confidence rose immeasurably and it could not resist the temptation to show off a bit.

"Could I possibly be of any assistance?" it asked. "What's the first letter of the magic word?"

"It begins with an 'r,'" said Gawaine weakly.

"Let's see," mused the dragon, "that doesn't tell us much, does it? What sort of a word is this? Is it an epithet, do you think?"

Gawaine could do no more than nod.

"Why, of course," exclaimed the dragon, "reactionary Republican."

Gawaine shook his head.

"Well, then," said the dragon, "we'd better get down to business. Will you surrender?"

With the suggestion of a compromise Gawaine mustered up enough courage to speak.

"What will you do if I surrender?" he asked.

"Why, I'll eat you," said the dragon.

"And if I don't surrender?"

"I'll eat you just the same."

"Then it doesn't mean any difference, does it?" moaned Gawaine.

"It does to me," said the dragon with a smile. "I'd rather you didn't surrender. You'd taste much better if you didn't."

The dragon waited for a long time for Gawaine to ask "Why?" but the boy was too frightened to speak. At last the dragon had to give the explanation without his cue line. "You see," he said, "if you don't surrender you'll taste better because you'll die game."

This was an old and ancient trick of the dragon's. By means of some such quip he was accustomed to paralyze his victims with laughter and then to destroy them. Gawaine was sufficiently paralyzed as it was, but laughter had no part in his helplessness. With the last word of the joke the dragon drew back his head and struck. In that second there flashed into the mind of Gawaine the magic word "Rumplesnitz," but there was no time to say it. There was time only to strike and, without a word, Gawaine met the onrush of the dragon with a full swing. He put all his back and shoulders into it. The impact was terrific and the head of the dragon flew away almost a hundred yards and landed in a thicket.

Gawaine did not remain frightened very long after the death of the dragon. His mood was one of wonder. He was enormously puzzled. He cut off the ears of the monster almost in a trance. Again and again he thought to himself, "I didn't say 'Rumplesnitz'!" He was sure of that and yet there was no question that he had killed the dragon. In fact, he had never killed one so utterly. Never before had he driven a head for anything like the same distance. Twenty-five yards was perhaps his best previous record. All the way back to the knight school he kept rumbling about in his mind seeking an explanation for what had occurred. He went to the Headmaster immediately and after closing the door told him what had happened. "I didn't say 'Rumplesnitz,'" he explained with great earnestness.

The Headmaster laughed. "I'm glad you've found out," he said. "It makes you ever so much more of a hero. Don't you see that? Now you know that it was you who killed all these dragons and not that foolish little word 'Rumplesnitz.'"

Gawaine frowned. "Then it wasn't a magic word after all?" he asked.

"Of course not," said the Headmaster, "you ought to be too old for such foolishness. There isn't any such thing as a magic word."

"But you told me it was magic," protested Gawaine. "You said it was magic and now you say it isn't."

"It wasn't magic in a literal sense," answered the Headmaster, "but it was much more wonderful than that. The word gave you confidence. It took away your fears. If I hadn't told you that you might have been killed the very first time. It was your battle-ax did the trick."

Gawaine surprised the Headmaster by his attitude. He was obviously distressed by the explanation. He interrupted a long philosophic and ethical discourse by the Headmaster with, "If I hadn't of hit 'em all mighty hard and fast any one of 'em might have crushed me like a, like a—" He fumbled for a word.

"Egg shell," suggested the Headmaster.

"Like a egg shell," assented Gawaine, and he said it many times. All through the evening meal people who sat near him heard him muttering, "Like a egg shell, like a egg shell."

The next day was clear, but Gawaine did not get up at dawn. Indeed, it was almost noon when the Headmaster found him cowering in bed, with the clothes pulled over his head. The principal called the Assistant Professor of Pleasaunce, and together they dragged the boy toward the forest.

"He'll be all right as soon as he gets a couple more dragons under his belt," explained the Headmaster.

"The Assistant Professor of Pleasaunce agreed. "It would be a shame to stop such a fine run," he said. "Why, counting that one yesterday, he's killed fifty dragons."

They pushed the boy into a thicket above which hung a meager cloud of steam. It was obviously quite a small dragon. But Gawaine did not come back that night or the next. In fact, he never came back. Some weeks afterward brave spirits from the school explored the thicket, but they could find nothing to remind them of Gawaine except the metal parts of his medals. Even the ribbons had been devoured.

The Headmaster and the Assistant Professor of Pleasaunce agreed that it would be just as well not to tell the school how Gawaine had achieved his record and still less how he came to die. They held that it might have a bad effect on school spirit. Accordingly, Gawaine has lived in the memory of the school as its greatest hero. No visitor succeeds in leaving the building to-day without seeing a great shield which hangs on the wall of the dining hall. Fifty pairs of dragons' ears are mounted upon the shield and underneath in gilt letters is "Gawaine le Cœur-Hardy," followed by the simple inscription, "He killed fifty dragons." The record has never been equaled.